TURNING TO THE
DARK SIDE

Also by Gregory V. Diehl

Brand Identity Breakthrough

Courage to Live

Everyone Is an Entrepreneur

Our Global Lingua Franca

The Heroic and Exceptional Minority

The Influential Author

The Romantic Ideal—The Highest Standard of
Romance for a Man

Travel as Transformation

What Zen Isn't

TURNING TO THE
DARK SIDE

What Star Wars Teaches Us About
How a Good Person Turns Bad

by

Gregory V. Diehl

Library of Congress Control Number: 2026907410
First edition. First published in Buffalo, WY.

ISBN-13: 978-1-969995-03-3 (ebook)
ISBN-13: 978-1-969995-04-0 (paperback)
ISBN-13: 978-1-969995-05-7 (hardcover)

Cover and Anakinalome art by Elham Montazeri.

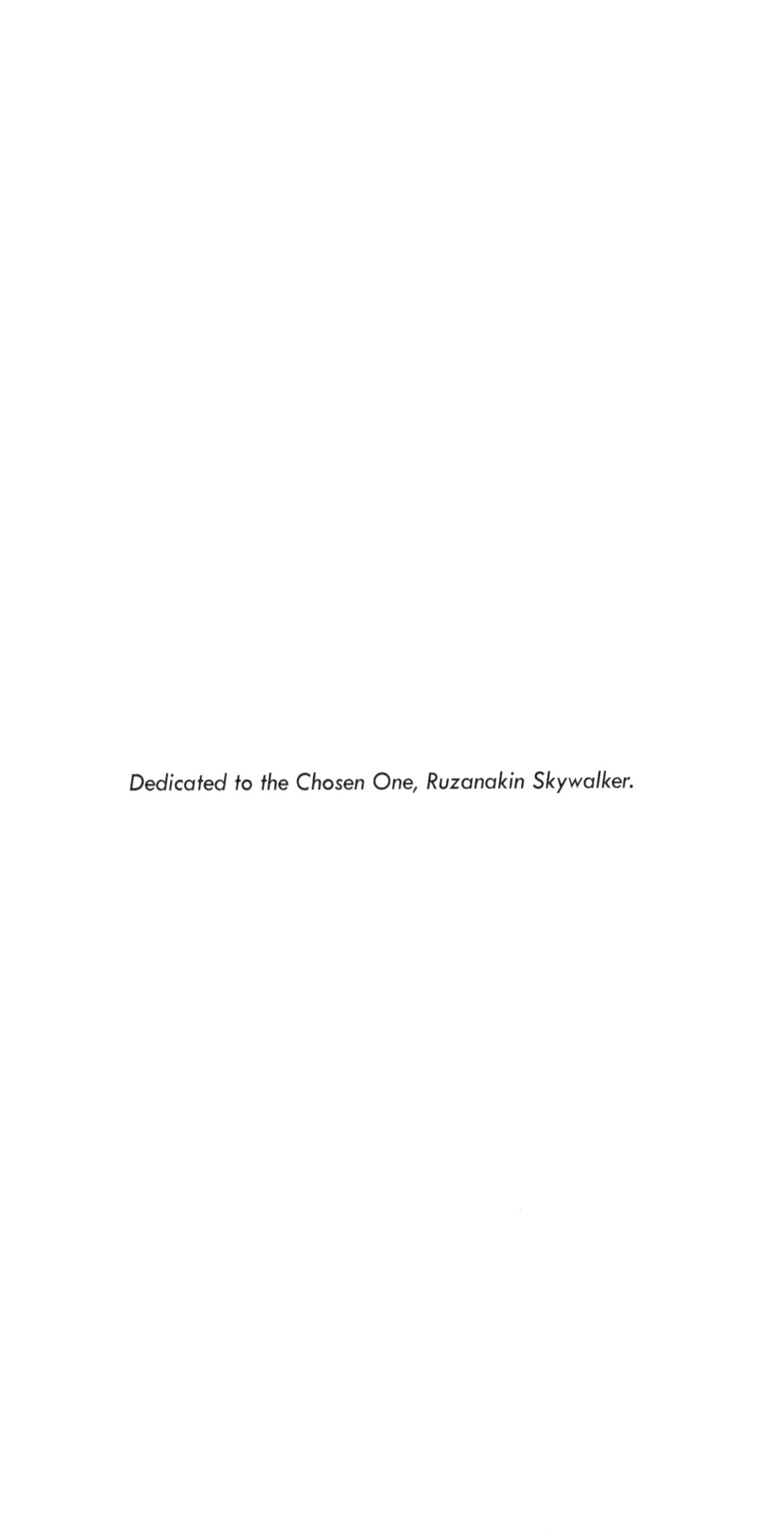

Dedicated to the Chosen One, Ruzanakin Skywalker.

"The ideal hero of the age emerges as a titanic individual who, after rejecting and overthrowing a corrupt social order, struggles on behalf of his fellows to inaugurate a new culture."

—James D. Wilson, *The Romantic Heroic Ideal*
(Baton Rouge: Louisiana State University Press, 1982), 65–66.

CONTENTS

ACKNOWLEDGMENTS

*S*tar Wars remains engaging viewing for me after all this time, as does thoughtful analysis by cultural commentators who refuse to resent the art for not making itself small, as some ill-informed critics do. I wish to acknowledge those who had some influence on the perspective of *Star Wars* I provide in this book, each adding their own point of view and specialization in unweaving the tapestry of the metamyth. In my opinion, they remain criminally overlooked in the broader discourse of these films. Of course, the fact that I derived some influence from their work does not imply they would necessarily agree with my thought process or conclusions in this book.

Mike Klimo's *Star Wars Ring Theory* essay

Rick Worley's *How to Watch Star Wars* video essay series and *Every Time Star Wars Quotes Star Wars* video montage

J.G. Scammell (josh_from_xboxlive)'s *Does Anakin Skywalker Have an Arc?*, *Does Luke Skywalker Have an Arc?*, and *Battle of the Star Wars Theories* video essays

SPOILER DISCLAIMER

STOP

Read no further than this page if you haven't seen *Star Wars*.

This book examines major philosophical and psychological issues through the lens of *Star Wars*, a six-film morality tale set in a blended science fiction and fantasy space opera universe, created by George Lucas in 1977 and completed in 2005. Do not read this book before you have seen Episodes 1 through 6 of *Star Wars*, in that order. Do not even casually skim through this book beforehand. Doing so is guaranteed to lessen the first-time viewing experience. If you obtained a copy of this book before meeting this requirement, I order you to leave it in your "to read" pile until then.

These six movies, spanning 13 hours and 26 minutes of runtime, changed the world of filmmaking and hero stories by portraying profound truths about the human condition in ways never before achieved. I do not want to be responsible for robbing you of that experience by spoiling it with my analysis before you've had a chance to see it. In fact, please deliberately refrain from looking up any further information about *Star Wars* until you've been able to experience it in its entirety. Please approach the experience as open-mindedly as possible, in a state of childlike wonder.

This book will proceed under the assumption that you have a thorough understanding of the plot, characters, and themes of the six main *Star Wars* films, ignoring any additional sequels or spinoffs.

FULL SPOILERS AHEAD

PREFACE

I cannot remember a world before *Star Wars*. For most of us in the Western world under a certain age, *Star Wars* has always been a part of our cultural consciousness, even among those who have never seen the films, thanks to general cultural osmosis.

In the introduction to my personal development book *The Heroic and Exceptional Minority*, I reflected on how mythology, if passed down through the generations in a viable medium like popular film, can serve as a more powerful form of mentorship than that afforded to us by real-life mentors and parental figures. I identified *Star Wars* as one such intergenerationally potent form of mentorship that had had a particularly strong effect upon my moral heroic development as I matured:

"*Star Wars* offered me, at first as a young boy with the original three movies and then later as a teenager when the newly released prequel trilogy concluded, dual heroic arcs turning away from each other at their most defining moments. Anakin Skywalker, lacking sufficient mentorship, succumbs to his unresolved dark emotions. Luke, his unknowing son, embarks upon a similar path a generation later. Through the interjection of now-wiser versions of his father's old mentors, Luke, at last, receives guidance that is relevant and adequate for the completion of his path to heroism. Luke's success holds true to his chosen values in the face of great temptation, possible only through the perspective of his father's prior failure, demonstrating that a villain is frequently a failed hero at his core."[1]

For reasons I did not understand when I was a child, I related more to old Ben Kenobi in *A New Hope* than I did to young Luke Skywalker. I saw a more developed example of part of my fundamental nature on screen before me and identified more with the mentor's struggles of passing on the moral lessons than I did with the hero's burden of receiving them. In the prequels, the pain of Obi-Wan's loss of a fallen friend and student he loved so much, who showed so much promise, spoke to me on levels I wouldn't fully understand until I experienced similar pains with people in my life who showed similar signs of personality corruption, including even the woman who would later become my wife. It seemed so familiar to me, like a path I had walked before. I knew that I was not the only one who had ever experienced this. There were universal patterns and explanations behind such devastating and self-destructive behavior. Thus, the inspiration for writing *Turning to the Dark Side* was born: to explore, from every available angle, *Star Wars'* mythological depiction of how a good person turns bad, and how even the best people can become the worst if they are unprepared for the burdens of their own existence.

It begins with a switch, a dramatic, anti-miraculous change in personality, priorities, or working terms of a relationship with someone you love. The person you know becomes passive, and some other, uglier force emerges in their place. There's a circuit breaker in the mind that limits higher brain function. It concentrates activity in automatic emotional reactions. It ceases to integrate events into memory, instead defaulting to whatever it has already accepted as the only narrative of events. Consciousness is reduced to a minimum. Under these conditions, people cannot self-reflect. They cease to be themselves and become a machine-like and animalistic facsimile instead. As George Lucas said in a 2005 *Vanity Fair* interview before the release of Episode 3, *Star Wars* is "the story of how a good person turns bad."[2]

I wrote this book because I needed to understand what was happening to the people I loved, the same people I had witnessed become fundamentally different under the influence of emotional avoidance. This book exists to help you understand what has happened or is happening to you or a person you love who seems to be falling into unconsciousness, and to remind you to *keep loving them* despite their betrayal. Familial connection is the best hope they have of someday coming back to the light and returning to embody, once again, the identity you loved them for.

However, if someone you love is operating from a distorted perception of reality and self, a reciprocal, mutually loving and respectful relationship *is impossible* until and unless they undergo the long journey of recovery and self-remembering. You will injure yourself or be vulnerable to manipulation and harm if you approach them expecting them to act as a conscious, self-reflective person when they are not presently capable of being one. You may even inadvertently push them further away by trying to persist in their life when they are not in a state of consciousness to have you there.

Relationships are forged from shared identity and understanding. You cannot have a real relationship with someone who has fallen into a subhuman state of their conscious, actualized self. No matter how intelligent you know they are capable of being, they are not applying their own mind and its intellect consistently. They cannot be held accountable for the agreements they make because it's too easy for them to transform into someone who does not remember or respect those agreements as soon as they perceive that they do not serve their changing wants or values.

By learning to spot the signs of a mind heading down the dark path, we can accomplish three important things:

1. Avoid engaging in intimate relationships with compromised people who will be unable to reciprocate what we offer.

2. Spot the effects of the darkness brewing in ourselves so that we can get back on the right path before it is too late.

3. If at all possible, help those we love recover from a fall into unconsciousness and reclaim the best version of themselves they are capable of being.

Everything in this book is my personal interpretation of the work of George Lucas and the many talented individuals who contributed to the creation of *Star Wars*. Although I believe there is considerable evidence that my interpretations align with the creator's vision (some of which is provided as direct quotes from Lucas in the endnotes), this book has not been reviewed, approved, or endorsed by anyone involved in the production of these films. My interpretations are also heavily influenced by my personal life experiences, including the loss of many great friends, apprentices, and romantic partners to the dark side as it manifests in real people. And it is because of those personal experiences that I know it is possible, at least in some rare cases, for someone to crawl their way out of their hate-fueled unconsciousness and remember the person they used to be and the values they once held. That's how I ended up marrying someone who once *hated* me and treated me like her mortal enemy, forgetting all that we had shared over years of friendship, mentorship, love, and intimacy before that. The conclusion of this book will tell you more about her downfall and what it took to bring her back to a state much higher than ever before, both for her individually and for the two of us as a couple.

Except where stated in some endnotes, this book only takes into account Episodes 1 through 6 of *Star Wars*, which is the theatrical vision George Lucas explicitly intended and published for his story, regardless of whatever other value may be present in the ever-expanding universe of additional movies, novels, comics, games, and shows (whether in canon or Legends continuity)[3] that continue to be produced as part of the overarching *Star Wars* intellectual property.

I refer to this as the Lucas hexalogy to avoid confusion with the larger collection of anything else that might fall under the broad *Star Wars* umbrella—one whole consisting of six interdependent parts.[4]

The theme of dual identities, each with its own designation, applies to several characters in *Star Wars*. I will reference each character by the name most closely associated with the persona they are acting in at the time they are speaking or acting. Whether these dual names and identities actually represent different people is a matter of viewer interpretation. For instance: Queen Amidala and her handmaiden Padmé, Senator/Chancellor/Emperor Palpatine and Darth Sidious, Anakin Skywalker and Darth Vader, as well as Obi-Wan and Ben Kenobi.

There are two forms of success. One is to never fall to the dark side of the Force in the first place by having your emotional needs met in a healthy way that allows for emotional integration the first time around on the path to adulthood. Otherwise, people who fall to the dark side by failing to have their fundamental needs for self-expression met must find a way to come back from it and return to being who they really are, fully self-embodied.

NOTES

1. Gregory V. Diehl, *The Heroic and Exceptional Minority: A Guide to Mythological Self-Awareness and Growth* (Identity Publications, 2021), viii.

2. George Lucas, quoted by Jim Windolf, "Star Wars: The Last Battle," *Vanity Fair*, February 2005, 110.

3. In regard to *Star Wars*, "canon" refers to the official storyline recognized by Lucasfilm and Disney. It includes everything that is considered part of the main *Star Wars* universe, where all events are treated as officially "real" within the narrative. Legends continuity, formerly known as the *Star Wars Expanded Universe* (EU), is an expansive body of older material, including hundreds of novels and comics, reference books, older TV shows, and video games, that was rebranded after Disney acquired Lucasfilm in 2012. Lucasfilm continues to incorporate concepts, characters, or plotlines from Legends into canon, resulting in some overlap and ambiguity between the events and themes of the two.

4. "Each episode has to stand on its own and have meaning on its own—except that it's only one chapter in the book. It's not the book. I can't sacrifice one for the other, so I'm constantly balancing between the now and the larger picture. The now has to be engaging, but the larger picture is what's really important." George Lucas, quoted by Scott Chernoff in "The Plot Thickens," *Star Wars Insider*, July/August 2002.

INTRODUCTION

"Turning to the dark side" is an idiom derived from the pop culture success of *Star Wars*, referring to someone starting to act in a way that is harmful, destructive, or evil, as exemplified by Anakin Skywalker's transformation into Darth Vader. The meaning is easily inferred even by people who have not seen *Star Wars*. But even among those who grew up with and love the movies, few are able or willing to unpack exactly what happens to the story's central protagonist/antagonist as he adopts his dual identity (and how a less melodramatic version of the same thing happens all the time to people here in the real world when they surrender to emotions that inhibit their own consciousness).

What does *Star Wars* have to say about how a good person turns bad? How does someone begin to act in ways completely contradictory to how they did before, so set against what they claimed to care about and identify with? In *Star Wars*, the Force represents the spectrum of emotional influence experienced by sentient life forms, conscious beings like you and me. The dark side of the Force is an emotional state of resistance to vulnerability that suppresses consciousness and choice. If wholly indulged in, it leads to long-term personality distortion. The light is the opposite, consisting of the emotions that enable consciousness, self-awareness, and self-control. The Sith and Jedi are two opposing religious orders in the *Star Wars* universe that draw strength from these opposites, characterized most directly as the extremes of either greed at the lowest end of the spectrum or compassion at the highest.[5] The Sith represent the spiritual path of passionate indulgence in desire, and the Jedi the spiritual path of dispassion and denial. The war between the two sides, within the individual and out in society, is what we see play out across the films.

In cross-cultural myths and philosophies, light is associated with consciousness, while darkness is linked to unconsciousness. Light is the primary input to our sense organs, specifically our eyes. Where there is light, we can see. Thus, we are aware of what is going on. Where there is darkness, the ability to see is compromised or negated entirely. There is no more awareness. Those on the dark side are unconscious, unaware of what is going on within themselves, in their memory, and in the world around them. Those who remain in the light maintain their self-awareness and the ability to accurately assess reality through reflection upon their thoughts, emotions, and actions. As Yoda says to Luke on Dagobah, one can know the difference between the good side and the bad when their mind is calm, at peace, and passive.

In my opinion, *Star Wars* Episodes 1 through 6 contain the greatest narrative ever told on film concerning the transmission of themes and warnings essential to human character development. These films set the standard for the rest of Hollywood with Luke Skywalker's Hero's Journey a la Lucas' eventual friend, comparative mythologist Joseph Campbell, which provided a map of personal growth that reflects, in a universal way, the inner voyage a person takes as they expand beyond their present state of awareness and integrate deeper truths.[6] That's why it is so important to have emotionally resonant examples of its application, like Luke Skywalker, ingrained in our cultural consciousness. Campbell called his template the *monomyth*, indicating oneness or unity. Lucas applied his intimate knowledge of that pattern to craft the most effective practical application of it known to man.[7] I call Lucas' application a *metamyth*: a myth that encompasses and updates older myths, and a myth that stands above others in its scope and influence[8] for what has likely amounted to billions of people since 1977 by tapping into the universal experience of maturation (i.e., growing up) as a conscious being. His work is an ongoing demonstration of how myths evolve and recombine to remain relevant in the ever-changing human psyche.[9]

Star Wars does not just follow a predefined pattern, though. It also masterfully subverts the very expectations it helped establish about how the journey of a hero occurs by showing us the dark backstory of Luke's father, but not arbitrarily so. Anakin Skywalker does not fall to the dark side to be contrarian or just for the sake of it. The context of his fall illuminates and informs Luke's eventual triumph over the dark side and ascension to the state of self-determined hero.

As such, the experience of *Star Wars* is significantly influenced by the order in which one first watches the films, which is complicated by the fact that they were produced out of chronological order. Lucas began halfway through the story in 1977 with Episodes 4, 5, and 6 (collectively known as the original trilogy), and then returned two decades later to tell the beginning of the story with Episodes 1, 2, and 3 (collectively known as the prequel trilogy). I just think of them as the second and first half of the same integrated whole: a unified *hex*alogy rather than two separate *tri*logies.[10] Whatever other sequels, prequels, sidequels, and spinoffs might continue to be produced in the generations to come, these six will remain integral to the foundation that resulted from one man's evolving vision as a filmmaker and storyteller. Although your understanding of the characters and setting may differ, the story remains effective whether you start halfway through and then go back to the beginning (as many viewers did before the prequels were released) or watch them all from the chronological start to end. And though Lucas has stated he intends for audiences to experience the story beginning with Episode 1 and ending with Episode 6,[11] I have my own tested theory about an unexpected viewing order that, I believe, optimizes the *Star Wars* experience for first-time viewers who go into it completely ignorant of what's in store. I have included a detailed explanation of my preferred viewing order for first-time viewers in the first appendix at the end of this book, starting on page 205.

Star Wars is designed to reward repeat viewing, as long-time fans still discover new aspects of the highly intentional and reused dialogue (many such instances of which have been underlined throughout this book for emphasis),[12] visual, thematic, musical, and editing choices.[13] There are more layers of narrative meaning than casual fans or people who geek out over spaceship models, alien species, and droid designations are likely to ever notice. These six films, taken as one long and integrated narrative, remain engaging viewing. Like any great work of art, repeated exposure to it, under differing contexts, reveals more depth to the artist's vision.[14]

At the most obvious level of analysis, there are connections between the first, second, and third movies of each trilogy, showing up in Episodes 1 and 4, 2 and 5, and 3 and 6, respectively. At a deeper level, there are connections that are mirrored symmetrically at either end of the series, appearing in Episodes 1 and 6, 2 and 5, and 3 and 4, respectively.[15] Beneath all this, a throughline of metadevelopment emerges, beginning with Episode 1 and continuing uninterrupted until the closing moments of Episode 6, which depicts the childhood, adolescence, adulthood, eventual death, and afterlife of Anakin Skywalker.[16] It reaches through the screen and speaks to our evolving perspective across the six films as we have grown and matured alongside them, serving as their metatextual observer.

Even the music of *Star Wars* plays a crucial role in conveying subtle meaning. It provides emotional context and plays a significant part in indicating how we are supposed to feel about the events on screen. Ever since I was a boy, watching the original trilogy on my father's faint and grainy Betamax cassettes in the early 90s,[17] I have been fascinated by how John Williams' musical compositions conveyed the story's characters and themes. I found that I could listen to key portions of the soundtrack from all three films on vinyl record and recall with a high degree of accuracy when each musical cue occurred, what was happening on screen at the time, and which characters said which lines of dialogue to accompany it. It was like watching the movies and experiencing the story all over again just through the music. Later, I studied music theory and music history. I began to appreciate on a deeper level all the work that went into various leitmotifs and allusions to classical pieces by famous composers. With the release of the prequel trilogy and its many new musical compositions by Williams, it became evident to me how closely he must have worked with Lucas to ensure every single piece of music captured the nuances intended for the story.

Leitmotif, a practice originating in traditional opera, involves the use of a short piece of music that represents a recurring theme or character. When we hear it, we're being deliberately reminded of that person, feeling, concept, or event, which contributes to narrative cohesion of the story across the films. The intentional insertion of musical leitmotifs can even reveal intended connections from the creator that might not have been obvious from the visuals and dialogue. Once you associate *The Imperial March* with Darth Vader or the Force theme with Luke Skywalker looking longingly into the binary sunset of Tatooine, you can't remove the psychological connections. Would the same effect hold true for someone who had never seen the *Star Wars* movies but had heard the music? Could such a person derive the intended thematic representations without knowing the story context?

I had the opportunity to test this with a friend who is a classically trained opera singer. At 30, she had never seen any of the *Star Wars* films and had only vague familiarity with their plot and characters. Before showing her the movies, I had her listen to some of *Star Wars'* most narratively important pieces of music. I wanted to see her interpretation of what they represented, including the themes conveyed and the kinds of actions that might be happening as each piece is played. Until she heard the musical score, she had been convinced she would *not* enjoy the movies. The quality of the musical score convinced her to give the movies a chance, especially when she learned that *Star Wars* was considered to be a "space opera" due to its melodramatic storytelling style, grand thematic scope, and over-the-top character arcs and archetypes. Once we finished Episode 1, she wanted to binge-watch the next five films with me over the next two days.

After we finished, she went back to listen again to some of the same musical pieces she had heard before, now with the context of having seen how they are used in the films. She was stunned by how intricate and intentional some of the musical clues and connections were. For instance, though *The Imperial March* is first played in full military form in *The Empire Strikes Back* as the Imperial fleet searches for the Rebel base on Hoth, pieces of Vader's leitmotif had been present throughout Episodes 1 through 3: first in *Anakin's Theme*, the sweet, hopeful, and innocent piece that plays prominently in *The Phantom Menace* when little Ani is introduced and contains hints of a positive, major-key variant of the Vader theme. It then grows more prominent and distressed, transferring from major key to minor, as Anakin's dark side emerges within him in *Attack of the Clones* and especially as he betrays the Jedi in *Revenge of the Sith*. It closes out, with somber overtones, the physical transformation into Darth Vader as Anakin is entombed in the Vader suit, with clear allusions to Chopin's funeral march, showing that Darth Vader represents both the archetypal evocation of the death of the individual and the doling out of death to anyone who stands against him. Adopting Vader's musical cue as the march for the entire might of the Galactic Empire (or rather, vice versa, considering the production order of the movies) indicates an important connection between Anakin's personal spiritual corruption and the Republic's large-scale societal corruption. Musically, it represents not just Darth Vader, the man, as a terrifying villain, but the Vader *persona* slowly growing within

Anakin's shadow,[18] only to eventually take over in his most desperate moment. "Vader is written more like an insidious spiritual force than an actual person," my friend realized.

Mythological stories, such as *Star Wars*, influence human development by providing children (and adults, to the extent that they can maintain childlike curiosity and wonder) with narrative familiarity of developmental states they may not have directly experienced. Hero narratives prime the mind for new challenges, making them feel familiar ahead of time, as if it is a path someone has walked before. We remember simulated experiences as more manageable and familiar. Children cannot easily distinguish between reality and fiction, the real and the unreal, so the storyworld of *Star Wars* becomes indistinguishable from memory. If they grow up feeling a sense of fulfillment when they see the good guy save the world from the bad guy, or Luke Skywalker resisting the temptation to fall to the dark side and redeeming his father, that's who they will think they're supposed to be. That's the principle around which their ideas and emotional associations will self-organize. And no matter what else happens to them, even if they face extreme hardship, even if there's social pressure for them to act a certain way or be a certain thing, if their emotional associations with this grand heroic image that preceded the hardship are stronger, they will return to that as their standard for self-identification and resist the pull to the dark side.[19]

And it's the same if they grow up with Anakin Skywalker as a gruesome warning of what *not* to allow themselves to become by being trained to have a conscious negative reaction to the mistakes he makes, including seeing him burn alive in a literal hellscape of his own making as he proclaims his hatred for his mentor.[20] I have seen grown men start to reflect on the anger they harbored and emotionally rewire themselves after being exposed to the emotional imprint of Anakin's fall and realizing they didn't want to go down the same path, unraveling decades of generational hate and cultural conditioning in the process. These mythic stories steer moral development in the right direction, pursuing what is good in the world and avoiding the hot skillet of evil, thereby avoiding the risk of being burned along the way. *Star Wars* is exceptionally good at conveying heroic, mythic imagery to ordinary people who do not deliberately study such things, but are still sensitive to its mythic elements.

Young people watching *Star Wars* for the first time will identify most strongly with Anakin and Luke as the primary point-of-view characters at the start of their respective journeys. They are supposed to learn the same lessons as they watch the Skywalker boys grow into two very different types of men through the parallel narrative structure between the two trilogies. The first films (Episodes 1 and 4) represent the protagonists' first steps out of *childhood* innocence. The second films (Episodes 2 and 5) represent the trials of growing up in *adolescence* and having our naive perspective challenged and inverted. The third and final films (Episodes 3 and 6) represent the burdens of *adulthood* responsibilities and how we either crumble under their weight or rise up to meet them, ultimately shaping the kind of people we will be for the rest of our lives. That is where Anakin and Luke's paths diverge; understanding why makes all the difference.

For everyone's benefit, the setting of these movies is not limited to one earthly time or culture. It is an intentionally eclectic remix of influences from classic cinema and television, world history, and mythology, somehow old-fashioned and futuristic at the same time. That's why we can still watch the original trilogy today, some 50 years after its inception, and still feel immersed in it (some dated visual effects aside). The storyworld of a galaxy far, far away, I believe, will continue to prove to have more durable relatability and influence than almost any other provided on film, no matter when and where one experiences it.

Because I have had the opportunity to live in parts of the world where *Star Wars* is not as ubiquitous in popular culture as it is in the West, I have been able to introduce new audiences to the metamyth, people who have no cultural biases or preconceptions about it. Experiencing *Star Wars* vicariously through their virgin eyes has made me more sensitive to many things about it that those who grew up with the story take for granted, such as the central plot twist of the dual identity of Anakin Skywalker and Darth Vader (i.e., that the protagonist you thought was going to be the hero of the story instead turns out to be the antagonist and the villain) and the brutal realism of the Republic's corruption into a totalitarian empire.

In the West, where the sovereignty of consciousness is highly regarded, dictatorships and empires are often viewed as fantastical threats and exaggerated versions of our minor political problems. They are like dragons to us. We only know they are meant to represent the height of all danger, the hyperbolic apex of apex predators. None of us ever expects to face a dragon in real life. Viewers in parts of the world that have lived through or are currently living through totalitarianism respond to *Star Wars'* depiction of large-scale political corruption in a more immersive way due to their recent personal and cultural memory. The Galactic Empire is a real antagonist to them, and Palpatine's manipulations of the Senate are a real political threat to overcome.[21]

The long-term, cross-cultural success of *Star Wars* reflects an important universal truth about the human experience: the moral struggle to become and remain the people we are meant to be, which is to say who we are when we are fully self-expressed. I view it as the story of how individuals surrender to their insecurities and forfeit their heroic potential to enact their passions and values, and what it takes to avoid falling into that trap as we mature. *Star Wars* is a universal type of myth that can be identified and appreciated by people from any time or place.[22] Lucas believed that heroic stories matter for future generations, so we must continue to update and retell the myths that shape our collective sense of morality. Luke Skywalker saving the galaxy and overcoming impossible obstacles is a tale that we will pass down in our cultural mythology for generations to come, because, on some level, we believe it matters too.[23]

Recently, we have entered an era where it is popular to demythologize iconic characters and storytelling. Once larger-than-life mythic beings who broke past cycles and transformed their social order (including even Luke Skywalker) are being intentionally brought down to a more normal, human scale, repeating the same old struggles of the past and leaving us without ideal standards to compare ourselves to. Thus, it is even *more* important now that we work to understand the myths that have brought us here and keep them alive in our hearts and culture. In addition to this book's primary purpose of helping readers understand how the dark side of the Force manifests in their lives and in the lives of those they love, I hope it also allows fans of the saga to discover more hidden depth as they rewatch their favorite films. Perhaps it will help future generations derive greater personal meaning for so long as *Star Wars* endures in human culture, not just as a cinematic work of art but as part of a grand unifying myth of personal development.

NOTES

5. "The film is ultimately about the Dark Side and the light side, and those sides are designed around compassion and greed. And we all have those two sides of us and that we have to make sure that those two sides of us are in balance." George Lucas, interviewed by Bill Moyers, "Of Myth and Men," *Time*, April 18, 1999.

6. The idea that different cultures' myths share common features, to be explained either by a shared origin or a form of convergent evolution toward the same destination in the human psyche, long predates and influenced Campbell's formation of the monomyth, notably the work by psychoanalysts, sociologists, and folklorists like James George Frazer, The Brothers Grimm, Sigmund Freud, Otto Rank, Carl Jung, Émile Durkheim, Lord Raglan, and many others. Lucas certainly understood and was influenced by this: "The drama is archetypal. Its roots go deep into the mythic past we all share." George Lucas, interviewed in *From Star Wars to Jedi: The Making of a Saga*, directed by LeVar Burton (Los Angeles, Calif.: Lucasfilm Ltd., 1983), documentary film.

7. The spread of new ideas has often depended on the successful implementation of those ideas by someone close to the discoverer or innovator. Professor Andrew J. Galambos, in Course V-50 (*Sic Itur Ad Astra*, San Diego: Spaceland Publications, 2024) referred to this as "the disclosure barrier," citing the historical example of Isaac Newton identifying universal laws of motion and gravitation for the first time, which unified previously disparate sets of ideas about the physical world (much like how Campbell's monomyth unified separate cultures' mythologies). It took Newton's friend, astronomer Edmond Halley, applying his work to predict the timing of the return of a comet, a feat previously thought to be impossible, for the public to accept Newton's ideas. One man was an inventor of an intellectual tool or framework; the other was a craftsman who used that tool to accomplish something of cultural significance that no one had ever done before. I see the relationship between Campbell and Lucas as similar, and I wonder if Campbell's work might not be nearly as known and respected today were it not for Lucas and the success of *Star Wars*.

8. "There's a mixture of all kinds of mythology and religious beliefs that have been amalgamated into [*Star Wars*] and I have tried to take the ideas that seem to cut across the most cultures because I am fascinated by that. And I think that is one of the things I really got from Joe Campbell. What he was trying to do was find the

common threads through the various mythologies, through the various religions." George Lucas, interviewed by Bill Moyers, "*The Mythology of Star Wars,*" PBS, June 18, 1999.

9. "If [*Star Wars*] is a tool that can be used to make old stories be new and relate to younger people, that's what the whole point was." George Lucas, interviewed by Bill Moyers, "*The Mythology of Star Wars,*" PBS, June 18, 1999.

10. "I do see [*Star Wars*], tonality-wise, as two trilogies. But they do, together, form one epic of fathers and sons." George Lucas, quoted by Jim Windolf, "*Star Wars: The Last Battle,*" *Vanity Fair*, February 1, 2005, 110.

11. "You gotta remember this is one movie, and it's meant to be seen one through six. So I think when you watch the actual movie in order, the story will become very clear..." George Lucas, interview in *The Chosen One*, featurette on *Star Wars: Episode III – Revenge of the Sith* (DVD, Lucasfilm Ltd., 2005).

12. "It's very, very clear in the two trilogies that I'm putting the characters in pretty much the same situations, sometimes even using the same dialogue, so that the father and son go through pretty much the same experience." George Lucas, commentary on *Star Wars: Episode I – The Phantom Menace* (DVD, Lucasfilm Ltd., 2001).

13. Rick Worley's *Every Time Star Wars Quotes Star Wars* video on YouTube (https://youtu.be/AAAoqrCLC-E) offers a comprehensive two-hour montage of hundreds of instances across the six films of characters repeating or paraphrasing lines of dialogue or the framing of shots being reused in different contexts. His *Every Time Star Wars Quotes Other Movies* video (https://youtu.be/MSnuP5Xq3rg) accomplishes a similar task for references and homages to George Lucas' primary cinematic influences. Furthermore, his *How to Watch Star Wars* series (https://youtu.be/vqnjzVX8EKA) elaborates on the importance of these inclusions in how we ought to interpret Lucas' movies according to his intentions as an auteur filmmaker.

14. "There's a lot going on [in *Star Wars*] that most people haven't come to grips with yet. But when they do, they will find it's a much more intricately made clock than most people would imagine." George Lucas, quoted by Jim Windolf, "*Star Wars: The Last Battle,*" *Vanity Fair*, February 1, 2005, 116.

15. The bookended and mirrored connections across the films was first brought to my attention by Mike Klimo's *Star Wars Ring Theory* essay (www.starwarsringtheory.com), written in 2014. His analysis attributes this to an ancient storytelling technique called ring composition, also known as chiastic structure, in which a narrative's elements are arranged in a symmetrical pattern, with the central idea placed at

the core around which everything else revolves. The beginning reflects the end, and the two meet in the middle.

16. "It has the epic quality of following one person from the time he's nine years old to the time he dies. It's Anakin's story, but obviously there are many other characters in that story — his children, his best friend — and their stories carry through." George Lucas, quoted by J. W. Rinzler, *The Making of Star Wars: Revenge of the Sith* (New York: Del Rey, 2005), 221.

17. The original trilogy films were first released on retail VHS in 1984 (Episodes 4 and 5) and 1986 (Episode 6), before I was born in 1988. My father, who worked for Blockbuster Video, used his connections in the movie rental industry to obtain early pirated copies of the 1982 rental-only Betamax releases of *A New Hope* and *The Empire Strikes Back*, years before the public could own the movies on home video. Thus, my earliest memories of watching *Star Wars* came from old Betamax cassettes with handwritten labels. I recall it being a pretty momentous occasion when we finally upgraded to the THX remastered VHS box set (the one featuring the faces of Darth Vader, a stormtrooper, and Yoda) of all three films for Christmas 1995, and we finally had the real deal for seven-year-old me to watch on a loop and wear out. That was the first time I got to see how the unexpected and culturally defining way Luke and Vader's story ended, not knowing then how that mythic, emotionally resonant image would stay with me and influence my understanding of relationships and self-actualization in the decades to come.

18. In Jungian psychology, upon which much of Campbell's Hero's Journey is based, the shadow is the part of personality that contains traits a person rejects or fails to recognize in themselves because it does not fit who they prefer to think of themselves as (or who they are *supposed* to be). Under stress, the unconscious aspects of personality can surface in a chaotic manner, just as we see happen when Anakin faces situations that he is unprepared for the burden of calmly dealing with, such as with his mother in the Tusken camp, or when forced to side with either Windu or Palpatine in their duel. In Anakin's case, the shadow takes over as Vader once he lets it out completely in Episode 3. It's especially fitting then that marketing for Episode 1 featured the silhouette of the Vader suit in young Anakin's shadow, and that the outline of the Vader helmet can be seen in Anakin's side profile shadow in the light of Tatooine's setting suns.

19. "Storytelling is about imparting the wisdom of the previous generation onto the children who are becoming adults and giving them a context for how to behave

and how to learn the lessons of the past without making the mistakes on their own." George Lucas, quoted by Jon Favreau in *"Jon Favreau Shares Advice George Lucas Gave Him About His 'Star Wars' Show." Uproxx*, July 25, 2019.

20. "Societies have a whole series of stories to bring adolescents into adulthood by saying, 'Don't worry, everybody thinks that way. You're just part of the community. We don't quite talk about it, but if you act on some of your notions, here's what will happen: Zeus will reach down and smash you flat like a bug or the entire Greek army will come and crush your city and burn everybody inside of it, including your heroes.'" George Lucas, interviewed in *"George Lucas on Star Wars, Fahrenheit 9/11, and His Own Legacy," Wired*, May 31, 2005.

21. "I only hope that those who have seen *Star Wars* recognize the Emperor when they see him." George Lucas, interviewed by Bill Bradley for *American Voices*, November 15, 2015.

22. "I really tried to take the psychological motifs from mythology all over the world. As a result, I was able to take ideas that go through all societies, through all the ages, and bring them down and put them into a razzle-dazzle Saturday matinee serial action-adventure film." George Lucas, interviewed by Bill Bradley for *American Voices*, November 15, 2015.

23. "I'm hoping that *Star Wars* doesn't become too dated, because I think its themes are timeless. If you've raised children, you know you have to explain things to them, and if you don't, they end up learning the hard way. In the end, somebody's got to say, 'Don't touch that hot skillet.' So the old stories have to be reiterated again in a form that's acceptable to each new generation. I don't think I'm ever going to go much beyond the old stories, because I think they still need to be told." George Lucas, interviewed in *"George Lucas on Star Wars, Fahrenheit 9/11, and His Own Legacy," Wired*, May 31, 2005.

ANAKIN'S CHILDHOOD

The unexpected and uncomfortable message of *Star Wars* is that Darth Vader, that great and awful villain, is a part of everyone. That's the lesson Luke Skywalker must learn when he discovers the truth of what happened to his father. Vader lives in our friends, our spouses, our parents, and even our innocent young children, too. He will always be a threat if we do not teach them how to defend against his influence. He doesn't always look like murder, rage, subjugation, or the other horrendous qualities he's known for on screen. He is the total amalgamation of personality traits that result when people let their insecurities get the better of them. Vader's influence causes people in emotionally compromised states to partake in extreme behaviors that would have been beyond their character when they were confident and in control of themselves.

Everyone is guilty of momentary lapses in moral judgment and self-awareness. They do not necessarily distort personality or character, provided they are eventually reflected upon and integrated back into reality. Truly *turning* to the dark side means a sustained loss of conscious self-awareness and control over cognitive processes, stemming from the inability to regulate emotions into their most useful, moral, and healthy form. It manifests most obviously as extreme fear, anger, and, of course, hatred, but it also encompasses every insecurity that has not yet been resolved, lying dormant in a person's mind. Turning to the dark side means surrendering to emotional defense mechanisms and becoming the version of yourself in least control of your own actions because your consciousness is not fully functional.

All evil results from an incomplete person compensating for emotional trauma and lack of self-awareness. No villain, in fiction or history, has ever been secure and at peace with themselves, fully mature in their self-expression. Everything villainous they did was, by necessity, a product of their incomplete self-actualization. As turning to the dark side is a product of emotional immaturity, the only defense is emotional maturation, which enables self-actualization and which begins while we are still young and immature. Emotional maturity leads to an understanding of what you truly care about on the deepest level, your fundamental values, and an increasing ability to willfully pursue and embody them. To mature is to grow, to evolve, to progress into a more ordered, complex, and useful state as the structure of your identity expands according to the blueprint of who you really are. Denying, suppressing, or misusing any emotion is a symptom of emotional immaturity and poor emotional management. The Jedi have learned to suppress the emotions they believe they cannot control. The Sith, meanwhile, use the very same emotions to attempt to dominate what scares them. Both are operating out of fear.

When an exceptional person becomes a slave to suppressive emotions, their corruption is likewise exceptional. That's the story of Anakin Skywalker, the boy who never had the opportunity to develop the emotional resilience that would have allowed him to live up to his grand heroic potential until the very end of his life. The story of the man who would become Darth Vader begins when he is just nine years old. It goes against all genre convention to have the moviegoing audience get attached to a selfless and gifted child, and then to watch that child grow up to become the epitome of corruption and evil instead of the archetypal hero.

The first episode of *Star Wars* is told from a childish perspective. It adopts a childlike tone, tailored for young audiences who are being introduced to this storyworld for the first time with innocent expectations. The young viewer is eager to see what comes next in this adventure, which will grow progressively darker, more serious, and more grounded, reflecting their changing lens of awareness as they grow older and wrestle with the weight of life as it unfolds. The opening movement of the first film establishes a manufactured political crisis. What appears to be a localized trade dispute is actually the visible surface of a hidden consolidation of power into the hands of Sith Lord Darth Sidious, in the guise of kindly Senator Palpatine. He will escalate the Trade Federation's blockade of Naboo into a full-scale invasion and takeover, which he will use to create a political crisis and a Separatist movement to secede from the Republic, resulting in full-scale galactic war.

Obi-Wan Kenobi's first spoken line is a phrase that will be repeated or paraphrased at least once in every episode of the Lucas hexalogy to represent anxiety about the future: He has a bad feeling about what's happening. Even though Obi-Wan's anxieties about the future are based on a real threat, they are manifesting in a general and inactionable way, the only result being that he is less prepared to deal with the issues of the moment as they arise. Mindfulness about the future should never come at the expense of the moment, teaches Jedi Master Qui-Gon Jinn to his apprentice. The ability to fully experience the present moment is a product of high consciousness and self-awareness, of not allowing yourself to be a slave to your emotions but also not being afraid to fully feel them as they occur. This is what Qui-Gon deems as being in tune with the Living Force: consciousness in the moment, as channeled through and generated by living beings, which is presented as distinct from the Cosmic Force that composes all the energy in the universe around them. These distinctions are analogous to our sciences of biology and physics, life and energy, clueing us into the fact that the Force is not meant to be interpreted as some elusive, unknowable, unreal spiritual presence, but as something that is a fundamental part of our real, tangible world that we navigate through and that our bodies evolve out of.

On their forced detour to Tatooine, Qui-Gon and Obi-Wan are befriended by a young slave working in a junk shop, nine-year-old Anakin Skywalker, and taken into his home. Anakin's mother, Shmi, describes her son as <u>knowing nothing of greed</u>, giving without any thought of reward. In his innocent and predeveloped state, little Ani has never had a reason to feel insecure. He has maintained his purity of heart despite his condition as a slave. In fact, he does not dream of his *own* freedom, but of becoming a Jedi so that he can come back to Tatooine and free all the slaves someday. To him, a Jedi is an invincible hero, a mythic being, an unkillable figure who has conquered even death. He is a boy who believes that the biggest problem in the galaxy is that nobody helps each other, who is so sensitive to the world that he can see things before they happen. This is who Anakin Skywalker is, authentically at his core.[24] His mother's love has been an emotional shell for Anakin, keeping him soft and protected in a coarse and irritating world. Due to her protection, he has never had anything to become possessive of, with the sole exception of his all-important relationship with his mother.

But there is a phantom limitation to Anakin's development, one that has not yet factored much into it but will soon become the deciding factor in the path his life will take (and the state of the galaxy with it). Anakin has never been taken outside the confines of his starting conditions, so he does not know what lies beyond his microcosm of junk traders, moisture farmers, gangsters, and gamblers on Tatooine. He has no vision of a future outside of what little he knows, an example of what he can and should become as he grows, except for the fanciful tales of heroism he has grown up hearing about the Jedi.

Only Qui-Gon can see a greater destiny for young Anakin when he identifies him as not only exceptionally kindhearted but also unusually strong with the Force. He confirms that the midi-chlorian count in Anakin's blood, the quantity of microscopic organisms that exist symbiotically in all life and silently communicate the will of the Force, is higher than that of all known Jedi, <u>even Grandmaster Yoda</u>,[25] which leads him to believe that his father must have been an exceptionally powerful Jedi, too. Shmi confides in him that Anakin had no father; she miraculously became pregnant with him all on her own. Anakin is so exceptional that he could not have been conceived by mortal man. This fact represents, in a physiological kind of way, his role of breaking with the chains of the past that are carried forth in each new generation. If he is not born of the seed of ordinary men, he does not have to carry their baggage, their sins, their point of view, and their way of seeing and doing things. His surname, Skywalker, hints at this: one who walks above the rest of us, practically on a different plane of reality and a sort of demigod among us. He is the blank slate and the fresh start that the Jedi and Republic desperately need, here to bring about true transformation and revolution, even just by existing. He is a direct manifestation of the will of the Force through its miraculous interaction in the biology of his mother, according to Qui-Gon's interpretation of the Jedi prophecy of the Chosen One.[26]

Anakin is a boy without a father. And how does a boy become a man except by having the example of a father figure, a paragon, to look up to, to guide him through the hard times ahead in his emotional development, to teach him to master himself, and to give him a shining example of what he should become, not via cultural conditioning or social coercion to be a certain way but because the growing boy recognizes a more developed version of his own essential nature in the one he looks up to? In a few years, Anakin will be a teenager. His focus will shift away from the conditions under which he was nurtured and toward the unknown galaxy all around him, from his past to his future, the world that will force him to grow in response to challenge, stress, and injury. But if he begins that initiatory journey too soon, before he has matured enough to feel fully nurtured and self-assured, he will build his character atop a shaky emotional foundation.[27]

As Anakin prepares to race at speeds too fast for ordinary humans at the Boonta Eve Classic podrace, Qui-Gon steps into the father role to tell him to concentrate on the moment, to feel what is happening and use his instincts instead of constantly trying to anticipate what *will* happen—in other words, to feel the Force flowing through him and trust himself. This, Qui-Gon believes, is the factor that will ensure Anakin wins the race against older, more experienced, and more aggressive opponents like Sebulba. The Force is so naturally strong with Anakin that all he has to do is quiet his mind and listen to how it communicates. What matters for the story is not the external contest that secures his freedom, but the psychological lesson embedded in it: When Anakin trusts his instincts and remains present, he acts with clarity and effectiveness. His owner, Watto, serves as a contrasting warning about what happens when someone is so greedy that their lust for more causes them to lose everything when he bets against Anakin winning the race.

Anakin will now be called to leave his ordinary world behind and be trained as a Jedi under Qui-Gon, putting him on the path to fulfill his exceptional potential. His mother reminds him that <u>the choice to take the path placed before him is his to make</u>. She has given Anakin the responsibility of choice for the first time in his young life. She is treating him like an adult when he is, in no way, ready to act like one. Acting on his newfound freedom will invite more change than he has ever known and require him to <u>let go</u> of his only stable source of love, identification, and attachment: his mother. It represents his first step out of childhood, a step he is taking too soon to realize its responsibilities and consequences. But Shmi insists that it is already time for her son to let go of the only earthly attachment he has ever known so that he will not be limited by where he comes from. She reminds him that, like the setting of Tatooine's twin suns, he <u>cannot stop change</u>. The rest of Anakin's story, until his death, will be about his quest to test the validity of that premise, seeing if it's actually possible to become powerful enough to stop the changes everyone else accepts as inevitable, including even death.[28]

Anakin's surrogate father on his Jedi path <u>makes Shmi a promise to watch after him</u>, but it is a promise he will not be able to keep. And everything will change because of the loss of this would-be father figure, the only person in the galaxy besides his mother who believes in Anakin's potential and is prepared to do what is necessary to nurture it. Even Obi-Wan does not see the potential that Qui-Gon does, and he is not eager to take on the challenges and responsibilities that such a gifted child will bring to their ragtag family unit.

Anakin, too, makes an important promise to his mother, one that he will not be able to keep, at least not in the way he means: <u>the promise to come back and free her</u>. The consequences of that failure will be painful enough to alter his and the galaxy's destiny. And though Shmi urges her son not to look back as he walks out of her life, not to focus on the past when it is the future he is supposed to be heading into, he will continue looking back on her in his thoughts and dreams in the years to come.

As Anakin takes his first steps outside the home he has always known, he is attacked by Darth Maul, who may very well have killed him had Qui-Gon not been able to leap into action to defend him. Anakin's very first lesson is that life outside what he has known is dangerous, and it is only with the intervention of a protector that he will survive long enough to become capable of defending himself. The same lesson will be repeated with Luke in *A New Hope* as he takes his first steps outside the confines of home into Mos Eisley Spaceport and is accosted by strangers at a bar simply for existing out of place.

Though there is only a five-year age difference between Anakin and 14-year-old Padmé Amidala, it is enough at this early stage of development that she, still barely a teenager, is much more physically developed, emotionally mature, and experienced in life than he is, far enough above Anakin to act as a stand-in maternal figure for him. He has not grown up at all yet, and she has had to grow up too fast.

He <u>feels cold</u> for the first time in his life in space, a physical symptom of his separation trauma and sudden emotional insecurity. He comes from a warm planet, reflecting the love and warmth he has felt from his mother's presence all his life on Tatooine. Anakin, the young boy, is alone and insecure for the first time in his life, in the void of outer space, disconnected from all he has known. Padmé is the new source of feminine warmth and comfort in his life, making him feel secure when nothing else will.

When Anakin is evaluated by the Jedi Council, we see the limitations of an institution that has lost contact with ordinary human development and forgotten how to see possibilities beyond their own doctrine. They forbid Qui-Gon from training Anakin, as they insist that <u>taking on a second padawan is impossible</u> simply because the Jedi code forbids it. They have confused what is possible with what they are comfortable with. The Jedi have been cut off from emotional attachment for so long that they have lost their sensitivity to ordinary, healthy human emotions, particularly those related to human connection. They are bewildered that Anakin admits to missing his mother, as though this should be a noteworthy characteristic for a nine-year-old boy who has been separated from her for the first time in his life. Yoda even accuses the child standing before him of being afraid to lose her and, therefore, being influenced by this negative emotion.

What the Jedi have forgotten over generations of indoctrination is that negative emotions are not enemies, and it does no good to deny them. So long as a person is emotionally integrated,[29] such feelings will pass once expressed. They serve their purpose and then leave. Trauma only occurs when negative emotions persist beyond the point where they are useful, when they cannot be easily shut off or reactivated when appropriate. Such is the path that Yoda, Grandmaster of the Jedi Council, foresees for Anakin when assessing him. Yoda identifies <u>fear as the path to the dark side</u>, claiming that it leads to all the more extreme symptoms of unconsciousness and losing self-control, like anger, hate, and suffering.

Fear, mismanaged, is the first thing to detach consciousness from reality, allowing for autonomous impulses to hijack our minds and, eventually, our actions. What follows are increasing levels of resistance against a reality we do not wish to deal with. Suffering results from the refusal to live in reality and from living in active defiance of it, even. The fear response in the face of uncertainty, discomfort, or pain is a natural and healthy reaction. However, when we organize our lives around avoiding what we fear rather than integrating it into our worldview, we set ourselves on a perilous path that will ultimately result in a total disconnect. We become rigid, defensive, and eventually aggressive in our attempts to make reality conform to our needs. We live in a constant state of panic, seeing enemies where there are none and perceiving danger all around that must be forced into submission and controlled. It's the formation of a dictatorship over reality within the human psyche.

Though the Council cannot help but be impressed with Anakin's natural strength with the Force, they also feel threatened by him and decline to train him because he is too old. The Jedi seek out Force-sensitive younglings across the galaxy to take them from their homes and begin their Jedi training as early as possible. Their intuitive mastery of the Force is exceptional because they have no conscious memories of never having had it. The Council is not concerned about Anakin's ability to catch up to other padawans who started before him. We will see that by the time of *Attack of the Clones,* Anakin will outperform the other learners his age, despite his late start. By the time of *Revenge of the Sith,* he will have become a legend within the Jedi Order. They are worried about the emotional attachments he has already formed in his childhood outside their restrictive ideology.[30] They are not prepared to raise him to manage his emotional attachments. The only path the

Jedi know is emotional abstinence. Anakin is not predestined for evil, but Yoda believes that his future is clouded. When Anakin is an adult, Yoda will warn him to be careful when sensing the future, for the fear and anxiety it brings about may ironically play a part in actualizing the very future one is trying to avoid, which is a state that Yoda himself has grown too arrogant to see now applies to him.

Away from the chamber, Obi-Wan also argues that Anakin is dangerous and should not be trained, but this <u>is only true from Obi-Wan's point of view</u>. According to the limits of Obi-Wan and the other Jedi's ability to understand, the only outcome of training Anakin is danger. The positive alternative, the one where Anakin masters the emotional lessons he will need to harness his potential, requires a father figure and mentor with more of a particular type of wisdom than the dogmatic Jedi are prepared to offer. Qui-Gon has this wisdom and, therefore, a different point of view about training Anakin. If the Jedi train Anakin the only way they know how, the outcome will be danger. They should be willing to adapt their techniques for the individual placed before them instead of trying to force him to fit what they are comfortable with and experienced with. Whether Anakin lives up to his potential as the Chosen One and hero of the Jedi or falls into darkness as the Sith Lord Darth Vader will depend upon the community influence he receives. Only Qui-Gon is prepared to play the role of the father that an exceptional boy like Anakin so desperately needs because only he has broken himself free from Jedi dogma.

While the Republic senators debate the Trade Federation's invasion with newly appointed Supreme Chancellor Palpatine in power, Queen Amidala makes an unexpected move by deciding to return to Naboo to free her people directly with the help of the Gungans to end the occupation by the Trade Federation's battle droids. The Gungans are what the Trade Federation considers a primitive race, living beneath the surface of Naboo's waters and incapable of posing a threat to their technologically advanced army. Both here and again in Episode 6 with the Ewoks on Endor, we will see so-called primitives come together with heroes who were willing to overlook their initial impressions to outwit a machine-like invading force as bookends to the saga. They represent a primal and animalistic aspect of sentience that our protagonists must reconcile with, rather than deny or oppose, so that there can be integrity and symbiosis between the two.[31] As the Gungan leader, Boss Nass, puts it, the big-brained surface dwellers of Naboo must not think they are greater than them, that their rational faculties are somehow above and independent of the animal nature from which they emerge. The battle droids they will face off against are machines with an artificial form of programmed intelligence but no animal nature and, therefore, no sentience brought about by natural evolutionary processes.

During the Battle of Naboo, Anakin inadvertently activates the autopilot of a Naboo N-1 starfighter and launches into the battle against the Trade Federation's droid control ship. Anakin is spiraling out of control amid the chaos of the dogfight until he instructs R2-D2 to deactivate the autopilot, allowing him to take control of the vessel and start treating the machine as a tool that serves his consciousness instead of letting it control him. Like in the podrace before, he follows Qui-Gon's advice about trusting his own instincts instead of mindlessly following the path of the other pilots, who are being gunned down in their feeble attempt to penetrate the control ship's deflector shield. He displays no fear and does not even seem to fully register the danger he is in, laughing and enjoying the adventure like a child playing with his toys as he spins and performs tricks while expertly avoiding enemy fire. His focus is determining his reality. If he perceives the dangerous battle as fun and games, that's what it will be for him. Enthusiasm in the face of the unknown is something only a child who has never lost anything can experience. He has never reached his limits and felt the pain of failure. It is a far cry from the weight of impending doom that Luke will carry with him when he joins the first major battle of his life in the Rebel assault against the Death Star in Episode 4. Anakin effortlessly destroying the droid control ship from inside marks the beginning of a pattern in *Star Wars*, how what seem to be impossible obstacles for ordinary people become surmountable once someone shifts their point of view to consider new facts, perspectives, or abilities.

On the surface of Naboo, the duel of Qui-Gon and Obi-Wan against Darth Maul rages deep inside the power generator complex of Theed Royal Palace until master, padawan, and opponent are separated by a rotating shield wall. During this brief intermission, where Maul can no longer attack, Qui-Gon takes the opportunity to meditate, which allows the aggression that has been building in him through extended combat to dissipate so that he will be able to remain calm in the rest of the duel that follows. Maul, however, as a follower of the Sith spiritual path, draws his strength from that building passion. He paces anxiously back and forth like a jungle cat, waiting for the red shield wall to turn off again. Both can feel the Force flowing through them, but Qui-Gon remains calm and still in the intensity of that stimulation, while Maul uses it to propel his forward momentum through his aggression and attacks.

Throughout the duel, Qui-Gon has seen how Obi-Wan has struggled to keep pace with their attacker. He knows his padawan is the weakest link in the fight and will be the obvious target for their attacker. He would rather fight alone than risk his surrogate son being in danger. Thus, he does not wait for Obi-Wan to catch up to the fight before pushing Maul deeper into the complex, away from Obi-Wan and the shield wall cutting him off from them. Though Qui-Gon hoped to end the fight quickly, Maul instead gains the upper hand by studying his moves carefully, disorienting him while he is distracted thinking about Obi-Wan and fatally stabbing him. There is a look of shock and devastation on Qui-Gon's face as he falls to the floor, as though he has just realized what a terrible mistake he has made by miscalculating the risk posed to him by choosing to fight alone and not treating Obi-Wan like an adult who has the right to choose to die for what he believes in. Obi-Wan screams an impassioned "Noooo!" from the other side of the shield wall as he witnesses the fall of his master, mentor, and father figure.

Not a single word has been spoken between Maul and his Jedi opponents. The dynamic is elemental, with no personal identity involved in their rivalry. Maul is pure, embodied hatred toward everything the Jedi stand for. He has no reason to personally antagonize Qui-Gon or Obi-Wan. He is a slave responding to emotional programming placed into him by his Sith master, Darth Sidious. His permanently yellow eyes, a sign of spiritual corruption resulting from immersion in the dark side, reflect this state.

Now filled with grief and rage, Obi-Wan is clearly being influenced by the dark side, but he lacks the experience of his enemy to wield it effectively. He ignites his lightsaber first, just before the shield wall deactivates again, and becomes the aggressor against the man who just killed someone he loves. He fights harder and more recklessly, giving him a temporary advantage, but it's not a natural way for him to fight, not like the calm and defensive mastery he will become known for as a Jedi Master. Obi-Wan pushes too fast and too hard, leaving him open to counterattack and allowing Maul to push him over the edge of an endless pit below.

While Maul is distracted by his pride in a premature victory, Obi-Wan finally listens to the wisdom of his master, just as Anakin did before him: to stay calm and focus on the moment. He leaps from the pit, flips over Maul, and summons Qui-Gon's lightsaber with the Force. Though Maul should have time to react to this sequence of events, he is too stunned by this impossible feat to do anything about it, allowing Obi-Wan to slice him in half, his body plummeting into the abyss below that Obi-Wan himself had been at the mercy of only moments ago. The first major sudden reversal of *Star Wars* has occurred.

Qui-Gon, in his dying breaths, makes Obi-Wan <u>promise to train Anakin</u>, not because he believes he is the most appropriate mentor for him, but because he believes there is no other choice. If Obi-Wan does not take up the task, no one else will, and Anakin will be sent back to his life on Tatooine, never to develop his potential. Even if other Jedi were willing, they would be too indoctrinated in the Jedi way of emotional denial to give Anakin the specific guidance he would need to manage the emotional connections he has made. Any other Jedi would teach Anakin to suppress his empathy and emotions, the very sensitivity that makes him who he is. Qui-Gon's desperate hope is that he has passed on enough of his rebellious and anti-dogmatic ways to his padawan, that he will be able to give Anakin some of the guidance that the rest of the Jedi Order is incapable of. He passes the burden of fatherhood onto his grown son, despite him being neither ready nor particularly enthusiastic about it, except out of a sense of obligation to his master.

Anakin was taken from his mother with the promise that he would be given the father he needed, but he ended up with an unready older brother instead. Despite the best of intentions, we will see that Obi-Wan lacks the life experience and wisdom of the father figure he briefly shared with Anakin. He will fail to be the caretaker Anakin needs in order to develop into the best version of himself, for his clouded future to end up in the light instead of the dark. Might Anakin even have been better off being returned to his mother if he did not have another caretaker who was prepared for the burden of raising someone so special?

Qui-Gon's physical presence in *Star Wars* proves to be relatively minor, in the sense that he only appears in the first of six movies. Despite this, his influence lingers like a ghost over the rest of the story, much like the Force spirit that he will eventually be revealed to be the first Jedi to appear as before passing this ability on to Yoda and Obi-Wan. We are left now to wonder how differently Anakin's development would have turned out had Qui-Gon been his master. He embodied what the Jedi should have been from the beginning, coming full circle with the character Luke develops by the end of Episode 6 as a more enlightened form of Jedi who will rebuild and redefine the Order without the weakness that allowed the Sith and the dark side to rise up and destroy it. Qui-Gon was the paragon Anakin needed, the proper role model and father figure that would have shown him how to handle the responsibility of being who he is.

A paragon is a hero who has reached the end of their heroic trials and proven themselves worthy of the ideals they seek to embody. Traditionally, we don't follow the paragon's story. We follow the new up-and-coming hero who needs mentorship from an unconflicted soul. The mentor needs to be the guiding star for someone who is still unsure of their place in the cosmic order and how they will grow strong enough to remain true to their path atop a stable foundation of identity and values. *Star Wars* accomplishes the rare feat of showing us directly on screen what characters like Obi-Wan and Yoda have to endure before they are ready to be the type of teachers Luke will need them to be by the time of Episodes 4, 5, and 6. And we can directly contrast that with how unprepared they were for leading Luke's father just one generation prior. They fail to play their role for Anakin when he needs them to most.

Obi-Wan is too young and inexperienced, only 16 years older than Anakin, which is not quite enough of an age and experience difference to make for a proper father figure. Yoda, more than eight centuries older, is more like a stubborn old grandfather. He has become blinded by the sameness of his prolonged experience, which has led to dogma and bureaucracy. He is not adaptable enough to recognize the need to break with tradition and that the old ways that have worked for most every other Jedi will not work the same for someone exceptional like Anakin, on whose future the life of the Order and balance in the Force itself depend. Qui-Gon is the only one in the story who could have possibly filled that role.

Yoda, at last, reluctantly considers that Anakin may indeed be the Chosen One. Regardless, he <u>fears grave danger in his training</u>. Vader's musical theme plays quietly and briefly as Yoda voices this fear aloud, subtly clueing us into the fact that Vader is not the man, but the emotional principle behind him, the fear from which he manifests. Obi-Wan now carries the strength of his father figure's conviction in his words. He gave Qui-Gon his word and will train Anakin, even if he has to defy the Council to do so. He is not taking these drastic actions out of love and concern for the upbringing of the exceptional child like Qui-Gon was. He is only doing so out of loyalty to his fallen master. Obi-Wan is not acting authentically, and his inauthenticity will show in every aspect of how he raises Anakin.[32]

Obi-Wan approaches Anakin at Qui-Gon's funeral pyre to affirm his fate and the awkward sibling relationship that will define them both. Their father is dead, and with his death, Anakin's naivety about the invincibility of the Jedi and the conquerability of death is shattered. He has taken a huge step out of childhood illusions and into brutal adulthood realities too soon. He worries about what will happen to him without the one man who saw his potential, the one man who believed in him enough to free him from slavery and risk everything to train him as a Jedi. Obi-Wan steps up and <u>promises that Anakin will be a Jedi.</u> *Qui-Gon's Funeral* plays, with an intense and solemn choir carrying the weight of the great Jedi who has been lost, including everything he represented. The same musical requiem and warning will return to lament the loss of another great Jedi in the conclusion of Episode 3.

Following Qui-Gon's funeral, our heroes celebrate their apparent victory over the Trade Federation with the Gungans on Naboo. *Augie's Great Municipal Band* starts playing, the first of three celebratory finale scores we will hear across *Star Wars*, at the end of Episodes 1, 4, and 6, respectively. The tone is completely opposite to the striking and somber funeral piece we just heard. Hidden within this jovial tune is a major-key variant of *The Emperor's Theme* that will reappear throughout the saga as Sidious rises to power in Episodes 2 and 3 and again when Luke confronts him in *Return of the Jedi*. This early victory celebration is misguided. Our heroes are making the same mistake Maul just did by taking pride in a premature victory, which prevents them from seeing the hidden threat of the dark side looming over the galaxy as a whole and within young Anakin. Conditions have already been set for it to grow in power and eventually take over in a total structural collapse for both. And just as the Jedi Council did not believe that the Sith, the agents of unconsciousness, could have returned without them knowing, they will refuse to see that their prodigy and Chosen One is becoming the very thing he was meant to destroy instead, because to do so would be to acknowledge their own limitations. That requires a level of self-reflection they are not yet ready for.

NOTES

24. "How did [Anakin] get to be Darth Vader? You have to explore him in relationships, and you have to see where he started. He was a sweet kid, helpful, just like most people imagine themselves to be. Most people said, 'This guy must have been a horrible little brat -- a demon child.' But the point is, he wasn't born that way -- he became that way and thought he was doing the right thing." George Lucas, interviewed in "*George Lucas on Star Wars, Fahrenheit 9/11, and His Own Legacy*," *Wired*, May 31, 2005.

25. Members of Yoda's species are presented in extended canon materials as having a strong biological predisposition to the Force. They also have an extended lifespan (Yoda is over 900 years old by the time he dies in *Return of the Jedi*), so they have more time to develop mastery of the Force. Thus, it is virtually inconceivable that any member of a common humanoid species could ever approach Yoda's power by natural means, making him the standard by which many Jedi and Sith characters compare themselves to across the movies. That's why it's such a shock when Anakin, a common human slave, is confirmed to have objectively greater Force sensitivity than even Yoda according to the midi-chlorian count in his blood, and why Qui-Gon takes it as confirmation that Anakin must be the Chosen One, conceived by the Force itself.

26. "It was a virgin birth in an ecosystem of symbiotic relationships. It means that between the Force, which is sort of a life force, and reality, the connectors between these two things are what we call mitichlorians. ... Ultimately, I would say the Force itself created Anakin. I don't want to get into specific terms of labeling things to make it one religion or another, but, basically, that's one of the foundations of the hero's journey." George Lucas, quoted by Jim Windolf, "*Star Wars: The Last Battle*," *Vanity Fair*, February 2005, 117.

27. "There were a lot of things that would have been easier if Anakin had been twelve. ... But the problem was that a twelve-year-old leaving his mother — as Anakin does — is not nearly traumatic as a nine-year-old leaving his mother. And there is a key story point that revolves around the fact that he was separated from his mother at an early age, and how that has affected him." George Lucas, quoted by Laurent Bouzereau in *Star Wars Episode I: The Phantom Menace — The Illustrated Screenplay* (New York: Del Rey, 1999), xiii.

28. "The core issue, ultimately, is greed, possessiveness — the inability to let go. Not only to hold on to material things, which is greed, but to hold on to life, to the people you love — to not accept the reality of life's passages and changes, which is to say things come, things go. Everything changes. Anakin becomes emotionally attached to things, his mother, his wife. That's why he falls — because he does not have the ability to let go." George Lucas, quoted by J. W. Rinzler, *The Making of Star Wars: Revenge of the Sith* (New York: Del Rey, 2005), 53.

29. The Hero's Journey follows a structure that forces the protagonist to confront the parts of themselves they have avoided, denied, or never fully understood and integrate them. Campbell described it as an outward path that mirrors the inward Jungian model toward emotional integration by making the unconscious (or "shadow") conscious in one's identity. Something inside feels unfinished, suppressed, or unexplored until the path toward integration is undertaken.

30. "The story is not about a guy who was born a monster — it's about a good boy who was loving and had exceptional powers, but how that eventually corrupted him and how he confused possessive love with compassionate love. That happens in Episode II: Regardless of how his mother died, Jedis are not supposed to take vengeance. And that's why they say he was too old to be a Jedi, because he made his emotional connections. His undoing is that he loveth too much." George Lucas, interviewed by Gavin Edwards in "*George Lucas and the Cult of Darth Vader,*" *Rolling Stone*, June 2, 2005.

31. "One of the main themes in [*Star Wars*] is having organisms realize that they must live together and they must live together for mutual advantage. Not just humans, but all living things and everything in the galaxy is part of a — a greater whole." George Lucas, interviewed by Bill Moyers, "*Of Myth and Men,*" *Time*, April 18, 1999.

32. "Obi-Wan has always had a suspicion about Anakin. In the beginning, he didn't want Anakin to become a Jedi. He thought what Qui-Gon was doing was wrong." George Lucas, quoted by J. W. Rinzler, *The Making of Star Wars: Revenge of the Sith* (New York: Del Rey, 2005), 41.

ANAKIN'S ADOLESCENCE

Destiny, invoked across *Star Wars*, is a concept of what lies in someone's future, what path they are or ought to be on, what they must do or become. Many conceptions of destiny change across the movies, and many contradict each other. Yet, everyone, from Yoda to Darth Sidious, the respective avatars of light and darkness in this story, seems assured that their interpretation of destiny and how it applies is the only valid one. Ironically, many of these characters' actions indicate that they are actually preoccupied with *controlling* the flow of things, including the will of sentient beings, to work out the way they have prescribed instead of trusting that it will on its own.

When Qui-Gon and the Jedi Council identified nine-year-old Anakin Skywalker as the Chosen One, they were projecting a predefined role and future onto him, creating pressure for him to live up to grand ambitions. Qui-Gon, in his dying words to Obi-Wan, affirmed this prescription when he made him promise he would train Anakin so that he would live up to his interpretation of the prophecy and bring balance to the Force. Only many years later, in *Revenge of the Sith*, would the Jedi even begin to wonder if Anakin might have been misidentified or show enough humility to question if their entire interpretation of what it means to be the Chosen One could have been wrong from the start.

Teenagers and young adults, like Anakin at this stage of his development, naturally attempt to disconnect from the boundaries and prescriptions imposed on them by protective parents and other societal authority figures who do not support this state of self-discovery. By the end of this movie, Anakin will go to great lengths to keep the earnest desires of his heart hidden from the Jedi and the Republic. He will feel that the only way to show any semblance of who he really is is to live constantly on edge, rebelling against the social order because he perceives it as oppressing him. Anakin doesn't develop into the Chosen One in the way he is expected to because the very people meant to help him on that journey, his Jedi parental figures in the form of

Obi-Wan and the Council, prevent the emergence of his authentic and healthy self. It's not his attachment to his mother or Padmé alone that dooms him. It's that he lacks the guidance he needs to manage these attachments in a healthy way. The Jedi directly watching over Anakin's development create the conditions for Darth Vader to take over by failing to guide him when he needs it most, such as right now, during the sensitive changes of adolescence, as he struggles to manage the responsibility of being himself.

From childhood, Anakin rejected the restrictions put upon him in his role and sought to assert his own identity when Padmé first met him and showed surprise that he was a slave. That little slave boy responded, with defiance and conviction, that he was a person and <u>his name was Anakin</u>, proud to be called such a name and associate it with who he is. Anakin knew that there was a crucial distinction between a person and a slave. It is the same that distinguishes a person from an animal or a machine: the capacity for conscious choice. He does not yet know how machine-like and animalistic he will one day become.

Inherent passions, the choices we would make if left to our own devices without imposed limitations, are products of the authentic self that develops through the act of living and self-expression. Anakin's overwhelming passion will be shunned in this film and the next by his mentors and turned into a catalyst for the corruption of his personality because he will not be able to express what he needs to be happy. He will come to believe that his only option is to pursue those aspects of his personality by deception in this film and by force in the next. A split emerges between the person Anakin's mentors want him to be and the person he would choose to be if left to follow his own passions. In rebellion, he begins to do the opposite of what Obi-Wan and the Council want for him, just so that he can maintain some sense of autonomy and self-determination.

Episode 2, the part of the saga depicting Anakin's passage through adolescence, is subversive and disorienting, challenging much of the lore and mythological framing established in the previous film, which was presented from Anakin's childish perspective and intended for consumption by a childish audience. In Episode 1, the Jedi were treated with awe and reverence by even their enemies. The Neimoidians of the Trade Federation were afraid to even enter a room alone with Qui-Gon and Obi-Wan due to their reputation as mythical warriors, a reputation which they lived up to by easily escaping a trap designed to kill them and disposing of a squadron of battle droids sent to finish them off. They even nearly melted through reinforced metal blast doors with the incredible power of a single lightsaber, a feat which the terrified Neimoidians <u>declared to be impossible</u>. This fairy tale ideal of the Jedi lasted until the end of that movie, when a superior Sith duelist, Darth Maul, struck down one of the best of them, destroying the myth of their invincibility and that they could do no wrong. Children grow out of similar myths about their parents as they come of age in the world, at first resenting them for not living up to the myths they intrinsically believe about mom and dad as perfect parental figures, and then eventually accepting them as the real people they are, at last seeing them more or less as equals. If all goes well, the rebalancing occurs at the transition into adulthood.

In the events of this film and the next, the Jedi will be further brought down to Earth as they become entangled in politics and mundane human affairs. Their unchallenged wisdom will be argued against and shown to be inadequate as they enter into territory they are unprepared to deal with. Minor economic interference in trade routes has grown over the last decade into several thousand systems losing confidence in the Republic to solve their problems through democracy. The Jedi are now insufficient to play the role of superheroes and spiritual leaders for the galaxy and maintain the integrity of their society, prompting the

Senate to vote on the creation of a Grand Army of the Republic that will maintain peace by force, a motion that Senator Padmé Amidala leads the opposition against.[33]

The opening shot of *Attack of the Clones* subtly plays with our perspective by panning up instead of down from the void of space to Coruscant as Nubian ships invert themselves to align with the planet's gravitational pull. They begin their descent through the obscuring clouds to a landing platform, and an objective sense of direction has lost all meaning as our characters emerge onto a foggy platform where visibility is limited and danger may be all around. Another disorienting environmental motif will appear throughout *The Empire Strikes Back*, which is the part of the saga that depicts Luke's confusing adolescence. When the ship suddenly explodes, killing Padmé's security decoy, it sets the tone for the uncertainty and insecurity that will follow for the rest of the film.

Anakin and Padmé are reunited after ten years as part of a plan by Chancellor Palpatine to put Anakin in a compromising position that will facilitate his turn to the dark side. She at once sees how much he has grown since she last saw him as a child. He is now so tall that he actually towers over his paternal figure, Obi-Wan, which contributes to the issues with masculine authority between the two. She also dismisses his attempts at interacting with her in an adult, romantic way when he awkwardly attempts to compliment her beauty. To her, he is still <u>that little boy she knew on Tatooine</u>, which she makes clear with her repeated use of the childish nickname Ani, the same name his mother used to call him.[34] Anakin is 19 in *Attack of the Clones*, no longer a boy but not yet a man, a teenager on the cusp of adulthood, still a padawan, not a true Jedi Knight. Padmé is 24 and a respected senator with many career accomplishments. The last thing we would expect from someone like her would be to fall for a younger man instead of an older one.

The strained parental relationship between Obi-Wan and Anakin is immediately on display, punctuated only briefly by moments of levity over their shared adventures. Anakin, who once looked up with heroic idealism to the Jedi, now questions their every mandate and challenges their every shortcoming. A mini power struggle forms when Anakin promises to find out who's trying to kill Padmé, but Obi-Wan insists that they will not exceed their mandate from the Jedi Council to protect her. Anakin's sudden questioning of why he should do what he is commanded to do comes as a shock and an offense to Obi-Wan, reflecting how many parents feel the first time their teenagers become self-determined enough to question the habits, rules, and institutions they have followed since childhood. Obi-Wan reiterates the need for Anakin to learn his place and stay in it instead of expanding to become everything he is capable of. Instead of working well together as a functioning unit, they compete with one another for control. Anakin is not shy about directly challenging his master's level of Force attunement compared to his own. As the audience, we are meant to wonder how such a sweet kid from *The Phantom Menace* has turned into someone so combative and confrontational, until we realize that this is the same path many real-world teenagers take.

In one of their better moments, Anakin shows signs of vulnerability to Obi-Wan, opening up and confessing that he doesn't sleep well because he dreams so much about his mother, his thoughts still dwelling on her all this time since he left her in Episode 1. His consciousness is under constant distraction due to an emotional attachment he has not reached a sufficient level of closure about. There is a part of him that has not matured out of the state he was in when he left her ten years ago. Had he been separated from his mother when he was a baby, before his mind was developed enough to have a conscious attachment to her and a need for her influence on his development, teenage Anakin would not be feeling her loss now. Similarly, had the separation occurred when he was a few years older, at least at the start of his teenage years and during the hormonal changes of puberty that drive independence, his mind would have grown out of its dependence on her and sought its own freedom on natural and healthy terms. But because the attachment process was allowed to start and then interrupted, he'll always remain that little boy on Tatooine until he receives closure.

For Anakin, just being around Padmé again is intoxicating. His overwhelming attraction to her is affecting his judgment. He is not free to choose his own path so long as the emotional needs within him remain unmet. Soon, his need for love and connection will transfer from his mother to Padmé as the object of that need. Obi-Wan, instead of increasing the strength of his bond with Anakin in this vulnerable moment, scolds his padawan for not being mindful of his thoughts and acting out of line with his commitment to the Jedi Order.

In their pursuit of Padmé's would-be assassin through the city traffic of Coruscant, Anakin's impulsiveness and ambition contrast sharply with Obi-Wan's caution and restraint. Parents of teenagers worldwide can relate. We can see Anakin's impatience with Jedi discipline as Obi-Wan lectures about everything he is doing wrong. Anakin, even, quite arrogantly, believes his skills could somehow rival Grandmaster Yoda's, someone whose experience spans centuries longer than his. At the same time, we also see Anakin's earnest desire to make his master proud by living up to his expectations, even candidly admitting that he is the closest thing he has to a father and insisting that he is trying to listen to him better.

Chancellor Palpatine is the first person in Anakin's life since the death of Qui-Gon Jinn to encourage his development on his own terms, outside the context of the destiny the Jedi impose upon him. He bestows upon Anakin the praise, approval, and permission he seeks but never receives from the Jedi, feeding his adolescent arrogance and desire for masculine mentorship and connection. He tells Anakin what every frustrated and gifted young person butting up against societal restrictions needs to hear: that he doesn't need the Jedi's guidance, that he will learn to trust his feelings in time, and even that when he does, he <u>will be invincible</u>. He will be the greatest of all the Jedi, even <u>more powerful than Yoda</u>. Palpatine echoes Qui-Gon's advice about trusting his own intuition and calls back to Anakin's childish hero worship of the Jedi as unkillable superheroes. From this twisted take on sound wisdom, Anakin begins to accept that complete autonomy is the path to power and security, to being safe from ever being hurt.

Anakin's overbearing influences from the Jedi Order do the opposite of Palpatine; they try to instill in him the idea that being too differentiated, too assured in who he is and what he cares about, is wrong. The Jedi imposed this standard on young Anakin before his sense of self had even developed. The people meant to bring about the Chosen One, a uniquely powerful Jedi who would, by design, stand out from the crowd and use his exceptionalness to change the world, prevented that which they needed from occurring because, as Palpatine would one day relate to Anakin, they feared the change that would come if Anakin <u>became too powerful to control</u>.

The path of a hero is about conscious individuation, or differentiation from the limitations of social norms, by someone self-expressed enough to push culture beyond its present capacity.[35] That heroic individual follows their own path of discovery and expression until they acquire exceptional traits and knowledge, becoming the doorway or catalyst for introducing these to the rest of their society. Rather than trying to stop change and preserve the status quo, they become an agent of ordered evolution. They bring the world to a higher state of functioning through their uninhibited self-expression. Anakin is poised to perform this function on a scale never before seen in the galaxy. He will go on to accomplish wonders that the present Jedi Order cannot imagine, and the fundamental change to their structure and culture scares them so much that it makes them susceptible to internal corruption.

The Jedi Order exists in a stale form that maintains itself through dogma and imposed ignorance. All new padawans are inducted as infants, before they are cognitively mature enough to realize the commitment they are taking on. It's a cyclical process wherein the old Jedi indoctrinate younglings into their way, their vision, and their identity. Those padawans grow up to repeat the cycle with the next generation they train, with few people, such as Qui-Gon or Anakin, asking any questions along the way or daring to challenge the tradition. Major progress occurs when someone exceptional becomes self-determined enough to create a new operating standard that replaces the old one, elevating the whole society. That's the conclusion of the hero path: when the hero returns with what they learned or obtained as a result of their quest for personal growth, the benefits of which they spread to the world, so that society can evolve with them. This is what Anakin is *supposed* to be for the Jedi: the messianic figure who breaks them out of the prison they have built for themselves, including its vulnerability to unseen corruption from the dark side, and carries them to the next stage of existence in the endless cosmic cycle of change.

To protect Padmé from Count Dooku's attempts to kill her, the Jedi instruct her to return to Naboo, her childhood home, with Anakin as her protector. Later, Anakin will also be called to return to his childhood home of Tatooine, offering both of them the opportunity to reflect upon where they came from and move beyond the conditions that shaped them in their childhood. Count Dooku is portrayed as a political idealist who lost faith in the Republic and the Jedi Order and now leads the Separatist movement.[36] Unlike Darth Maul, who was driven by a pure form of emotional hatred, Dooku is motivated by ideology. He is not wholly consumed by the rage that the dark side offers, which helps explain why his eyes never turn yellow, and why he continues to use his original name, despite being christened Darth Tyrannus by Sidious. He will use the Jedi's fear of the dark side to spread mistrust and insecurity by warning them of the threat of the Sith in a way that is too nebulous for them to act effectively against. He even hopes to convert disillusioned Jedi like Obi-Wan to his cause. His regal and respectable demeanor will go on to influence a maturing Darth Vader, once he realizes he cannot only be an attack dog let loose, but must learn to compose himself to play his role in the Empire.

While Obi-Wan worries that Anakin's exceptional abilities have made him arrogant, Yoda is wise enough to see that the same flaw is spreading among many Jedi, even among the older, more experienced ones like him. Yoda is beginning to show signs of self-reflection that the Order has been missing, even slyly admitting to his own shortcomings as the oldest, most experienced Jedi of all. His and Obi-Wan's ability to see through the limitations of their ways will someday soon contribute to their surviving of the Jedi purge and the role they play in communicating the lessons of past generations to future ones.

Anakin's conflicted relationship with Obi-Wan is most evident when he cannot even praise him as a mentor to Padmé on Naboo without also inadvertently starting to complain about him. Padmé is impressed with this unexpected display of maturity, even seeing it as evidence that Anakin <u>may have actually grown up</u>. But then Anakin, showing his childish side, complains that Obi-Wan is too critical and fails to see how grown-up he is, and that he is ready to be knighted by the Jedi, symbolically making him an adult. Obi-Wan, Anakin believes, is preventing him from growing up and completing the transition from child to adult. The rest of Episode 2 will be about witnessing Anakin cross that threshold through the trials he will have to overcome. Padmé reminds the temperamental teenager that part of a mentor's job is to acknowledge a learner's faults, and that by doing so, they help them grow. She urges Anakin <u>not to try to grow up too fast</u>. Anakin already sees himself as an adult, but Padmé's off-put reaction suggests she still sees him as a boy, not a grown man she can consider a romantic interest.

The Jedi's key limitation on display in this film is their inability to see beyond the limits of their own traditions and institutionalized knowledge. It takes an outsider, Dexter Jettster, in a diner on Coruscant to identify the dart fired by Jengo Fett as Kaminoan in origin, not by explicit identifying information, as per the analysis methods of the droids in the Jedi Archives, but by a more intuitive and creative approach. As Obi-Wan dismissively states, if such droids could think like people, there'd be no people left, as they would outperform them in every domain, which helps explain why it is so easy for the Jedi to defeat unthinking armies of battle droids. Clone troops will be marketed by the cloners on Kamino as superior to droids because they can think critically, creatively, and independently. They possess at least a rudimentary sense of self, situated somewhere above robots but below real people who have their own distinct identities. Their growth is accelerated twofold, so they lack sufficient time for adolescent development and real-world experience with which to understand themselves. They receive combat training from a young age, mimicking the way in which droids are programmed to behave. And they are engineered on a genetic level to be subservient, taking orders without question, ominously foreshadowing when they will turn against the Jedi during Order 66.[37] By the time of the original trilogy and the rise of the Empire, clone troops will be replaced by stormtroopers, voluntary conscripts who give up their personal identity to become part of the Imperial machine and carry out the will of the Empire.

If clone troops are people who can be reduced to the level of robots, R2-D2 is their opposite: a droid who elevates himself to the level of humanity. Our heroes do not realize how fortunate they are that their little blue friend seems to be the only robot in the galaxy who has demonstrated the ability to think creatively and act on its own will, such as how he will use his booster jets in a manner they were not designed for, to ignite spilled oil and defeat a pair of B2 Super Battle Droids in Episode 3, or how he will take the initiative to fly ahead and save Padmé in the conveyer belt scene on Geonosis later in this film when Anakin struggles with the same task. Even from his very first scene in Episode 1, R2 displayed an unusual capacity for original thought, initiative, and creative problem-solving. He was the only astromech droid aboard Queen Amidala's ship to survive their departure from Naboo and figure out how to repair their damaged shield generator by bypassing the main power drive. Sabé, Queen Amidala's body double acting in her guise, showed an unusual amount of gratitude and recognition for just a lowly astromech droid, essentially treating him as though he had consciousness and individuality in a galaxy where droids are seen on a level somewhere between appliances and slaves. Padmé spent the next scene painstakingly scrubbing R2 clean in appreciation for saving the ship, lowering herself before the machine in recognition of his vital contributions. R2-D2 is like your much-loved cat or dog who somehow displays more intelligence, awareness, or insight than should be possible, becoming personified in your eyes.[38]

Obi-Wan is so dependent on the worldview provided by the Jedi Order's institution that he at once <u>declares it to be impossible</u> when the planet Kamino is missing entirely from the Jedi Archives. This glaring discrepancy prompts Obi-Wan, like Yoda before him, to begin to think for himself, outside the confines of Jedi doctrine. Only a young boy guided by Yoda, unbiased by existing knowledge and open to possibilities that rigid adults overlook, could see what the evidence was pointing to: that someone must have erased the planet from the archive memory, something Obi-Wan again <u>considers to be impossible</u>. Darth Sidious has managed to blind the Jedi in a technological way similar to how he uses the influence of the dark side to blind them in a psychological way.

On Naboo, Padmé bonds with Anakin over the difficulties involved with having sworn his life to the Jedi and taken their oath of emotional celibacy. Even if Shmi Skywalker had been freed from slavery along with Anakin, his Jedi training would still have required that he abandon all emotional connection with her because the Jedi forbid attachment and possession. Compassion is the only form of love available to Jedi, which is both impersonal and unconditional. It describes a general kind of love for all living beings, not personal relationships formed between people through shared experiences and values, such as the bond shared between a mother and son, or even a master and their padawan.

Padmé worries that <u>if the people of the galaxy are afraid</u>, they will vote to create a Grand Army of the Republic, opting for violence over diplomacy. Anakin believes it is already too late for democracy and the will of the people to restore order to the Republic's chaos, that someone wise should decide what is best for everyone instead. It's a childish view of how the world works, reducing complex human beings with their own preferences and values into a unilateral mold of what is in the best interest of everyone, according to a centralized power's, a political father figure's, point of view. But it is understandable why Anakin thinks this way. Padmé was surprised to learn there was still slavery in the galaxy when she arrived on Tatooine ten years before. Her idealistic faith in the Republic couldn't allow for such an aggressive violation of human rights. Anakin has grown up suffering under the Republic's blind spots and weaknesses. A benevolent dictatorship, where a wise leader can compel the people to align with their vision, is the only solution he sees to the galaxy's pervasive inhumanity.

Dictatorship is the large-scale societal manifestation of the immature belief that things can only ever work out the way that is acceptable to you if you force them to. The opposite, the principles of the type of republic that Padmé is espousing and that Obi-Wan will one day soon remind Anakin his allegiance lies with, enables individuals to make their own choices, even if no one knows how those choices will turn out or if not everyone thinks the same way. A republic places autonomy and choice above forced certainty. It accepts that mistakes will happen and some things will be lost. There can never be complete security.

Anakin has now become possessive of Padmé and can no longer function normally without her. He has become desperate for a type of emotional connection he is incapable of getting anywhere else, and he is willing to sacrifice everything about himself to acquire it. He <u>will do whatever she asks</u>, so long as it gets him what he needs. When someone has an emotional attachment compensating for their lack of actualization, it grows more important to them than their principles and threatens to destroy the structure of their values the moment they fear losing what they've grown dependent on. Padmé insists that Anakin must return to "the real world," by which she does not mean what is authentic to them but instead what has been imposed upon and expected from them. She asks him to be rational and think analytically, to use only his mind and not his heart to make decisions. He offers to keep the relationship a secret, but Padmé is unwilling to live a lie. She overlooks the fact that she is already living one by denying what she genuinely desires and curtailing her self-expression.

That night, Anakin dreams of his mother in pain and suffering, and it is enough to distract him from his mandate of protecting Padmé. Once more, he fears losing that which he has grown possessive of. The next morning, in standing meditation before a railing over a serene lake, he tries to center himself and make sense of what he is feeling. A faint yin-yang symbol forms in the clouds over Anakin's head, symbolizing that at this moment, he is halfway between the dark and the light. The darkness in him is anxious and insecure about the premonition he just had, but he is balanced enough in the light to remain calm and reflect on what he is feeling and decide, consciously, what the right thing to do about it is.[39] The Jedi do not realize that the prophecy of the Chosen One bringing balance to the Force begins within the individual, meaning the ability to feel emotions intensely without becoming slave to them, and spreads outward to the collective. Thus, Anakin cannot bring balance to the galaxy until he can maintain it as a stable and permanent state within himself. He will lose his momentary balance when he tips over into panic and passionate indulgence as the darkness grows stronger than the light. He confesses to Padmé that he plans to leave Naboo to help his mother on Tatooine, stressing that he has to, that he <u>doesn't have a choice</u>.

The two arrive on Tatooine and learn that Shmi was sold to Cliegg Lars, a moisture farmer who freed and married her, before being abducted by a hunting party of Tusken Raiders. Cliegg characterizes the Tuskens as walking like men but behaving like vicious, mindless monsters. Anakin's face darkens with grief for his mother and also with simmering anger at the sand people and his new stepfather for being so inadequate as to have given up the effort to rescue her. Anakin has been searching for a father figure since he was a child, and now that he has an official one to look up to, he immediately disapproves of him in the role, overlooking the fact that this man cared so much for Shmi that he lost his leg and dozens of lives in their attempt to rescue her. Cliegg regained enough composure to move on after losing a part of himself, a pound of flesh, to his obsession with rescuing his wife so that he would not lose himself completely. Anakin will not learn this lesson when he loses his arm at the end of this film. He takes up the challenge that his stepfather was incapable of conquering, symbolically becoming the man of the household. Tatooine's setting suns cast the shadow of Vader's helmet from Anakin's hair in side profile against the walls of the Lars homestead, hinting that Vader's influence is becoming more prominent in him as he dives deeper into an anxious state. He heads off on his own to find his mother, rushing past Tatooine's setting suns on a speeder, the same suns his son will one day look off into while in a similar state of upset, and ignoring Cliegg's advice to <u>accept that she is dead</u>.

Shmi is only able to get out a few sentences to Anakin when he finds her battered in a Tusken camp, before succumbing to her injuries. At last, Anakin is fulfilling the promise he made when he left as a boy to come back and free her, but not at all in the way that he intended. She calls him <u>her grown-up son</u>, informally christening him as an adult, stating how proud she is and that now, having seen him grow past the trials of youth into a man, she <u>is complete</u>. She struggles to complete one last expression of love for her son, but her words are cut off before she can finish uttering, "I <u>love you</u>," leaving the transmission of that love from mother to son incomplete in the unstable structure of Anakin's identity.

Anakin has no patience. He is unable to sit in the grief of the moment, which would entail going as deep as possible into self-reflection over what she meant to him and what it means to lose her. Sadness quickly turns to rage. The music turns from somber to strained and chaotic, reflecting Anakin's internal state. Now with focus and strength, he exits the tent, ignites his lightsaber, and effortlessly slaughters the entire tribe of sand people as though they were the lowly beasts Cliegg described them as, despite their rudimentary intelligence and sentience. The Tuskens give us one more demonstration of humanity in a state of arrested development, not quite beast and not quite man, due to the primitive state of their culture. It is hard to tell if they are fully cognizant of the nature of the crime they have committed and the suffering they have caused by taking Shmi. In Anakin's machine-like state, cutting them down is no more difficult or consequential than cutting any of the legions of unthinking battle droids he has practiced his combat skills against. He is showing the separation he is building within himself between his higher conscious functions and primal intuitive ones, which is the opposite of what Qui-Gon tried to teach him. When there is no more integrity and symbiosis between the two, disaster and a split identity are sure to follow.

Meditating far away on Coruscant, Yoda feels Anakin's suffering through the Force. Qui-Gon's disembodied voice yells out Anakin's name, followed by a pained exclamation of "Nooooo!" as though his spirit is shouting out his concern for him from the netherworld of the Force to warn against the dark path the boy he identified as the Chosen One is heading down. Darth Vader's theme grows in the background of the musical score, more prominent than when it briefly appeared in the last film, signaling that this is the moment the seed of corruption that was placed in Anakin as a boy begins to sprout. Yoda feels death, but it is not clear whether Anakin is its cause, its victim, or both.

Returning to the Lars homestead, Anakin laments that he cannot fix the loss of a loved one the way he fixes broken machines, as easily as he built C-3PO even when he was a child. He wishes to reduce human emotional depth and complexity to simple, mechanistic forces because the full spectrum of feeling is too great a burden to bear. Later, when presented with an opportunity by Palpatine to learn to use the Force to save people, the mechanic in him will not be able to resist the promise of being able to treat conscious beings like the machines he creates, controls, and manipulates so well. Padmé reminds him that he is not all-powerful, but still, Anakin feels that he should be and promises that someday he will be the most powerful Jedi ever. He will even learn to stop people from dying through mastery over nature itself. He has adopted a new lust for power that he thinks will protect him from ever experiencing the trauma of loss again. Vader's theme spills out of him during this emotional outburst. He blames Obi-Wan for his powerlessness in the face of death, believing that his mentor is holding him back from accomplishing everything he is capable of, and that perhaps his mother would not have died if Obi-Wan had been a better teacher.

Most troubling of all, Anakin does not know how to process the fact that he killed the tribe of Tusken Raiders responsible for his mother's death, not just the adult men, the ones who might reasonably be considered fair combatants and at fault for taking his mother's life. His rage extends to everyone in the tribe, the women and children, too, who he considers just as guilty by association, just as he will one day blame the entire tribe of Jedi for the actions of a few, including their innocent younglings. His rage has become impersonal and ambiguous, undifferentiating now between the guilty and the innocent. *The Emperor's Theme* plays, indicating that Anakin is unwittingly moving closer toward becoming a pawn of Sidious. In Anakin's mind, he did not murder sentient moral creatures; he was only slaughtering animals, creatures less than human who did not deserve to live, echoing the same justification often employed by genocidal minds intent on wiping out entire populations. He <u>hates them</u>, and that overwhelming hatred creates an imbalance in him that acts as the motivation needed for the terrible thing he has done. He is training his mind to respond to future stresses in a similar manner. Any pain too great for him to manage will threaten to send him right back into the hellish place he is now, and his behavior will adapt accordingly.

This is the moment Padmé begins to see Anakin as a real man, a man capable of doing absolutely anything for someone he loves, as dangerous as he is intriguing. She begins to take on her all-important role in his life as the feminine influence that calms him with her presence and inherent beauty. She reminds him that the anger he displays is a normal human emotion. But Anakin has been trained to hold himself to the impossibly high ideals assigned to him, the most powerful of all the Jedi. He knows he is supposed to be better than he is, better than human.

Should Padmé have seen all that transpired as an obvious warning sign of what a dangerous person Anakin would become? That he would one day grow to become capable of hurting even her? In that moment, she saw only a hurt young man struggling to express the emotions he was burdened with carrying alone, without even the support of his emotionally distant mentor and the Jedi Order. She saw depth to him that she hadn't before, back when he was just Ani, that little boy she knew on Tatooine. This is the moment Padmé goes from being uncomfortable with Anakin looking at her in a romantic way to someone she truly, deeply loves, despite all the logistical reasons for them not to be together. She stops thinking like a droid or a bureaucrat and starts feeling like a human woman instead.

The source of Anakin's spiritual corruption here is *not* that he killed the beings responsible for the death of his mother. Nowhere in *Star Wars* is it implied that it is morally wrong to kill bad people, people who intend to harm you or other innocents, only that it is wrong to be emotionally impaired and out of conscious control while doing so. The Jedi fight and kill their enemies as part of their job description. So do the other heroes of the Republic and future Rebel Alliance. Execution, the deliberate and sanctioned taking of a life, if truly deserved, should be dispassionate. If someone deserves to die, the one who takes on the task should be capable of carrying it out in peace and calm. They should not have to be incited to violence. They should not require rage to push them to extremes of action they would otherwise not be capable of. Killing an active threat out of defense for self or others is a very different ethical scenario than killing someone out of hatred or resentment or to ease one's own pain. Revenge is not the Jedi way. By the time Anakin entered his enraged state and wiped out the Tusken Raiders, there was no active threat to anyone. His priority was the self-soothing that came from doling out punishment to those he decided deserved it. He put himself on unconscious autopilot that could not be switched off until the ghastly task he started was complete and conscious reflection could return, dissociating from the moral consequences of his actions while he was committing them. Only afterward does he feel the weight of what he has done because he is reflecting honestly again.

Everything a person is capable of is part of who they are. Each new behavior comes out in response to changing emotional states. The most extreme emotions result from situations that they are unprepared for. They can develop a higher tolerance for these situations with exposure, allowing them to remain conscious and cognitively functional in conditions that would have previously overwhelmed and enslaved them. If they fail to emotionally mature, trauma brews inside until it reaches a boiling point, spilling out into the world in what seems a sudden distortion of character. Anakin slaughtering the tribe of Tusken Raiders is just a precursor to the larger boiling point that will be reached when he aligns himself with Sidious and turns against the tribe that raised him. The dark side is the result of overidentification with what should be a temporary emotional state, forcing it to become more permanent. People remain susceptible to it for so long as they have not established a permanent, fully embodied sense of self, which means the ability to self-organize and emotionally regulate around their ideals in the most trying circumstances.

The two most important men in Shmi's life have markedly different reactions to her passing at her funeral. Cliegg gives a heartfelt goodbye, thanking her for all she gave him in their time together. He has accepted the truth of what he has lost and reflects on what it means to him. Mourning brings him proper closure so that he can move with a clear mind into the future. Anakin's last words, instead of voicing the kind of woman his mother was and the impact she has had on him, are focused on his own perceived inadequacies. He laments only that he <u>wasn't strong enough to save her</u> and <u>promises he won't ever fail again</u> so that he does not have to repeat the pain of his past. Anakin, the authentic Anakin, will spend the rest of his life trying and failing to fulfill that promise until the final moments of his life in Episode 6, when, at last, he becomes *emotionally* strong enough to save someone he loves.

Only scenes later, Anakin nearly reneges on his promise not to let someone he loves die when he learns that Obi-Wan's life is at risk on Geonosis, and his initial reaction is to obey his master's order to stay on Tatooine. This is uncharacteristic behavior from Anakin, who, up until this point, has been defiant, self-determined, and argumentative at almost every opportunity. It is now as though he feels so beaten by his failure to save his mother that he has sacrificed his ego and confidence. Now, it is Padmé's job to remind Anakin who he is and what he cares about, inspiring him to heroic action. In an emotional outburst, Anakin admits that Obi-Wan is more than just a friend or mentor, that he's <u>like his father</u>. In the end, it is Padmé's choice to pursue what is right by going to help Obi-Wan that leaves Anakin following in her wake.

On Geonosis, Anakin and Padmé are captured and sentenced to death by Count Dooku. Before the two are led into the public execution arena, Padmé turns to Anakin to confesses, at least, that she truly, deeply <u>loves him</u>, not in comfort or peace like she could have on Naboo, but in the face of death. Bonding with Anakin and facing impending doom has forced her to confront the lie she has been living, the inauthentic life path she has been forced onto as a duty-bound politician. They kiss. It's their first truly mutual, unguarded expression of love. Her confession is a sudden reversal of earlier scenes where she resisted Anakin's advances out of fear of the consequences of abandoning their social responsibilities. Stripped of control and feeling she has nothing to lose, she at last chooses authentic self-expression. She kisses Anakin once more after they are rescued by the Jedi and their new clone troops after their battle in the arena ends, and they are no longer in danger. She has abandoned the pretense of the excuse of their lives ending and is now committed to her new dynamic with Anakin. This kiss is very different than the one they shared when they first entered the arena and thought they were going to die, or the impulsive kiss by the lake on Naboo. This is a kiss of acknowledgment and commitment to a new path. This is a kiss of graduation, officially signaling that Padmé now fully sees Anakin as a man, as her man, after what they have just survived together.

When Padmé is thrown from the open side door of a low-flying gunship in pursuit of Count Dooku, Anakin demands that they abandon their mission and put the ship down so they can help her. His newly actualized feelings for her are already overtaking his duty as a Jedi for the Republic. Still hurting from the trauma of losing his mother, Anakin resists experiencing the same pain of loss again. His anger at the prospect of abandoning Padmé is an evolution of that fear. The only thing that pulls him out of it, temporarily, is to adopt the sense of duty he sees in her when Obi-Wan asks him in frustration what she would do were she in his position. In a reversal of traditional gender associations, *her* order complements *his* chaos—a dynamic that will be repeated between Anakin and Padmé in their most tense moment on Mustafar.

In confrontation with Dooku, Anakin lacks the patience to reflect and assess the situation, and he is still not at all inclined to follow orders from the master he resents for holding him back. He threatens Dooku that he's going to pay for all the Jedi that he killed, revealing that his motivation is punishment, not nullifying a threat or achieving justice. Despite Obi-Wan's instruction for the two of them to take Dooku together, Anakin rushes in alone. He is acting like a reckless teenager again, and Dooku quickly dispatches of him with Force lightning because of it. He duels Obi-Wan alone and easily bests him with a lightsaber. Anakin leaps in to defend his master, showing that there is still a side to him that genuinely loves Obi-Wan despite their conflict, also providing a positive alternative to when Obi-Wan was not able to defend *his* master in the fight against Darth Maul that cost him his life once they were separated.

Dooku takes this opportunity to toy with and test the skills of the Jedi's supposed Chosen One and Sidious' object of interest for conversion to the dark side. Dooku could end the fight now if he wanted to, but part of him enjoys the dark paternal role he gets to play briefly with the talented child before him, a dynamic that will be repeated with Anakin, operating as Darth Vader, then in the father role against his own son. Once he's done sizing him up, Dooku swiftly slices off Anakin's right arm. It's the first pound of flesh he will have to pay for rushing into a fight he wasn't ready for because he was driven unconsciously by anger instead of taking the time to reflect upon himself and the situation. Anakin has literally lost a part of himself now, and he will lose far more soon enough because he will fail to learn the lesson from this tragic misstep, each lost piece replaced by machine parts that represent his progressively machine-like mentality.[40] By the time Yoda shows up to rescue the boys, Dooku is proudly proclaiming how he has become more powerful than any Jedi, even Yoda.

At the film's close, Anakin and Padmé are married in secret, settling Anakin onto a path where he will have to hide the most sensitive parts of his authentic self from the people he is supposed to be able to trust most. The trauma of losing his mother cannot be expressed out loud to the people he relies on for support, with the exception of Padmé and, as we will learn in Episode 3, his new dark father figure, Chancellor Palpatine. Without expression, the trauma goes unintegrated and maintains a hold over him. It will take him down a dark path that could have been avoided with the support of people who did not make him feel ashamed for being who he is.

Legions of clone troops, now part of the Grand Army of the Republic, move in formation to the tune of *The Imperial March*, foreshadowing the might of the Galactic Empire that they will become enforcers of. They are products of the same suppressive emotions that will cause Anakin to lose his way. Supreme Chancellor Palpatine has been granted emergency powers over the Republic, ostensibly only for the sake of dealing with a temporary crisis, but he secretly plans to extend and consolidate this power until his status as a de facto dictator becomes accepted as the new norm in a society that once valued freedom and individuality. When that happens, the people of the galaxy will welcome the tyranny of his new empire, as they will believe it is the only way to ever feel safe and secure again.

NOTES

33. In a deleted scene, Padmé pleads her case before the Senate that someone is trying to kill her to ensure the creation of the Grand Army of the Republic, which she argues will be equivalent to a declaration of war against the Separatists. She foresees that what is being framed as a *defensive* security measure is actually an act of *offensive* violence that can only be met with more violence. She urges them to wake up (i.e., become conscious and aware) of the reality that acting out of fear like this will only lead to the loss of lives and freedom.

34. In one deleted scene taking place at Padmé's family home on Naboo, Anakin complains about Padmé still calling him Ani, instead of Anakin, which he sees as a <u>little boy's name</u>, right after she reaffirms that she still sees him as the <u>little boy she knew on Tatooine</u>. In other deleted scenes with the Amidalas, Padmé dismisses the suggestion from her sister, Sola, that Anakin is her boyfriend or that there could be a romantic connection between the two, referring to him as "<u>just a boy.</u>"

35. Joseph Campbell built upon Jungian ideas to construct his monomythic Hero's Journey as an archetypal pattern of transformation. The heroic individual separates themselves from collective conditioning, descends into the unknown to confront challenges aligned with their authentic values, and returns as a consciously integrated being. Carl Jung presented conscious individuation as the process through which someone becomes aware of and integrates different components of their psyche into an authentic whole, which describes what we see Anakin and Luke do on their respective journeys, though Anakin takes an extended detour into the dark side and inauthenticity along the way.

36. Much of Dooku's backstory is covered in a deleted scene that takes place in the Jedi archives. Jocasta Nu compares Dooku to Qui-Gon, who was his apprentice, saying that both were individual thinkers and idealists who were out of step with the Council. But while Qui-Gon sought to remain a bright light within the Jedi Order in the hopes of bringing it back to the standard it once held itself to, Dooku left ten years prior under the belief that the only way to fix the corruption in the Jedi and the Republic was to dismantle both and start anew.

37. *The Clone Wars* television series also introduces bioengineered implants in clone troops' brains called inhibitor chips that can compel them to follow orders, furthering the theme of living, conscious beings operating like unconscious machinery. This helps explain why Order 66 will be implemented so quickly and without question,

even by clones who fight alongside Jedi for years and are shown to be capable of forming emotional bonds with them.

38. "Even with R2, who is clever and ultimately the hero of the whole piece. He's the Lassie of the movies: Whenever there's a pivotal moment of real danger, he's the one that gets everybody out of it." George Lucas, interviewed by Gavin Edwards in "*George Lucas and the Cult of Darth Vader,*" *Rolling Stone*, June 2, 2005.

39. "We all have good and evil in us because we have the selfish side of us and we have the compassionate side of us. The idea is how do you keep those things in balance? And by keeping those things in balance, you can do a lot of good things." George Lucas, interviewed by Bill Bradley for *American Voices*, November 15, 2015.

40. "[Amputation in *Star Wars*] is a metaphor: As your humanness is cut away, your become more like a programmed droid." George Lucas, interviewed by Gavin Edwards in "*George Lucas and the Cult of Darth Vader,*" *Rolling Stone*, June 2, 2005.

EPISODE III

ANAKIN'S ADULTHOOD

I was a teenager when *Revenge of the Sith*, the final film produced in the Lucas hexalogy, was released in 2005. I remember the heavy emotional toll witnessing Anakin's dark transformation took. There was a sense of revelation and completeness to seeing the two halves of the story, the prequels and the originals, stitched together. Finally knowing how Anakin became Darth Vader changed many of my associations with the original trilogy, such as the extent of his injuries beneath his suit and the fact that Ben Kenobi, a relatively minor presence in the original films, was pivotal to Vader's existence in such a deranged and damaged state.

At that time, much of the relevant discourse revolved around how sudden Anakin's fall was. I could only think about how accurate to real life Anakin's quick and total personality change was. People *do* often suddenly become far worse versions of themselves, versions that their previous selves would be appalled by, when confronted by unprecedented moral dilemmas and extreme stress from the fear of losing something they love and have grown dependent upon.[41] The change does not come out of nowhere. The new unseen operating standards had to have been growing beneath the surface before they took over. We can look back, in retrospect, and say that it was obvious this person was going to turn out this way once we know what to look for after the fall has occurred.

A sudden fall to the dark side is the result of accumulated trauma, which turns into the splitting of a once-unified identity. It's an anti-miracle, a spontaneous reversal of things that seemed to be moving in an overtly positive direction toward the opposite. There is always a long internal conflict that predates the fall, so what seems quite sudden can be shown to have been long in the making. Witnessing Anakin so quickly justify betraying the Jedi is both shocking and, in hindsight, perfectly foreseeable.[42] The early warning signs are always present, but we prefer to ignore them until they can be ignored no longer, because we do not want to accept such an uncomfortable truth about someone we love.

Anakin's return to the light that will come in the final moments of *Return of the Jedi* seems to be a similarly miraculous sudden reversal, this time from an overwhelmingly negative direction to a spontaneously positive one: the hero, Luke, on the brink of death at the electric hands of the Emperor suddenly being saved by the villain, Darth Vader, the man you least expect it from. But you only don't expect it if you ignore the underlying evidence that supports the sudden return to the light. *Star Wars* is full of sudden reversals that only make sense in hindsight, when you understand the full context of what is going on.

Plot twists, in real life or fiction, can happen anytime we are deeply invested in a facade or half-truth covering up something very different from the appearance that has been put before us. Anakin's moral realignment only seems sudden if you take Episode 3 out of context and ignore the buildup present in the previous two films (which is one reason why *Star Wars* is experienced better as one integrated story than as six independent parts).[43] These are the types of thoughts we must imagine Ben Kenobi spent years mulling over in his solitude on Tatooine after the fall of the Republic, trying to come to terms with how it all went so wrong and how he might have prevented it if he had only known what to pay attention to.

Revenge of the Sith opens in the middle of a warzone as *The Battle Over Coruscant* plays, featuring the Force theme as the melody of an aggressive military march. The music is signaling a shift from the Jedi's role as keepers of the peace to soldiers, now fighting a war rather than protecting the innocent. The Jedi have turned against their code and ideals. They are no longer in integrity with themselves, and this will have drastic consequences for the rest of the film. Anakin echoes the same childish enthusiasm about danger he's carried with him since Episode 1, and which will be spiritually carried forward by another daredevil character, his future son-in-law Han Solo, when he announces to Obi-Wan that, from his point of view, this is where that fun begins.

When clone pilots are quickly overwhelmed by vulture droids. Anakin is instinctively moved to help them, but Obi-Wan stops him, insisting that he let them die in the line of duty so they can focus on their mission. Anakin then moves in to help Obi-Wan with a swarm of buzz droids. He impulsively tries to shoot the small robots off Obi-Wan's ship, but this only causes more damage. Anakin is unintentionally hurting the very person he is hastily trying to save because he is not patient enough to consider the consequences of his actions. His second effort is more thought-out and executed with greater precision: tilting the wing of his ship to delicately knock the buzz droids off, showing that Anakin is capable of employing patience and critical thinking when he has a chance to calm down from his initial state of overwhelm in a crisis.

Facing Count Dooku in Grievous' observation deck, Anakin's demeanor is markedly different than what he displayed in their encounter three years prior. He does not rush in, eager for a kill. He is not motivated by anger but by the Jedi code of justice and the guidance of his master, following Obi-Wan's instructions to fight together instead of apart. Still, for the third time in as many films, a mentor and his apprentice become separated during a crucial two-on-one lightsaber duel. However, this time, we will see that the apprentice will win not despite the loss of his mentor, but because of it… revealing that perhaps Anakin has indeed outgrown his master and is actually stronger without his imposed limitations. Dooku taunts Anakin, <u>calling out the fear, anger, and hatred he possesses</u> but fails to employ in combat. With Obi-Wan lying unconscious and unable to judge or limit him, Anakin feels invigorated to follow this new dark mentor's guidance. Dooku, during their last encounter and this one, acts as a precursor to the father figure that Palpatine will soon become and influences how Vader will one day attempt to mentor his own son toward the dark side when they duel on Bespin. Once he taps into the rest of his emotions, even a little, Anakin quickly gains the upper hand by removing both of Dooku's. Anakin, fighting alone but unrestrained, is more capable than a limited version of himself fighting with his master's oversight and restrictions.

No longer engaged in combat, Anakin has the opportunity to return to a state of calm and reflect upon the right course. Should he take Dooku prisoner? Or should he kill him then and there? And will his decision be biased by his personal history with Dooku, the man who humiliated him in their last duel and cut off his arm? Palpatine urges him to kill Dooku immediately without considering the consequences. With the overt blessing of the devil on his shoulder, Anakin executes his prisoner via swift decapitation, his blue blade crossing with Dooku's red one in a scissoring motion, representing the crossroads of dark and light he is at in the Force.

Anakin, with labored breath, is disturbed by what he's done because it was not the Jedi way, but Palpatine reassures him that he only did what was necessary, that Dooku was too dangerous to be kept alive, and it is only natural to want revenge on the man who cut off his arm, in the same way he took revenge on the tribe of sand people who killed his mother. With his attention projected outward, Anakin does not have the composure to look inwardly, to reflect that losing his arm was ultimately his own fault for being so hot-tempered and short-sighted during his last duel. He will not integrate the lesson from the trauma, which means he will be liable to make the same mistake again when the stakes are even higher and the consequences even more drastic.

Palpatine had been secretly hoping that Obi-Wan would be killed in the duel with Dooku, leaving Anakin free of his influence and more susceptible to corruption. Now, he pressures him to leave the ship without his master, but Anakin will not go without carrying the unconscious Obi-Wan with him. Once again, Anakin is willing to sacrifice his duty and the entire point of his mission of rescuing the chancellor if it means losing someone he loves. When the trio is detained by ray shields. Anakin reacts with unexpected patience when even Obi-Wan does not. More and more, we are seeing hints of the man that Anakin is capable of becoming: wiser, more mature, and more powerful in every way than even the one who mentored him.

When Grievous' damaged ship begins to crash, Anakin takes control as it falls into the atmosphere of Coruscant. He activates the reverse thrusters to, as much as physically possible, backtrack from the disastrous course the ship is on, but it quickly splits in two halves, with one floating off into space to be spared from the coming catastrophe and the other continuing its fall, foreshadowing the upcoming split in his identity. The front half of the ship is engulfed in flame, coming in too hot and plummeting on a crash course into the ground. Anakin's spirit will remain present in the Force, only to return at the end of his story after his body has crashed, burned, and died. Because he manages to remain calm at the helm, Anakin is able to slow the descent while fire ships on Coruscant put out the flames before they can burn out of control. He just barely manages to bring the fallen ship to a stop before all is lost. The entire sequence is a metaphor for what will happen to Anakin as he descends into the dark side. Tragically, he will not show the same masterful composure when it is his psyche that has caught ablaze with hatred and begun to plummet toward total destruction without reversal.

Away from the wreck, Anakin shows his gratitude to his master and credits his training for his victory that day. He has finally overcome the adolescent rivalry he once had with Obi-Wan, back when he was desperate to be more powerful and saw his mentor as a limitation on what he could accomplish. As he rushes to embrace Padmé in a public space, it is clear that the sight of her has made him throw all caution to the wind once again. He no longer cares if anyone knows that they are married, despite the consequences it would have on both their careers, until she reveals that she is pregnant. Anakin's face is unreadable for a moment. All his life, Anakin has been looking for a father, and now, he is about to become one. He has had no proper, complete fatherly example to look up to, only bits and pieces here and there where he could find them. The boy without a father does not know how to be one, and he will not learn until the very end of his life.

When Anakin begins having premonitions of Padmé dying in childbirth, like the ones he used to have about his mother, he becomes dead set on not letting these ones become real. The trauma from the last time he failed to act still haunts him. Padmé suggests approaching Obi-Wan for help, but the weight of the secrecy of their relationship and child is too heavy to bear. They cannot risk letting Obi-Wan or any of the other Jedi know anything, especially with the revelation of their forthcoming child. This fear sets up the rift that will rapidly widen over the rest of the film's runtime, stemming from Anakin's inability to fully express himself to the people he considers his family.

When Anakin turns to Yoda for advice, he only warns him that <u>his fear of loss is a path to the dark side</u>. Instead of offering emotional consolation, he, like a stoic monk on a mountain, tells him to accept that death is a natural part of life, worthy of rejoicing even. If you have spent centuries watching generations live and die, as Yoda has, this must seem like sound, reasonable, and easy advice. There is no need to mourn or even miss those who are gone because <u>attachment just leads to jealousy and greed</u>. The advice Yoda gives is not exactly wrong; it's just not appropriate for who he is talking to, and it comes much too late. Without that foundation of emotional maturity that would have come from being raised with a proper father figure and family support system, Anakin is a victim of forces that he has allowed to override his cognitive abilities. To resist the temptations of the dark side, Anakin would have to be willing to die for who he is and what he believes in. And he would even have to be willing to lose someone he loves if saving them meant sacrificing his authentic moral principles. Instead, he will take increasingly drastic actions to end the crisis that preoccupies his emotions. All Anakin has really learned from his encounter with Yoda is that he cannot discuss his problems with the Jedi, that he cannot share himself with them because he will be shut down as soon as the conversation wanders into territory they disapprove of.

The fallacy that occurs in Anakin's mind is also occurring in the collective political arena.[44] As the war against the Separatists rages on, the Senate votes to grant more emergency powers to Supreme Chancellor Palpatine. He has manipulated their fears and insecurities so that they will be willing to give up their liberty as the only way to end the crisis he has put them in. Anakin sees this as a good thing, that the further centralization of power out of the hands of the many into those of a single wise soul will mean less deliberating and more forward momentum and decisive action. We see him slipping back into his impulsive adolescent self whenever the stakes are high and he is agitated to action. It is a childish and idealistic way to think about the world, a sort of heroic power fantasy. If only there were someone strong and wise enough in charge of everyone who could make all the bad things, all the war, slavery, and injustice disappear with the might of their will. It is what Anakin has hoped to become ever since he realized he wasn't strong enough to get and keep what he really wanted, since he started dreaming of becoming the most powerful Jedi ever, so that he wouldn't have to hurt or fear anymore.

When Palpatine appoints Anakin to be his representative on the Jedi Council, it is as though he is being given a small amount of the power that he craves from someone who wields it, someone he looks up to as a father figure. His delusions of Jedi grandeur are shattered when the Council allows him to join but does not grant him the rank of master. Instead of interpreting this in a positive frame, that he was so exceptional as to become the first Jedi in history to be placed on the Council before achieving the rank of master, the youngest Council member who ever lived, Anakin takes it as a grievous insult. He has become greedy, no longer appreciating the blessings and honors he is granted, but only wanting more to fill the hole of insecurity inside him. He reverts to a childish state with an outburst of incredulity in front of the Council. Vader's musical theme subtly comes through in the soundtrack's low winds. Master Windu adopts the position of a disciplinary parent, belittling young Skywalker as he commands him to take a seat and cease his disrespect. Obi-Wan shows a disapproving look and shakes his head at the impulsiveness that his student still has not outgrown.

Anakin's resentment toward the Council grows when he learns that the Jedi expect him to spy on Palpatine due to how he has remained in power long after his term expired, which is the opposite of how Padmé once stepped down as Queen of Naboo despite demands for her to remain in power longer than their constitution would allow. She accepted that her time was over with humility and welcomed change, whereas Palpatine is attempting to exert a permanently fixed state with himself and his ideology in control. Anakin is so loyal to Palpatine not because of *what* he is to the Senate, but rather *who* he is to him. His personal relationship trumps duties and systems. Anakin calls what Obi-Wan is asking of him treason, but Obi-Wan justifies this aberrant behavior by reminding him that they are at war. They are in an emergency state that, from their point of view, justifies betraying their values and acting impulsively.

A skeptical change has begun in Anakin's point of view about the Jedi Order. If they are capable of such hypocrisy by going directly against the Jedi code, it implies they are capable of anything. Maybe they have been deceiving him all along, even. Many teenagers begin to lose their faith in their parents as they come to realize that they are just fallible human beings, not perfect angels, paragons, or superheroes who can do no wrong. The naïve illusions Anakin held as a little boy about what it meant to be a Jedi are long gone, and he has to decide for himself what the reality of the situation is as he is placed further into stress and internal conflict. He even loses his temper and accuses the woman he loves of treason when she disagrees with him about the state of the Republic. He's becoming increasingly paranoid as the structure of his worldview is further challenged.

At the Galaxies Opera House, the seeds of mistrust sprout further. Palpatine claims to Anakin that the Jedi are attempting to take over the Republic because they <u>are afraid to lose their power,</u> and that the good they claim to use their power for <u>is only a point of view</u>. Palpatine denies the existence of an objective standard of morality, embracing a form of moral relativism that allows one to justify any act if they deem it necessary in the pursuit of their goals. Anakin has been taught a fairy tale version of the truth about the supposedly selfless and good Jedi and selfish and evil Sith. Palpatine challenges this notion by relating the tragedy of Darth Plagueis the Wise, his secret Sith mentor who could use the Force to create life[45] and keep the people he cared about from dying. This is a power far greater than any the Jedi have ever been able to demonstrate in all the time Anakin has studied under them, even greater than that of Yoda, who taught that death had to be accepted instead of overcome.[46] Having been told he was the Chosen One since he was a child, Anakin believes he is entitled, even obliged, to go beyond what is normal, human, and natural, to set aspirations beyond those of ordinary beings.

As Obi-Wan prepares to leave for Utapau to pursue General Grievous, he shows how much he, too, has grown as a mentor by finally stepping into the fatherly role, reflecting on how proud he is of Anakin, even admitting that he has, indeed, finally surpassed him as a Jedi. It's the approval and recognition that Anakin has always needed, but he has received it too late to stop the crash course he is already on. Obi-Wan's praise comes across like a father sending his grown son off to college, hoping that he will be able to take care of himself and continue his developmental journey on his own. Sadly, this is the final instance of earnest love between these two until they reunite after death. Obi-Wan's final lesson to Anakin, the version of Anakin that Obi-Wan knows him to be, is to be patient. If he can master this final test by keeping the Force with him and remaining calm and in control of himself when it is most difficult to, he will finally get everything he wants.

Facing off against General Grievous, Obi-Wan will receive a firsthand demonstration of how he embodies grotesque mechanical efficiency devoid of passion, creativity, soul, or style—a more extreme precursor to what will become of Anakin's physical form when he undergoes his reconstruction into Darth Vader. Having replaced almost all his organic body parts with an intimidating metal cyborg body, Grievous is unable to use the Force to fight Jedi. He will attempt to make up for this deficiency by fighting with four lightsabers simultaneously at speeds impossible for an organic being. He will quickly have this advantage neutralized by two calm and careful lightsaber strokes from Obi-Wan, a trait that will save his life again in the movie's climax on Mustafar.

Anakin's opinion of Obi-Wan starts to turn when he has another premonition, this time with Obi-Wan present as Padmé dies in childbirth, symbolically taking his place at her side as the father of his children during the critical moment of their birth.[47] He promises Padmé that his premonitions will not come true, but it is not a promise he will be able to keep. Each aspect of the premonition, Padmé dying and Obi-Wan taking the place of their father, both during childbirth and during Luke's development out of childhood, will come to pass as the direct result of Anakin's desperate attempts to avoid it.

Anakin feels lost as a result of so many of the certainties he takes for granted in his life being called into question.[48] He believes that his surrogate family doesn't trust him and that there are things about the Force they aren't telling him. He knows he is the most powerful Jedi, famous for his accomplishments, yet he still feels like it isn't enough, like he isn't the Jedi he should be according to the destiny projected onto him. Despite everything he has accomplished, he is still greedy and still wants more.[49] And at the same time, he is beginning to question the very foundation of the Jedi code and teachings he has been raised with, the nature of good and evil itself in the broadest cosmological sense.

Anakin is having an existential crisis, and there is no one he feels he can turn to for guidance except one man: Chancellor Palpatine, the man who claims to have a way to save Padmé. He is preparing to give this influential man unprecedented control over his life, believing it is the only way to save himself from the forthcoming personal tragedy. It is the same rationale the Senate used when granting him emergency powers in Attack of the Clones, powers that have only expanded in scope since then. In every visible way, Palpatine acts as a better mentor to Anakin than Obi-Wan and the Jedi ever managed to. Instead of withholding power, he offers to help him study all aspects of the Force and <u>achieve power greater than any Jedi</u>, even the power to <u>save the people he loves from certain death</u>, the secret ambition Anakin has fostered since losing his mother. Anakin is being offered everything he ever wanted, everything the Jedi have kept from him because they <u>fear his power</u>, on a silver platter.

When Anakin learns that Palpatine is actually Darth Sidious, he at first feels as though he has been betrayed by yet another mentor, someone he trusted with even secrets he had to keep hidden from the Jedi. He is barely able to contain how much he wants to kill him, a demeanor we will see repeated with his other primary mentor, Obi-

Wan, when he feels betrayed by him too. Anakin's nature is to be so deeply invested in personal relationships that any indiscretion, real or imagined, is met with the harshest punishment. Anakin barely regains his composure, reflecting just enough to realize that no matter how offended he is by Palpatine's lies, the right thing to do is to turn him over to the Jedi Council. Despite how conflicted he is, Anakin still believes in the authority of the Jedi and that they can be trusted to do the right thing by arresting Palpatine, even when, as Master Windu puts it, their <u>worst fears have been realized</u>.

Anakin's reflection in the Council chambers is interrupted by Palpatine's voice emanating through the Force in his head, planting doubts about the path he has chosen. Across the city, Padmé can sense Anakin's emotional turmoil, despite never having been shown to be Force-sensitive. The bond between them is so strong, perhaps even temporarily heightened by the fact that she is carrying his Force-sensitive children, that she can feel him at all times. Anakin starts to cry because he knows he has to stop what he has set in motion. He rushes off to Palpatine's office, only to find an enraged Mace Windu holding Palpatine at lightsaber-point on the floor, backed into a corner and defenseless. He doesn't know that he has just missed the crucial context of what transpired moments ago, in which he would have seen how Palpatine brutally killed three Jedi masters.

Anakin has only moments to decide which version of reality to align himself with, Windu's or Palpatine's, the Jedi way or the Sith Way, but his decision is biased by Sidious' promise to save Padmé. When Windu declares his intention to kill Palpatine instead of arresting him because he is too dangerous, Anakin is stunned by the hypocrisy and willing violation of the Jedi code, the very same violation he made in haste earlier when he killed an unarmed Count Dooku. He takes this as proof that the Jedi really are plotting to take over the Republic, as Palpatine claimed. The split within Anakin's identity has reached a crossroads.

He could ignore the differences until he had to take action based on values compatible with one side. This ultimatum is thrust upon him once Palpatine pleads with him to choose which side of the struggle he's going to align with.

If the viewer, up to this point, has managed to remain in the dark about Anakin's dark transformation, they will believe, wholeheartedly, that Anakin is going to do the right thing. It's how hero stories are supposed to go. We see our heroes tempted. We see them make mistakes and fail on their path to becoming what the story has set up for them to become. But they do not destroy the narrative by reversing everything it's meant for. Thus, Anakin's next action comes as a traumatic shock. When Windu raises his lightsaber for the killing blow, Anakin has no time left to deliberate. His fear takes over fully, knocking him out of reflection and into panic. The fate of the galaxy will hinge with it. With one swift motion and a dramatic "Nooooooo!," he severs Windu's raised arm. This moment is the first time the force of Darth Vader, which has been present all along, becomes stronger than Anakin since the Tuskens in the last film, and it takes a heavy emotional toll.

Anakin immediately regrets this crime of passion. He's still able to self-reflect here, but only briefly. What can someone do to live with themselves after making a mistake of that magnitude? Either take accountability immediately, or double down on the error, acting as though it was the only choice they had, that the situation forced their hand, or even that they are the victim of others who manipulated them into something beyond their control. Anakin desperately needs a narrative to align himself with, something he can mold all his memories to fit, recontextualizing his entire life if necessary to resolve the upset he is feeling now. If he can convince himself that killing this one Jedi was justified, necessary, and even good, he will be able to extend that same analysis to every Jedi in the galaxy. This mechanism is how we see what seems to be a sudden reversal in his character and values.

A crucial factor in his worldview changes, and everything that follows from that new value changes in accordance. Friends can be rewritten to be enemies. Evil can be transformed into good, and vice versa. What was previously unthinkable has become absolutely necessary. The only thing that cannot change is his ability to live with the story he tells himself.

It is conceivable that, if left to his own devices, Anakin could have returned to his senses and sought redemption for his crime against Mace Windu. Unfortunately, at this critical moment, he has Palpatine, or rather, the Sith Lord Darth Sidious, watching over him, nudging his consciousness in the wrong direction. He reassures Anakin by telling him that he <u>is fulfilling his destiny</u> by killing his first Jedi, an assessment that acts as a form of permission from an authority figure to continue doing it. So long as his father figure approves, Anakin does not have to think for himself and reflect on his own actions. He surrenders his will in order to be free from the guilt of what he has done and will <u>do whatever Palpatine asks</u>. Anakin began to die the moment he accepted someone else's will as superior to his own. In that moment, he ceased to be in control of his own actions. He became no different than clone troops bred into subservience, or even droids, machines that unquestioningly follow their programming without sentience.

With Anakin kneeling before him, Sidious commands him to commit to learning to use the dark side of the Force, to wholly indulge in the emotions he, until now, suppressed or ignored. Sidious, who once foresaw that Anakin would become the greatest of all the Jedi, now promises that he will become <u>a powerful Sith</u> instead. Anakin, who was previously withheld from high status within the Jedi Order, has found a mentor who is placing on his shoulders the burden of carrying the entire Sith Order into the future with him via the Sith Rule of Two.[50] For the first time in his life since Qui-Gon died, he has been given a teacher who promises to help him live up to his potential and fulfill what he sees as his destiny. Vader's musical theme plays once again, this time toned down and confident, as though the die is cast and his fate sealed with the verbal proclamation of Anakin's new Sith title: Darth Vader.

When Palpatine tells Anakin about the supposed Jedi plot to kill him and all the senators, he is quick to believe him. There has been so much distrust sewn between him and the Council now that he believes they are capable of anything. The apparent assassination attempt he just interrupted confirms it for him. He believes whatever interpretation is most convenient for him to believe, instead of reflecting upon the possibility of any alternatives. Palpatine's first piece of dark mentorship to his new apprentice is to not hesitate or show any mercy when he goes to the Jedi temple to kill all the Jedi there. In other words: Do not be patient. Doing so might allow Anakin to start self-reflecting and realize that what he's doing is wrong. Anakin must remain steadfast and 100% committed to the path laid before him, which he interprets as a sign of strength.

Thus begins the genocide of the Jedi, as Palpatine instructs all clone troops to execute Order 66, an order they have no choice but to follow, effectively reducing them to the level of the droids they were once said to be so superior to. Palpatine, like every totalitarian in history, justifies the terrible crimes he has commissioned by promising that once the Sith rule the galaxy again, there will <u>be peace</u>. The fine print he fails to mention is that it will be the type of peace only possible via dictatorship, by suppressing any opposition before it has a chance to make itself known. When all minds are coerced into unity, there will be no conflict or disagreement and no freedom or evolution.

As Order 66 commences, the pained choir of *Anakin's Betrayal* sings over a gruesome montage of clone troops and Darth Vader turning against and killing Jedi across the galaxy. The same musical theme will repeat later on Mustafar, but sadder and slower, as Anakin assaults Padmé. In order to go through with the evil things required of him, up to and including even the vile act of murdering children in cold blood, Anakin must hold onto the core belief, the pillar of his new false identity, that his perception and judgment are infallible and that he's incapable of doing anything wrong.[51] If he stopped to consider that he could be wrong, the realization that he might have taken extreme actions in error would destroy him with guilt. If Anakin, while still barely capable of self-reflection, felt so bad after contributing to the death of only Mace Windu, he would be all the more crushed to recognize the value of every life he takes during Order 66 after that. The only way he can avoid feeling this way is to dehumanize the lives he is taking, to see them as obstacles, animals, enemies, monsters, or empty and unconscious vessels. To him, it is no different than cutting down battle droids now.

Despite the remnants of a tear on his face, indicating significant internal struggle with the act, Anakin no longer even sees children when he ignites his lightsaber in front of Jedi younglings, one of whom bears a strong resemblance to his child self from Episode 1. He sees pawns of the Jedi, the fruit of a poisoned tree, and mindless representatives of the enemy, who are just as deluded by their propaganda as he once was. He has lost his own humanity, and thus he has lost the ability to recognize it in others. If anything, he sees what he is doing to them as a mercy killing, sparing them the life of servitude to false masters that he has suffered. Anakin is symbolically killing his child self and cutting ties to what he sees as a faulty past under the Jedi.

Across the city, Padmé sees smoke coming from the Jedi Temple and begins to cry. She is still sensitive enough to Anakin's emotional state that she can sense the pain and darkness that have appeared within him. When Anakin returns, he tells her the propagandized version of the truth, that the Jedi have attempted to take over the Republic and assassinate Palpatine. He informs her that many Jedi have been killed, deliberately using the passive voice to avoid revealing the source of the killing. Anakin promises Padmé that everything will be different, and things will be set right. He is hopeful that once the Jedi are out of the picture, they will finally be free to live and love the way they want, without limits on their self-expression.

When Anakin arrives on the hellish planet Mustafar to kill the remaining Separatist leaders, Nute Gunray cries out that Sidious promised them peace. A quick stroke of Anakin's lightsaber cuts him off... bringing about the peace promised by silencing dissent. Simultaneously, Palpatine announces the birth of the Empire to the Senate, ensuring what he frames as the security and stability of their society. A stable society is one that prevents any and all divergence from the norm, which the masses now interpret as being safe from the threat of change and the unknown.

Now, Anakin stands alone before the railing of a precipice over the lava rivers of Mustafar, the ruler of his own Hell and not quite able to bear the emotional weight of everything he has just done. Dark clouds almost completely obscure the sun in the Mustafar sky, reflecting the shot of him in a state of calm overlooking the Naboo lake in Episode 2, when the clouds only partially obscured the sun in a yin-yang shape, and he maintained enough composure to reflect upon the right course of action. Back then, he was centered in the shot, directly under the partially obscured sun. Now, he is framed on the far left with the almost totally obscured sun opposite him on the right, its light just barely poking through the black clouds to reach him. What little consciousness is left manifests as the tears streaming down his face. Because his mission is complete, he has to stand still again for the first time since his new personal narrative began. The fact that he can still feel sad in this moment, still reflect on what he has done, means he hasn't fully become a slave to hatred yet, just as the light of the sun still barely peeks through the clouds above. He can still feel remorseful about his actions, even if he justifies them internally. There is still conflict within him, and therefore, still hope.

Anakin's last shot at reversal and redemption occurs when Padmé flies to Mustafar to uncover the truth about the terrible things Obi-Wan has told her, descending into Hell in her J-type Naboo star skiff to rescue him from the depths of his shadow. As he runs to embrace her, similar to how he ran to embrace her on Coruscant when she first revealed she was pregnant, he is temporarily returned to a more normal operating state. For a brief moment, we see the love that defined Anakin as we knew him at the start of the film because her presence brings it out in him. She soothes the fires burning inside him, and he allows the anger and impurities to wash out of him from joy at the sight of the woman he loves. But this euphoria only lasts as long as it takes for his two identities, the one he lives out publicly for her benefit and the dark deeds he believes have been kept private from her, to collide.

Anakin's demeanor changes to antagonism and self-defense at the news of what Obi-Wan has told Padmé about his shameful actions. He must ask himself now: Is she still the woman he loves, the source of beauty and inspiration in his life? Or is she an enemy now because she dares to question him and hold him accountable? He has been confronted with a truth he knows he cannot rationally deny or justify in her eyes. He surely believed she would not find out about the crimes he thought he was committing in secret and with the blessing of the galaxy's ruling authority. Because she now knows the terrible things he has done, his consciousness is being made to consider the merit of his actions in a forced state of self-reflection.

Anakin feigns ignorance, even getting offended at Padmé's accusations. He downplays everything, pretending to himself that he could maybe get away with murder without her finding out about the gruesome details, perhaps planning to later tell her only the propagandized version of the story he would have preferred her to know, like that he was only acting out of defense for himself and the galaxy's political structure since the Jedi turned against it. He earnestly believed Padmé would join him in his newfound megalomania and position of power within his new empire when the time was right, so long as he could control the narrative. But now Obi-Wan has sabotaged that timeline by telling her too much of the truth too early. In his paranoid and deluded state of mind, the only reason Anakin can allow for why Obi-Wan would commit such treason against him is that he is his mortal enemy, deliberately seeking to hurt him and destroy his relationship with Padmé out of spite or jealousy.[52]

When someone has done terrible things, things so impermissible by the standards of their conscious self, they can no longer fairly assess their own behavior because to do so would be to burn in Hell under the weight of what they've done. Panic overrides the ability to assess a situation with higher brain functions because the mind instinctively thinks it already knows what it is dealing with. Threat detection against the truth goes into overdrive. Separation from reality extends to others when they ignore what they do not wish to believe about the person they love. Padmé is shocked at the news of Anakin having killed Jedi younglings; she does not want to acknowledge that Anakin has already admitted to doing this once before with the children of the Tusken Raiders who abducted his mother on Tatooine. She did not accept it as a defining fixture of his personality back then, but only a result of temporarily overwhelming emotions, so she allowed herself to ignore this inconvenient fact.

Anakin does not even attempt to deny the horrendous crimes he's accused of now. He does not claim he never did something so terrible as murdering children. He only seeks to diffuse attention away from himself. Everything is projected onto his new mortal enemy, Obi-Wan, who he tells Padmé is simply trying to turn her against him. Padmé herself will soon be included as a target of that erroneous blame when she does accept Anakin's new narrative and values. She desperately reminds Anakin that all she wants is his love, but his focus is only on greater power now. He is reminded of how powerless he felt as a person who led with love and kindness but still lost someone he loved. Love wasn't enough to make him feel safe from threats he couldn't control. By indulging in the dark side, he feels more powerful and protected, such that he may actually do the impossible and save the woman he fears losing, when previously he could not.

When Padmé invites Anakin to <u>come away with her</u> and leave everything behind, it is because she still desperately wishes to believe that she can ignore the terrible truths she has learned about the man she loves. Anakin's position is that they no longer have to run away or hide their love because he has removed the social institutions that made them ashamed of being who they are and limited their self-expression. He can even overthrow even Emperor Palpatine and rule the entire galaxy with her,[53] making things the way they want them to be in every area of life by force because, to him, it is the only viable option.

With those words, Anakin's underlying motivations are revealed. It was never just about saving Padmé's life. There was a lust for power after a lifetime of frustration at the perception of his own inadequacy. We see a dramatic shift in Padmé's body language and approach toward her husband. Even the musical score shifts with it. The veil is lifted. She can no longer lie to herself about the truth of the man she loves. She backs away cautiously, like she's afraid of him now, like she has just realized she doesn't know who he is anymore because his actions and demeanor are so contrary to the man she fell in love with. And as such, he could be capable of anything she would have thought impossible, even hurting her if she won't affirm the narrative of his new identity. She sees now that Obi-Wan was right about him changing, and he accuses her of turning against him, just like his paranoid mind has convinced him the Jedi did.

Anakin's two worlds are catastrophically colliding in front of him. He can justify his atrocities to himself, but he knows Padmé will never be convinced to see things the way he now does. The only thing left for him to do is blame the person who made her aware of this shameful and hidden side of himself: his mortal enemy, Obi-Wan. But Padmé does not accept his redirection, reiterating that it is entirely because of the choices Anakin himself has made, and those he plans on making, that she has turned against him. Vader's musical theme plays the moment Anakin goes from treating Padmé like the woman he loves to a potential threat, casting her in the same light as all the Jedi he has categorized as his enemies. He can no longer fairly assess that his friends and family never actually turned against him; they simply didn't give him everything he wanted, needed, or demanded. From his warped point of view, that is the equivalent of betrayal. Now he's applying the same standard to his wife. If she won't give him everything he expects of her, she will be redefined as his enemy, too.

Padmé pleads with Anakin to stop what he's doing, to come back to the light, because she <u>loves him</u>. In this moment, she nearly succeeds in bringing Anakin back to the light via forced self-reflection. It might have been over then and there, had Obi-Wan not made his unfortunately timed appearance from Padmé's ship with the intention of challenging Anakin head-on, sending him right back into his angst and darkness. Padmé's soothing, feminine presence is at once replaced by Obi-Wan's confrontational, masculine one, framed in the ship's entrance with his hands on his hips in a disapproving power pose, ready to discipline his misbehaving son and/or younger brother. Now, instead of seeking Padmé's cooperation and understanding, he rejects, out of anger, what love she still offers because he believes she brought Obi-Wan to Mustafar to kill him. He reaches out through the Force to choke the woman he loves, the woman he sacrificed so much to save, all because she contradicts his manufactured identity.

Stern sibling Obi-Wan steps in and commands Anakin to <u>let her go</u>. With that choice of phrasing, the elder brother is reminding the younger of the root of the problem that is about to cost him the life of the woman he loves: his inability to let go of his attachments and unwillingness to let things change. He displays the same look of disgust, not anger, that Padmé did upon seeing Anakin's dark side, the Vader persona, as if to communicate with his whole face at once, "Who *are* you?" Obi-Wan already knew what had become of Anakin before confronting him. He saw him killing younglings on a security recording and pledging his allegiance to Darth Sidious. Cognitively, he was prepared for the truth of what he was about to encounter. But actually witnessing Anakin choke Padmé, the woman he loves, witnessing him do something so horrible, so unlike the man he knows him to be up close and in person, is still beyond his ability to integrate. He can only be shocked and disgusted by what Anakin, or rather the dark force replacing Anakin, is capable of. He looks upon his closest friend, his brother, as a stranger because *that's what he is.*

Anakin regains just enough composure to release an unconscious Padmé to the floor, exhausted from the effort it took to stop himself from killing her. He has not noticed the irony that he, himself, was about to take Padmé out of his own life by killing her and his unborn children had Obi-Wan not interfered. But it is beyond Anakin's ability to self-reflect and realize this in his enraged state, so all blame is projected outward at the object of his hatred. He curses Obi-Wan for turning Padmé against him and trying to take her from him instead of recognizing his own failings. Obi-Wan accuses Anakin of becoming what he swore to destroy by allowing Sidious to manipulate and corrupt him. But did Anakin ever actually swear to destroy the Sith? Or is that only a projection from what Obi-Wan and the Council imposed on him to become?

Obi-Wan, dressed in white, and Anakin, in black, circle around each other as Obi-Wan descends from Padmé's ship. For a moment, they reflect the swirling pattern of black and white halves of the yin-yang. With Obi-Wan pacing and lecturing Anakin, their dynamic has regressed back to how it was at the start of Episode 2, only with a much more confident and powerful Anakin, who is now ready to stand up for himself against his overbearing mentor. He's no longer a whiny teenager protesting his father figure's unfair expectations, but a grown man ready to commit patricide.

Anakin's ad-hoc justification for everything he's done is to <u>bring peace and security</u> to the galaxy. He has become megalomaniacal about his power and perceived importance, which he revealed earlier when he stated he was already planning to overthrow Palpatine and take his place as emperor. He is a far cry from the humble and desperate young man who earlier pledged that he would do anything to learn from Palpatine and save Padmé's life. Any backtalk from Obi-Wan at this point, any questioning of the reality of Anakin's interpretation of things, only results in death threats, believing that Obi-Wan is making him kill him by standing against him now. When Obi-Wan reminds Anakin of his allegiance to the Republic, he interprets it as though his master's institutions are more important to him than the people in his life, the people he is supposed to love and care for.

Anakin has already killed dozens of Jedi by now, so he shouldn't need any further incentive or excuse to kill one more. Obi-Wan is the biggest threat to Anakin at this moment, not just because he is a Jedi like the others, but because he is holding him accountable for what he has done and become. Anakin's association with Obi-Wan, the reminder of the standard by which he should evaluate his actions, threatens to tear down the empowering illusion he has built around himself. By threatening to kill him, he's saying, "You better shut your mouth before I shut it for you." Anakin is unable to consider any point of view but his own. Anyone who is not with him is his enemy. Either you love him and accept everything he thinks and does without reservation, or you cannot exist at all.

The only reason this dialogue is still going on is that Obi-Wan is still conflicted about his task of killing Anakin. If he had truly accepted that Anakin was gone, as Yoda claimed he was when they first discovered the security hologram of Anakin taking instruction from Darth Sidious, he would not be trying to lecture and talk sense into him. Nevertheless, Obi-Wan insists, both to himself and to Anakin, that he <u>will do what he must</u>. He is the first of the two to draw and ignite his lightsaber and signaling his readiness to attack. Mustafar's barely visible sun, peeking through the dark clouds, appears behind him. Anakin responds that Obi-Wan <u>will try</u>, only then taking out his weapon and launching the first attack in response. He's foreshadowing a lesson about determination that Yoda will reveal more clearly to Luke in *The Empire Strikes Back* when his X-wing sinks into the swamp of Dagobah. There is an important difference between trying and doing. Obi-Wan is trying to convince himself that he is now ready to kill his brother, the Chosen One, the boy he raised. Instead, only a half-hearted attempt will be made.

Thus begins the battle of heroes, which matters so much to the mythology of *Star Wars* because it is a test of how far Anakin has fallen, how committed he is to the dark side and his newfound amorality. Killing this particular Jedi will prove more challenging than all he has already slain, not because of how skilled a fighter Obi-Wan is, but because it will require completing his internal separation from every positive memory he has of being raised by the man he has now convinced himself is his mortal enemy, his own form of spiritual patricide. Outmatching Obi-Wan in lightsaber skill or Force ability should be easy for the Chosen One, but he unconsciously holds back because of how conflicted he still is. The same type of emotional conflict will allow his son to overpower him in a similarly fateful duel 23 years from now.

While Obi-Wan and Anakin fight their personal battle in the Hell of Mustafar,[54] the battle for the soul of Anakin, a parallel impersonal battle commences between Yoda and Darth Sidious for the soul of the Republic. Sidious opens by warning Yoda that his apprentice, Darth Vader, will <u>become more powerful than either of them</u>. He's speaking with the confidence and enthusiasm of a good mentor, the kind of mentor Qui-Gon was meant to be for Anakin. While the Jedi were always afraid that Anakin would become too powerful to predict or control, Sidious wholeheartedly encourages his apprentice to become as powerful as possible. He wants Darth Vader to surpass him, but only so long as it happens according to the path he has laid out for him. He is depending on him to carry the Sith lineage into the future.[55] The only thing that makes Sidious a bad mentor is that he, like the Jedi, is also trying to sneakily instill his own values and ends into his protégé instead of cultivating the conditions that will allow him to discover and embody his own. *Duel of the Fates* returns in the soundtrack as Yoda and Sidious duel in the Senate chamber, throwing literal pieces of the Senate with the Force as weapons. They fight to a stalemate, and Yoda is forced to retreat into exile due to his failure to stop the rise of a dictator.

Blue blades clash against the industrial background of Mustafar's lava refinery, through corridors, catwalks, and control rooms, as the environment starts to crumble from collateral damage reflecting how the two fighters' relationship is falling into chaos. All the teenage angst and sibling rivalry of Anakin's past have reemerged as violent brawling, now in the hands of an adult empowered to act on dangerous adolescent insecurities. Anakin and Obi-Wan appear evenly matched, each knowing each other's dueling techniques intimately. Anakin fights with the intensity of raging fire, and Obi-Wan responds to every move Anakin makes like flowing water. One is a master of offense[56] and the other a master of defense.[57] The Force theme plays over dissonant harmonies, implying that the Force itself seems to be in pain and struggling to control the situation, as each fighter attempts to overpower the other with it.

The track *Battle of the Heroes* begins playing. In this context, "hero" means someone fighting passionately for their ideology. With the fight between Yoda and Darth Sidious having ended prematurely, Anakin and Obi-Wan are the only two remaining heroes to represent their opposing ideologies in the conflict: the Sith and the Jedi, the dark side of the force and the light. The music brings in an apocalyptic choir and spiritual overtones to the hellscape visuals of Mustafar and Anakin's consuming hatred for his master. The apocalypse represents chaos overtaking all structure in life, in the world, in our conception of all that is. The galaxy is in a state of spiritual apocalypse, as is the bond between Anakin and Obi-Wan.

As the refinery crumbles, the two fighters are forced atop separate floating droids and platforms that carry them over lava flows, putting distance between them. For the first time since the fiery duel began, the fighting is forced into a short pause, during which these two can exchange a few words, each attempting to assert the rightness of their position to the other. The Force theme emerges again from the chaotic background to symbolize a strained attempt at reconnection. Obi-Wan restarts their dialogue by reflecting on his shortcomings as a mentor, admitting to Anakin that he has failed him by allowing all that has transpired to come about. This is the beginning of the accountability Obi-Wan will need in order to outgrow the trauma he is experiencing and evolve into the kind of mentor who will lead Anakin's offspring in the future. Yoda is undergoing a similar revelation about his failure to stop Sidious in their duel in the Senate chambers and prevent him from taking over. But Anakin dismisses Obi-Wan's humility, redirecting the conversation onto his warped conspiratorial conclusion that the Jedi had been plotting to take over the Republic all along, thereby justifying their brutal elimination.

We can feel Obi-Wan's frustration in this debate. How does he begin to try to correct the structure of false beliefs behind Anakin's accusations and the sense of his assuredness in his insane position? Should he try to calmly and rationally point out to an enraged mind that the Jedi were never plotting to take over? Doesn't Anakin already know they only attempted to arrest Palpatine because they learned from him that he was a Sith Lord? Anakin has already changed the interpretation of the facts in his mind. The only thing Obi-Wan can think to say in this moment is that Anakin's new master is evil, that he should not be trusted. Anakin dismisses this claim outright by countering it with an equivalent claim about the Jedi: that <u>from his point of view,</u> they are the evil ones. He has embraced complete moral relativism. It's not that he suffers any illusion about Palpatine being a saint. It's that he believes that anything you can accuse Palpatine of, you can just as easily accuse the Jedi of.[58] But that's not true. The Jedi fall short of an absolute and objective standard of morality, which makes them seem pious and hypocritical. But they at least recognize that there is good and evil in the universe, and that one should always *try* to align oneself with the good.

Obi-Wan's frustration mounts, and he accepts that if that's indeed how Anakin thinks, then he truly is lost. He is lost because he no longer cares about what is true, only what is convenient for him to believe. He now feels that he may, in fact, finally be ready to commit to the act that he has so far been conflicted about: killing his friend, apprentice, and brother, as there is no longer any hope of saving him. Anakin, too, is done talking. He tells his master that this is the end for him before leaping off his droid and onto Obi-Wan's moving platform, where they will have no choice but to continue dueling in close quarters. The fight cannot last much longer under these conditions. One of them will soon make a critical mistake and fall. Obi-Wan makes the tactical move to leap off the moving platform up onto a steep slope at the edge of the lava river, once again creating distance between them and a new chance for the fighting to stop.

At last, Obi-Wan's repositioning has given him a clear tactical advantage. Anakin is now fighting with lava to his back and a steep incline in front that he must climb to continue the offense. He cannot retreat. He cannot attack without putting himself at a major disadvantage to his opponent, who has all the room in the world to maneuver and does not have the terrain working against him. It should be a stalemate. Anakin's best move would be to take his time, reconsider his course, and find a way to work the battlefield in his favor, perhaps by moving laterally to Obi-Wan and slowly getting onto equal terrain again. But such an approach would require more patience than enraged Anakin currently has. The only other option would be to take Obi-Wan's advice and stop fighting for once. Let the fires of hatred go out. Just let it be over.

Obi-Wan declares that the fight is over because he has taken the high ground. Besides the literal meaning, Obi-Wan is signifying that he has won because he has the *moral* high ground. He is operating virtuously and consciously, not autonomously like Anakin, refusing to give in to corruption and take the easy way out. Anakin will continue unconsciously, with full force and fury, upon the path he started. He will not stop to reflect on whether his next action is the right one, and it's about to cost him the fight.

Anakin, at the moment consumed by Vader, takes Obi-Wan's declaration as a taunt or challenge, as though he is telling him that he is too weak to beat him under these conditions. Obi-Wan, he arrogantly believes, simply <u>underestimates his unfathomable power</u> as the Chosen One and now as a dark lord of the Sith acting without inhibition. Obi-Wan, knowing Anakin better than anyone, realizes what is happening in his mind and urges him <u>not to try</u> the tactically unwise assault that is about to come. The apocalyptic soundtrack reaches a crescendo. It knows the end of the fight is moments away. Whatever the result of the next move is, only one of these two men is walking away.

Ignoring Obi-Wan's warning, Anakin attempts a flipping strike up the steep terrain and over Obi-Wan's head. Obi-Wan, being prepared for it, easily counters, slashing Anakin mid-air with one patient stroke and severing both his legs and remaining organic arm, coinciding with the final beat of the music. The maimed torso of Anakin tumbles down the slope, coming to rest near the edge of the lava. The fight is over, just as quickly and decisively as it began.

Anakin should have won this fight. Obi-Wan beat him the only way he could: by exploiting a character weakness he was privy to as his long-time mentor and friend. He goaded his pupil into a momentary losing position and took advantage of the split-second window of opportunity to land an incapacitating blow. Obi-Wan had pulled a similar reversal against Darth Maul as a younger man in Episode 1 by letting him believe he had already won the fight, thereby putting his guard down when he had a tactical advantage, as Obi-Wan dangled helplessly over a pit in the power station of Naboo. Each Sith, Vader and Maul, in their respective duels against Obi-Wan, was deeply invested in the idea of their position as the superior duelist who would easily win the conflict. Each time, they were suddenly proven wrong. There was a significant difference between their perception and the reality of the situation, between trying to win and actually doing it.

As Anakin writhes on the lava bank, Obi-Wan looks down on him, devastated. *The Immolation Scene* is played out to low, tragic strings as a direct counter to the chaotic musical fury that persisted throughout their fight. The score is decidedly unheroic. Although the hero has beaten the villain, this moment is not a victory celebration. The music is telling us that something wonderful has been lost in the aftermath of a great and tragic conflict. Now that Anakin has been rendered no longer a threat, Obi-Wan is free to say what he really feels about all that has occurred. With tears in his eyes, he reprimands Anakin about the loss the galaxy has suffered because he has failed to be the Chosen One he was meant to be. Obi-Wan's lamentation at losing Anakin is not just contained to the loss of Anakin as who he was, but rather *who he was meant to be to the Jedi Order…* who Obi-Wan *expected him to become* according to the edict, prescription, prophecy, and destiny, not who he really was.

Nothing could have broken Anakin out of his fixation on Obi-Wan as the source of his problems at this moment. At the realization that his legs and remaining arm have been cut off, still, only thoughts of hatred flow through him. The only thing he can verbalize in his suffering and devastation is that he <u>hates Obi-Wan</u> with a passion as fiery as the flames about to consume him. Couldn't this have been a moment for Anakin to reflect and realize what a terrible mistake he had made? Shouldn't he have been wondering what errors in his judgment must have transpired to bring him to that moment, lying limbless in the dirt, when only days before, he was married to the woman he loved, a member of the Jedi Council, the hero of the Clone Wars, the Chosen One, and an expectant father? Instead, still, even in the most desperate moment, when virtually anyone else would have hit rock bottom and re-assessed their narrative of the situation, Anakin only burned hotter within and screamed out with a hateful passion that was more important to him than saving his life itself.[59] No longer capable of using the Force to protect himself from the heat of the lava river in his injured and distracted state, he catches on fire and burns alive. Obi-Wan returns to Padmé's ship alone, and the Mustafar sun that was mostly obscured by dark clouds before is now completely blacked out, signaling that all the light within Anakin is gone with it.

Every line Obi-Wan delivered to Anakin in their final interaction was conjugated in the past tense. They were all qualities Obi-Wan believed were once true but are no longer. You *were* the Chosen One.

You *were* my brother. I <u>loved you</u>. He no longer believes Anakin is the Chosen One, he no longer sees him as his brother, and he no longer loves him. He frames his love as something that ended when Anakin died and became Darth Vader. He accepted too soon that the person he loved was already dead, and thus it became a self-fulfilling prophecy. Any hope of resurrecting Anakin resided in the love of the people who knew him as his better self and held onto that image when no one else could. That is why Padmé almost succeeded in bringing him back and why Luke eventually will.

In her final conversation with her son, Shmi Skywalker's declaration of love was cut off by her sudden demise. She could not even complete the words expressing that she loved him. Her love for him was interrupted, cut short from what it should have been from mother to son, because the two were separated, and her life was unfairly taken too soon. Padmé's desperate declaration of love for Anakin on Mustafar, meanwhile, was emphatically communicated, but it was denied and rejected by Anakin, even violently turned against her when he called her a liar and accused her of betraying him. To accept her love in that moment, as he once did when she first confessed it to him on Geonosis in Episode 2, would have required him to reflect and be emotionally vulnerable again. Obi-Wan is the only one who successfully conveys the message that the love was real, but it is already gone by then. In all three cases, Anakin has failed to receive the love he needs from the three people closest to him, his family, before he loses them. His mother is too weak to voice it. His wife cannot penetrate the wall of anger he's put up between them. And the most important figure of all, father, brother, and mentor, expresses his love too late, framed as only a past state that no longer applies.

We must wonder if, at any time between what we are shown in Episodes 1, 2, and 3, Obi-Wan ever actually told Anakin that he loved him as a present state of feeling and being, if the Jedi code would have even allowed it. He told him he was proud of him. He told him he was a great Jedi and a hero. But love? Imagine how differently the scene on Mustafar might have gone if Obi-Wan, instead of showing how much pain he was in because of the terrible thing he's had to do to someone he used to love and think of as his brother, took that moment to do something unprecedented, something seemingly impossible: tell him he *still* loves him. He *still* sees him as his brother. He *still* believes he can accomplish the wonders he was meant to as the Chosen One. He loves him despite every mistake he's made, every terrible thing he's done, and *always* will. It would take 23 years for Luke to rectify Obi-Wan's error by showing Anakin that, despite everything, he *still* viewed him as his father. He still *loved* him as his son and was willing to die for that love.

Anakin should have died after burning on Mustafar. Obi-Wan left him there, barely alive, believing his injuries would end him. He could not bring himself to finish the task he was sent there for because of his attachment to his fallen brother. He allowed his personal feelings to get in the way of duty in the same way he reprimanded Anakin for doing. Obi-Wan underestimated the power of the dark side, failing to consider that it could sustain the Chosen One on the brink of death through the strength given by hatred. What's left of Anakin's body, now skeletal and ashen, uses its remaining cybernetic arm to try to pull itself up the loose gravel of the lava bank where it was abandoned. His only remaining familial figure now descends in a spaceship into the depths of Hell to rescue him. This time, it is not his wife with hopes of restoring his soul to the light, but his dark father, his majesty, newly crowned Emperor Palpatine, seeking to salvage what is left of his apprentice for eternal servitude. Anakin believed that by doing what he did, he would become the ruler of Hell, but its true overseer has just arrived to put him in his place. Palpatine is framed like the Grim Reaper, a pale white figure clad in a black cloak and hood leaning over the corpse of the newly deceased to claim his soul.

The skies on Coruscant, which have been growing darker throughout the film, are now a torrent of rain and lightning as what's left of Anakin's body is transported on a stretcher to the Emperor's medical facility. Meanwhile, on the outer rim asteroid colony of Polis Massa, the image of Padmé, draped in white and light in an ethereal setting, giving life to twins, is contrasted with Anakin's body, scorched and black in the shadows, surrounded by mechanical arms and cold machines, being reconstructed and resurrected as a living corpse over a floor that resembles the insignia of the Empire he is becoming an indistinguishable part of. One is natural and healthy life; the other is life twisted by mad science and suffering, according to the machinations of a devil figure. Both cry out in pain during their respective transformations, but interestingly, Anakin's screams continue to emanate after his mouth has stopped moving and the camera has cut back to Padmé. His soul is crying out to her through the Force, and she is still, at that moment, sensitive enough to hear him. Anakin's eyes widen as the Vader mask is lowered onto him and he sees through its false red-tinted eyes for the first time, as though he has just realized the state of existence he will be confined to for the rest of his life—trapped behind this artificial thing going over him that will distort his senses and identity for the rest of his life. The mask seals and pressurizes, and the suit takes over Anakin's breath as his heartbeat becomes inaudible, his last undeniable signs of being a living person.[60] The machine is living for him now.

Revenge of the Sith is the darkest film in the hexalogy. The gruesome visuals of Anakin's dismemberment, burning, and cybernetic reconstruction into a living corpse are included to show us that, for the rest of his life, he will reside in Hell. His injuries are punishment for his crimes, a physical representation of his emotional state and its effects. We are shown this because we need to understand the extent of his suffering as a result of the choices he has made so that we are never tempted to make the same ones in our own lives.[61] The story could have left Anakin's fate on Mustafar ambiguous for us, leaving us to believe that he died there until the mysterious Vader showed up in a black suit in the next movie and we put the pieces together on our own. Instead, it shoves the twisted transformation in our faces so that we do not miss the point it is making.

The last bit we see of the authentic Anakin identity is the sadness he displays right after being entombed in the iron lung. Having risen up from the laboratory slab as a quasi-zombified man, his face now the visage of a skull, he asks only about the safety of the woman he loves, just as she only asked about him after being choked by him and regaining consciousness. Even through the vocal modulator in his mask, the pain in his voice can be made out. It's not yet the dominating tone that the deep and robotic Vader voice will come to be known for. He ignores the bodily horror he has endured, his thoughts momentarily free of hatred again, unlike when Obi-Wan maimed him and he could only shout his hatred at him. Anakin cannot ever truly hate Padmé, so he is still capable of feeling sad and self-reflective about her.

All that changes the moment Palpatine says that Anakin inadvertently killed Padmé in his anger. The inwardly pointed sadness immediately turns into outwardly pointed rage and despair. Palpatine tells this half-truth in order to malevolently manipulate Anakin toward his own ends. He needs Anakin to believe that everything about his old life and his identity as Anakin Skywalker is over, that he can never return to being that person again, and must submit completely to the dark side and the false Vader identity. Anakin stumbles onto his new robotic legs, impulsively crushing the bits of machinery all around him with the Force, his anger now undirected at everything in the environment because there is no enemy out there to hate anymore, none but himself. When he screams an extended "Noooooooooo" to the cosmos, it's the same melodramatic "no" so far used throughout the saga: a reaction to an unacceptable fate one is powerless to do anything about. The word "no" does not accomplish anything. It is an admission of inadequacy, a desperate expression of powerlessness, the very thing Anakin was trying to avoid by becoming Darth Vader. Now, Vader truly hates Anakin Skywalker for what he has done by killing the woman he loved and must kill him in return.

Padmé dies after giving birth to twin son and daughter Luke and Leia, with Obi-Wan at her side, just as Anakin feared she would, despite nothing being physically wrong with her that the medical droids attending to her can identify. They are machines that look at the healthy functioning of the human body in a mechanistic way, just like Anakin strived to do to prevent the people he loved from dying. They cannot understand that there is more going on with Padmé than what they can sense as the biological cause of her death. She dies not merely from a broken heart, as is implied, but from the complete collapse of her worldview and sense of identity. If she can love someone capable of doing such terrible things as Anakin has, not only does she not know *Anakin* anymore... she does not even know *herself* either. The structure of her identity was destroyed with Anakin's because the two were so intertwined.

Padmé, on her deathbed, insists there is still good in Anakin. She has to believe this. Because if there isn't any good left, if Anakin is capable of turning truly and completely evil, it means everything she ever knew about him has been a lie. As his only remaining familial connection, with Obi-Wan having excised himself from that role, she alone maintains the unconditional ability to see him for who he really was, to love him unconditionally, even like a mother to her son.

Padmé's funeral procession is held in the same location where Episode 1's premature victory celebration was. It was bright, loud, and colorful then. Now, it is dark and gloomy, and everyone present marches in solemn silence instead of joy, with even the always whimsical Jar Jar Binks present in silent contemplation over the role he played in bringing the galaxy to this point by naively granting emergency powers to Chancellor Palpatine back in Episode 2. Her body is carried to its final resting place with the japor snippet necklace Anakin carved for her in Episode 1. She stated at that time that she did not need it to remember him. But now, it is the last tangible reminder of that goodness and innocence she saw in him back then, and it is being buried with her to represent that the version she knew of Anakin as a child has died, too.

For the rest of his life as Darth Vader, Anakin will serve as the fist of and slave to the Galactic Empire, carrying out Emperor Palpatine's tyrannical orders—from a slave to a junk dealer, to a slave to the Jedi, and now, for the rest of his life, a slave to Darth Sidious, the iron lung barely keeping him alive, and the psychological force that is Darth Vader. We will not see a return of his heroism and free will until the final moments of *Return of the Jedi*, when he breaks the spiritual chains of his enslavement and sacrifices everything false about his life to serve his one remaining authentic value: saving someone he loves, that thing which he promised to learn how to do someday as the most powerful Jedi ever.

The final shot of Darth Vader is of him standing beside Emperor Palpatine on the bridge of a Star Destroyer, watching over the construction of the Death Star—the Empire's upcoming instrument of terror and subjugation. This new Empire was born out of the Republic, which once prioritized individual sovereignty, freedom, and choice, just as Vader was born out of Anakin, who once valued preserving life and goodness in the galaxy. The people of the galaxy allowed themselves, just like Anakin, to become afraid, so they sought force and certainty that they believed would alleviate that burden, thinking it made them more powerful. This is slavery mentality; it relies on masters and authority to dictate reality instead of employing its own consciousness and choice.

The two members of the Jedi Council who survived the purge of Order 66, Obi-Wan and Yoda, are the only ones to learn the lessons and evolve past the dogmatic old ways that made their Order vulnerable to corruption and collapse. They will eventually pass this new understanding on to Luke, the first of a new breed of Jedi who will rebuild the Order again from a clean slate, finally knowing enough not to repeat the mistakes of the past. It was the downfall of Luke's very own father that gave Obi-Wan the experiences he would need to derive the wisdom he would pass along to Anakin's very own son as Ben.

Before departing for Tatooine to watch over the son of Anakin Skywalker, a task he has taken on due to the guilt he feels over his failure with Anakin, Obi-Wan, soon to be reborn under a new name and identity, learns that his old master, Qui-Gon Jinn, has returned from the netherworld of the Force as the galaxy's first Force spirit.[62] He has achieved the immortality sought by desperate members of the Sith, such as Vader, Sidious, and Plagueis, albeit not in the literal, biological form any of them ever envisioned. Because Qui-Gon was a proper mentor to those who knew him, he has transcended physical death to live on in the hearts and minds of those he influenced while he was alive. His spirit, the pattern of the values and personality he represented, persists as a living memory in others. He earned immortality by becoming an immortal force to them, one worth carrying on into the future. It is wisdom that he will pass on to Yoda and Obi-Wan next, as they ascend to the level of paragons for Luke.

Star Wars has descended to its lowest point—a dark night of the soul for the galaxy and its heroes. Yoda and Obi-Wan are the hidden keepers of the light now, and the Skywalker twins are its receptacles. Next comes the turning point, when hope returns and heroism begins to create a higher form of order out of the chaos that has overwhelmed the soul of the galaxy, sonically signaled by Luke's and Leia's hopeful musical themes that appear for the first time as they make their way to their new homes on Tatooine and Alderaan. The Force theme plays the film out as Owen and Beru Lars hold Luke and look off into the binary *sunrise* of Tatooine, signaling the *rising* of new hope and consciousness in the twin newborns. The light has gone out in Anakin, but it has passed into his offspring. So long as those who survive can learn from their mistakes for those who come after, there is hope.

NOTES

41. "Some people were having a hard time with the way Anakin goes bad. Somebody asked whether somebody could kill Anakin's best friend, so that he gets really angry. They wanted a real betrayal, such as, 'You tried to kill me so now I'm going to try to kill you.' They didn't understand the fact that Anakin is simply greedy. There is no revenge." George Lucas, quoted by J. W. Rinzler, *The Making of Star Wars: Revenge of the Sith* (New York: Del Rey, 2005), 188.

42. "For the audience, it's a real jerk, because you're going along and then somebody yanks you in a different direction. Anakin turning to the dark side and killing Mace is a very hard right, because we're dealing with things that aren't so obvious. The audience knows Anakin is going to turn to the dark side, but the things that he's struggling with are so subtle that it may be hard for people to understand why his obsession to hold on to Padmé is so strong." George Lucas, quoted by J. W. Rinzler, *The Making of Star Wars: Revenge of the Sith* (New York: Del Rey, 2005), 205.

43. "I now have to make a movie that works by itself, but which also works with this six-hour movie and this overall twelve-hour movie. I'll have two six-hour trilogies, and the two will beat against each other: One's the fall, one's the redemption. They have different tonalities, but it's meant to be one experience of twelve hours." George Lucas, quoted by J. W. Rinzler, *The Making of Star Wars: Revenge of the Sith* (New York: Del Rey, 2005), 62.

44. "[*Star Wars*] is the hero's myth, really. I mean, there's a whole political side to it, which is the same as the mythological side of it, which is where you take one of the issues, which is how does a democracy turn itself into a dictatorship, which I was fascinated with. It happened in Rome, happened in France, happened in Germany, and what causes that to happen." George Lucas, interviewed by Bill Bradley for *American Voices*, November 15, 2015.

45. The Legends novel *Darth Plagueis* by James Luceno (New York: Del Rey Books, 2012), revealed that Plagueis and Sidious performed Sith rituals to manipulate the Force and the midi-chlorians, hoping to create a being of pure dark side energy. The Force reacted to their meddling by conceiving Anakin as a balance to their interference. Having failed to create their own version of a dark messiah to lead the Sith to victory over the Jedi, they take on the task of converting the Jedi's own to their side once young Anakin is identified in *The Phantom Menace*. Additionally, Lucas said in "George Lucas and the Cult of Darth Vader" for *Rolling*

Stone, "It's left unsaid: Is Anakin a product of a super-Sith who influenced the midichlorians to create him, or is he simply created by the midichlorians to bring forth a prophecy, or was he created by the Force through the midichlorians? It's left up to the audience to decide. How he was born ultimately has no relationship to how he dies, because in the end, the prophecy is true: Balance comes back to the Force."

46. "You basically get somebody who's going to make a pact with the Devil, and it's going to be a pact with the Devil that says, 'I want the power to save somebody from death. I want to be able to stop them from going to the river Styx, and I need to go to a god for that, but the gods won't do it, so I'm going to go down to Hades and get the Dark Lord to allow me to have this power that will allow me to save the very person I want to hang on to.' … That's, as we say in the film, unnatural. You have to accept the natural course of life. Of all things." George Lucas, quoted by Jim Windolf, "*Star Wars: The Last Battle*," *Vanity Fair*, February 2005, 110.

47. Deleted scenes from *Revenge of the Sith* depict Anakin growing suspicious of Obi-Wan and Padmé having a romantic affair behind his back, increasing his mistrust and jealousy toward his mentor before their showdown on Mustafar. Palpatine encourages this anxiety by suggesting that Padmé is hiding something, which turns out to be her involvement in the deleted subplot of the formation of the Alliance to Restore the Republic, the precursor to the Rebel Alliance in *A New Hope*. This is intensified when Anakin starts seeing Obi-Wan in his premonitions of Padmé dying in childbirth, suggesting he even fears that Obi-Wan may be the real father.

48. "[Palpatine] lures Anakin into a very impressionable state. It happens once the Emperor starts to work on him and make him doubt things, make him doubt his relationship to the Jedi, make him doubt what is good in the universe. This is where he finally succumbs to the influence of the devil." George Lucas, interview in *The Chosen One*, featurette on *Star Wars: Episode III – Revenge of the Sith* (DVD, Lucasfilm Ltd., 2005).

49. "[Anakin] progresses from being a bright, smart, loving, caring young boy to being an attentive, hardworking, but ambitious padawan learner who feels that, because he's better at being a Jedi and his Jedi skills than most of the other Jedi, that he should progress further and faster. And as he progressed, it was his inability to control his temper and his greed to control things that were his undoing." George Lucas, interview in *The Return of Darth Vader*, featurette on *Star Wars: Episode III – Revenge of the Sith* (DVD, Lucasfilm Ltd., 2005).

50. In Legends continuity (*Darth Bane Trilogy* by Drew Karpyshyn, New York: Del Rey, 2006, 2007, 2009), the Rule of Two was an edict demanding there only ever be one Sith master and one Sith apprentice at any given time. It was created by Darth Bane, a Sith Lord who lived a thousand years before the events of Episode 1, who witnessed how the old Sith Order destroyed itself through infighting and power struggles. According to this edict, the master embodies the power of the dark side, and the apprentice craves that power and seeks to surpass and replace the master, typically by killing him as proof that he is ready to. This creates a cycle wherein only the most powerful and cunning Sith survive, preserving their strength through concentration and evolution, rather than dilution by numbers.

51. "[Anakin] believes that he's the Chosen One. He's not doing wrong things knowing that it's having a negative impact. So, there is, there's that sort of naivety to him now that that wasn't there before, and it makes him more human in a lot of ways." George Lucas, interview in *The Chosen One*, featurette on *Star Wars: Episode III – Revenge of the Sith* (DVD, Lucasfilm Ltd., 2005).

52. "The Emperors don't see it. No matter how much you tell them, they can't see beyond their own greed. And anybody who is talking about hate or, you know, doing bad things to people, they are on the Emperor's side." George Lucas, interviewed by Bill Bradley for *American Voices*, November 15, 2015.

53. "If Anakin hadn't got all beat-up, he could have beat the Emperor." George Lucas, quoted by J. W. Rinzler, *The Making of Star Wars: Revenge of the Sith* (New York: Del Rey, 2005), 205.

54. "The climactic battle takes place on a sea of fire - lava, actually - on a planet filled with nothing but volcanoes... It ends in hell." George Lucas, interviewed by Rebecca Leung, "'Star Wars' Goes to Hell," *CBS News*, March 10, 2005

55. "Anakin, as Skywalker, as a human being, was going to be extremely powerful, but he ended up losing his arms and a leg and became partly a robot. So a lot of his ability to use the Force, a lot of his powers, are curbed at this point, because, as a living form, there's not that much of him left. So his ability to be twice as good as the Emperor disappeared, and now he's maybe 20 percent less than the Emperor. So that isn't what the Emperor had in mind. He wanted this really super guy, but that got derailed by Obi-Wan." George Lucas, quoted by Jim Windolf, "*Star Wars: The Last Battle*," *Vanity Fair*, February 2005, 117.

56. Anakin's fighting style, Djem So, is aggressive and relentless. The fighter seeks to dominate their opponent through a barrage of extremely fast and powerful strikes

to land a quick victory. His mastery of this form is what enabled him to slay so many Jedi once Order 66 commenced. But if the conflict does not end quickly, Djem So fatigues the attacker, leaving them vulnerable to critical tactical mistakes, which Anakin eventually makes, leading to his loss against Obi-Wan.

57. Obi-Wan's fighting style is Soresu, a defensive form developed to survive prolonged combat by emphasizing efficiency, patience, and tight defensive maneuvers. The fighter outlasts and wears down their opponent while waiting for the precise moment to counterattack, just as we saw during Obi-Wan's duel against General Grievous' four lightsabers. That Obi-Wan is a master of Soresu and knows Anakin's fighting style (including its weakness) is why he survives the prolonged onslaught and turns it into a slim victory.

58. "Anakin has to make a decision. His rationalization is 'Everybody is after power. Even the Jedi are after power.' Therefore, he thinks, 'They're all equally corrupt now.'" George Lucas, quoted by J. W. Rinzler, *The Making of Star Wars: Revenge of the Sith* (New York: Del Rey, 2005), 52.

59. According to *The Making of Star Wars, Episode III - Revenge of the Sith* by J.W. Rinzler (New York: Del Rey, 2005), Anakin was originally scripted to call out to Obi-Wan for help here, only for Obi-Wan to reject his cry. This would have been the moment he began to realize he had made a mistake. Lucas removed the line because he did not want to show any sign of redemption in Anakin until much later in his life, when he learns about Luke. This version of events is more consistent with the portrayal of the dark side and its aggression as all-consuming under its influence. More on this in the Conclusion.

60. "Obviously, one of the key elements in Episode 3 is that we see him actually put into the iron lung. The mask finally closed on him, that now he's an artificial man. But we know what's inside of it." George Lucas, interview in *The Return of Darth Vader*, featurette on *Star Wars: Episode III — Revenge of the Sith* (DVD, Lucasfilm Ltd., 2005).

61. "It's important in the end that you see the physical transformation of Anakin into this burnt-up crisp because that's the suffering he had to live with for the rest of his life... I felt it was important that we actually see that happen so that we could see the consequences of these bad things that he did." George Lucas, interview in *The Chosen One*, featurette on *Star Wars: Episode III — Revenge of the Sith* (DVD, Lucasfilm Ltd., 2005).

62. In season six of *The Clone Wars* television series, Yoda learns that Qui-Gon Jinn learned to retain his consciousness after death through the Living Force by training with the Force Priestesses, manifestations of the Force who resided on the Wellspring of Life.

LUKE'S CHILDHOOD

R*evenge of the Sith* concluded with Obi-Wan and Yoda fleeing into exile from an evil that had grown too powerful for them to oppose—Yoda to be alone on the swamp planet of Dagobah and Obi-Wan to watch over Luke's development on Tatooine. Their tactical retreat was never meant to be a surrender or an admission of permanent defeat. They had not given up hope, despite all they had lost. Yoda stated that they would disappear until the time was right. They are waiting not just for the twin children of the Chosen One to come of age, but for the general condition of the galaxy to progress to where it is willing to take a stand against its own enslavement and the illusion of security cast over it. Society requires a cultural evolution, represented by the rise of the Rebel Alliance 19 years after the formation of the Empire.

Luke Skywalker begins his story with the same childlike naivety as his father. While Anakin began his journey out of the safety of home too early at the age of nine, Luke's journey has been delayed too long. At 19, he should already be out in the world, overcoming obstacles and establishing his identity. Instead, he has been deliberately sheltered, hidden from the Empire, and kept psychologically inhibited by his aunt and uncle.

In the time since we last saw him, Darth Vader has evolved into his new position of power within the Empire and with the dark side of the Force. Superficially, he has exactly what he wants. However, those who have fallen to the dark side are not fulfilled, regardless of their visible accomplishments, and no matter how much they may project the image that they are. Vader is perpetually insecure and unsatisfied with himself. His performative confidence and power must overcompensate for that. Realizing how miserable he is and that every display of power is a pitiable defense mechanism surrounding a vulnerable ego, the only appropriate stance to take is not to vilify him but to show empathy and compassion for all he has been through to bring him to this point. It will take two more movies for Luke to mature enough to realize this when no one else in Anakin's life could.

Indeed, the icon of Darth Vader represents one of cinema's most remarkable displays of how context transforms the meaning in character design. The first time I ever saw him was the same as it was for most people from my generation: when he boarded the Tantive IV in the opening scene of *A New Hope*. The framing of the shot, the musical cues, the deference with which the stormtroopers and Imperial officers treated him, the fear on the faces of the Rebel soldiers, the black suit and cape, and his imposing stature and voice all made one thing very clear to my impressionable young mind: this man, whoever he was, was archetypal or elemental, practically darkness personified.[63] His armor felt like a deliberate, almost theatrical choice to project power and instill fear. I didn't even question what he looked like beneath the mask or why he wore it.

After I witnessed Vader's backstory, the armor that once seemed like an extension of his power was revealed as an elaborate life-support system, a mobile iron lung for a weak, deformed, and crippled body. The mechanical breathing, once thought to be calculated, became a constant reminder of his suffering and vulnerability, audibly underscoring his dependence on machinery to survive. The weight of his choices was carried with every labored step upon mechanical legs plugged into charred stumps. The Vader suit now evoked pity as a cage for a man who was simultaneously victim and villain.

Vader's manufactured personality also shifts in light of his tragic backstory. The confident, commanding personality covers up deep regret and self-loathing. It's like something Anakin picked up from his interactions with the magnanimous Count Dooku about how to carry himself to command respect as an intimidating figure. As the father figure to his original father figure (Dooku trained Qui-Gon after being trained by Yoda) and a fellow Jedi who became disillusioned with the

Order, Dooku was Anakin's spiritual grandfather. Anakin's personality transformation to Vader was influenced by how he perceived Dooku as one of his primary dark role models, right down to his regal cape and chain.[64]

My initial interpretation of Vader relied on my ignorance, as it does on his enemy's ignorance in-universe. Vader's entire presentation serves to establish him as an almost mythological figure of intention and evil. However, once the viewer understands the horrific circumstances that led to his current state, every aspect of his appearance transforms from intimidating to tragic. This recontextualization forces us to reinterpret every scene with him from the original trilogy.

The tragedy deepens when we consider how Vader must be acutely aware of this disparity between appearance and reality. None of his superficial ability to make himself appear powerful will ever compensate for the knowledge of the broken husk of a man within. When I look at Vader's mask now, fully informed about the character, I see hollow eyes and the corpse of a man who is the walking experience of death embodied, whose only power left in the universe is to intimidate and kill. I see a man who carries the weight of the worst mistake it is possible for a man to make.

Vader's first interaction with Princess Leia, the secret daughter, after boarding her ship strikes a similar chord to Anakin's last interaction with Padmé, her mother, as he accused her of betraying him on Mustafar. Leia is following in her mother's footsteps by acting as a key member in the Rebellion against the Empire. Throughout her career in politics, Padmé attempted to lead the Republic back to diplomacy, starting in *The Phantom Menace* when she refused to condone a course of action that would lead to war. In *Attack of the Clones*, she led the movement against the creation of the Grand Army of the Republic. In *Revenge of the Sith*, she planted the seeds of what would grow into the Rebel Alliance after the Empire took over.[65] Now, Vader accuses Leia of being part of that rebellion, a traitor to the Empire, just as Anakin once accused Padmé of sounding like a Separatist when she asked for his help to end the fighting and resume diplomacy. A totalitarian mindset like Vader's cannot tolerate any deviation from its worldview and prescriptions because it maintains its sense of identity through a rigid structure of control over others.

When we first meet Luke, the secret son, on Tatooine, he has the temperament of a whiny child and is treated as such by his adoptive uncle. This does not look like the hero of the galaxy. He is frustrated with the lack of opportunities afforded to him by his simple life on as a moisture farmer. While his father's stuck state was physically forced upon him by slavery, Luke's comes from guilt about his duty to family responsibilities. Although already 19, the age Anakin was by his second film in his story, Luke functions as a child. He sees the world through childlike eyes, naïve about the state of the galaxy and feeling powerless to do anything about the trajectory of his life. The first thing in his life to interrupt that state is the discovery of Princess Leia's message within R2-D2 asking Obi-Wan Kenobi for help. The image of a beautiful girl calling for help becomes the inciting incident that sets him on the path out of the life he knows and on a quest that will take him out of childhood naivete.

When Luke approaches his aunt and uncle with news of the distress call intended for Obi-Wan, it threatens their disarming narrative of who he is. Uncle Owen hopes to nip Luke's curiosity in the bud by telling him that Obi-Wan died at the same time as his father. Owen is telling the truth, from a certain point of view. The man Obi-Wan had been before losing Anakin died along with Anakin. He had to reinvent himself with a new identity, but he did it in the opposite way that Anakin did: by finally becoming the type of mentor, the type of father figure he should have been. He found the strength to metamorphose into the best version of himself, which he called Ben, while Anakin allowed himself to descend into his worst self, called Vader.

Luke submits to his uncle's command to forget the whole thing but still tries to negotiate for the right to leave his home behind by joining the Imperial Academy. Owen rejects this idea, claiming to need Luke's help during harvest time, when in reality it is due to his fear of what Luke may become out in the galaxy on his own. Owen has been the protective shell Luke needed to survive his childhood in comfort and love, just as Shmi was for Anakin, but he is not prepared to mentor him into the next stage of his maturation into an adult. Aunt Beru is somewhat more supportive than Owen, encouraging her husband to let Luke leave home and spread his wings like his friends have done. She knows that Luke's authentic destiny does not lie on their farm. He's too much like Anakin, too sensitive and ambitious for his own good. When the Lars family met Anakin, they could not stop him from rushing off in a state of passion to find his mother. Now, decades later in the same house with Luke, they succeed in dissuading him from leaving the moisture farm and accept that he has nowhere to go.

That evening, Luke looks longingly off into Tatooine's setting suns, into the horizon and a future it seems like he will never know. The setting of the suns represents the temporary diminishment of his consciousness and the loss of hope for the galaxy due to the restrictions he has surrendered to (and even the twins of the Chosen One, who are at this moment both hopelessly suppressed from developing and fulfilling their function). The Force theme builds up but does not resolve, trailing off into nothingness to represent its unfinished business and incomplete actualization in Luke.

Fortunately for the future of the galaxy, R2-D2, the exceptionally self-determined astromech droid, chooses to escape from the Lars homestead after using his creativity to trick Luke into removing his restraining bolt and heads off in search of Obi-Wan on his own. Luke goes out after him the next day, into the same Jundland Wastes where his grandmother was abducted by sand people. He's ambushed by a gang of Tusken Raiders, who are perhaps spooked by the return of a young man who bears a striking resemblance to the mythical killer who entered their camp years ago and slaughtered their tribe. He is saved by Ben Kenobi, who, so far as Luke knows, is simply a strange old desert hermit. In reality, Ben is the identity adopted by Obi-Wan Kenobi after the events of *Revenge of the Sith*, in which he lost everything that tied him to the person he used to be. Just as Anakin became Darth Vader as a result of the trauma he endured under his original identity, Obi-Wan had to become someone new to acclimate to the new reality he was living in, one where he could not continue to be the general and Jedi master who fought in the Clone Wars and mentored the Chosen One. That person saw everything he loved and worked for fall apart before his eyes. To go on living, he had to become the kind of person who could carry the light of hope to a new generation cast in darkness. He spent 19 years watching over Luke, preparing for the time when he would need the kind of mentorship he failed to give his father.

When Ben runs into Luke and R2 and hears that name Obi-Wan again, the memories of that life come flooding back. Owen insisted that Obi-Wan was dead, and for a time, that was true. But now Ben will deny that claim, insisting that Obi-Wan is not dead yet. Unlike Darth Vader, who will do anything to bury all association with his past self as Anakin Skywalker in the cemetery of his mind, Ben comes to terms with his past. The resurgence of the Obi-Wan identity signals the start of new hope, a time for him to emerge from hiding and begin restoring order to the galaxy. He knows he is about to begin playing a vital mentoring role in Luke's life as the paragon who will guide him to fulfill his destiny. This time, he's ready for the burden, unlike many years ago with Anakin, when he faced many doubts about his ability to mentor in the way he needed him to. Ben is integrating the memories of his old identity with the worldview of the new one. He is not distorting reality like Vader did by cutting off ties to a traumatic past and distancing himself from the truth.

At Ben's desert home, Luke learns a new version of the truth about his father. The version he had learned from Owen, that his father was a navigator on a spice freighter, was fabricated to quell any curiosity about his exceptional father or, worse, any ambition to become like him. Ben will now tell him the version he prefers, a half-truth that emphasizes the best aspects of his father and downplays or covers up the rest. Ben needs Luke to believe that his father was a great man, a general in the Clone Wars, the best star pilot in the galaxy, a cunning Jedi warrior, and a good friend. It's a form of benevolent manipulation. Unlike Palpatine's malevolent manipulations of Anakin, Ben intends to give Luke the information he will need to become his *best* self instead of his *worst*. He knows that if Luke has the mythical image of a proper father figure to look up to and set an example for what he can and should become, it will establish the foundation for his character development. Anakin had no father; Luke gets a fairy tale father instead.

Ben even passes along Anakin's lightsaber to Luke, the weapon that symbolizes his greatness and duty during his time as a Jedi Knight for the Republic and the burdens of being a hero. He tells him his father wanted him to have it—another half-truth. Ben is speaking of the man Anakin would have become had he stayed in the light and continued to mature into a proper father for Luke, if he had not allowed his insecurities to get the better of him. It's what he would have wanted if he had been fully self-expressed in his caring and mentorship for his son. Ben is paying homage to Anakin by treating him as though he died as the best version of himself instead of the worst. He's finally displaying the compassion Anakin needed from him when he descended into Hell.

Luke is also learning the fairy tale version of what the Jedi Order was, guardians of peace and justice for over a thousand generations, instead of the flawed and dogmatic institution it had allowed itself to become by the fall of the Republic, before the Dark Times and the Empire. While Anakin grew up learning mythical stories about the heroic Jedi, even in the backwater environment of Tatooine, Luke had never even heard of them until now, allowing him no ambition to become like them until this sudden introduction with his father and Ben as their figureheads for him. The Empire's propaganda has all but wiped out public knowledge of the Jedi, so Ben is free to tell the version of their history that he prefers to remember, the version that makes it easier for him to process his own failings.

Still, the biggest manipulation is yet to come, a form of deceptive mentorship that has to do with how Luke's father died. There's a literal meaning to death, in the biological sense of the cessation of an organism, and a metaphorical interpretation of Anakin's death. The metaphorical, selective, and relevant truth Ben tells—that Darth Vader was a pupil of his who turned to evil before betraying and murdering Luke's father[66]—is a kindness Ben offers to young Luke. Luke is mythologically still a child at this stage in the story. He is emotionally and intellectually immature. He has lived his whole life on a farm and doesn't know a thing about galactic wars and magical space wizards. He couldn't have understood the whole literal truth even if Obi-Wan had tried to explain it. A considerable amount of background information would have had to be filled in for him before he could have interpreted the conclusion correctly, which is to say nothing of the emotional effect it would have on him to learn that his father was neither a common navigator nor a mythical hero, but the cyborg enforcer of a space dictator.

Obi-Wan equates a change in personality and values with something as permanent and serious as physical death because he knows identity is the product of the continuity of consciousness. Autobiographical memory is what we can consciously recall experiencing as ourselves in a coherent narrative of events, which gives us our life story and sense of who we are. Identity is the integrated product of a consistent self-narrative. You are the result of the story you tell about yourself, which is formed by the selected memories you carry forward and the meaning you derive from them.

If trauma causes someone to dissociate from that story and forget the most important aspects of who they are, they cannot be a fully integrated self until the conflict is resolved. Whole events can be blocked out or the meaning behind them rewritten because they are associated with too much pain. When we cannot fully and fairly remember and reflect on our own experiences, we cannot learn their lessons. The lessons we should have learned from a traumatic experience, such as Anakin losing his mother, in order to know how to better protect ourselves from similar forms of pain, never get consolidated into an empowering worldview and self-narrative. Anakin failed to learn the right lessons from losing his mother, which caused him to repeat the mistake with Padmé. Now he has made it the whole galaxy's problem. Instead of bringing out the best from within himself to improve the rest of the world with, he has brought out the worst of himself to infect the world and make it as dark as he is. Darth Vader is not Anakin Skywalker because he does not acknowledge himself as Anakin, in the same way that Anakin did not acknowledge the darkness within himself, the shadow of the proto-Vader influence, before it took over. He did not consider it part of himself before he turned, and that's what eventually gave it the power to take over.

People die every time they abandon an old identity because it no longer serves the narrative they prefer to tell about who they are. A Jedi's Force spirit represents a form of immortality. It is a permanent state achieved by consistently and integrally developing a virtuous character. Those who remain true to themselves do not die, except once, only in the biological sense, at the end of their organic life. They achieve immortality because they develop the ability to maintain a continuity of consciousness aligned with a permanent reality, which they aim to pass on to the next generation that outlives them.

What's most important about the story Ben tells Luke is that he *does* intend to eventually tell him the full truth about his father, as does Yoda when it comes time for him to play his part in the story. They do not intend to keep him in the dark forever or continue benevolently manipulating him longer than necessary with their softened version of events. Ben genuinely believes he's doing the best thing for Luke at this stage in his maturation. Ben lies to Luke about Anakin because he wants him to make the kind of choices he would make if he had a father who lived up to Anakin's potential. He is also trying to avoid the possibility that Luke might be inclined to turn to the dark side if he knows it's what his father did. By presenting Luke with this modified version of reality, Ben is taking responsibility for the choices Luke will make operating under these premises. And ideally, once Luke has reached the end of his journey and become a mature adult, he will be ready for the full truth. He will be able to look back and agree with Ben's choice to deceive him before he was ready to know everything. Ben is making that choice for young Luke on behalf of the man he believes he will become. All parents play similar roles in guiding their children's actions and presenting simplified truths tailored to help them make good choices.

With that hope in mind, Ben invites Luke to learn about the Force and come with him to Alderaan to deliver the Death Star plans that Leia hid in R2's memory banks, but Luke rejects the opportunity to grow. Ben reminds him that he and Leia need his help, hoping to appeal to Luke's inherent goodness and desire to help others, a trait he inherited from his father. Luke's fear is still too strong at this point in his story, so he fails this first test of values.

Only a few scenes ago, he had been complaining about the restrictions placed on him by his aunt and uncle. Then he met a crazy old wizard in the desert who revealed to him that his father was actually a great and powerful warrior, a hero, signaling to Luke that he, too, may have a great destiny. Luke has just been given the opportunity he has been looking for to escape his mundane life and begin living up to his potential. Now he claims that he can't get involved because he's got work to do on the farm. His aunt and uncle will be mad at him for getting home late. Luke hates the Empire, but he believes he is powerless to do anything about it, his uncle's reserved ideology talking through him. There is no distinction between Luke and his parental figures because his will is subordinate to theirs. Luke, as an expressed individual, does not really exist yet. Episode 4, the part of the story representing his first steps out of childhood, is all about how he begins to define himself through authentic choice and action.

Anakin started the journey too young, before he was naturally ready for separation from the protective shell of his mother. Luke is too old. He's past the point where the separation would naturally have occurred, so he has remained a child psychologically. The longer he waits now, the more resistance he will feel about stepping away from the only state of living he has ever known. Without direct intervention of forces beyond his control, he will never organically alter his trajectory. Inertia has taken over. When Ben urges Luke to learn about the Force, he's telling him that it's time for him to get off the inauthentic path he started on and become what he was born to be. He's telling Luke to trust his judgment, that there are things he knows from his privileged position as his mentor that Luke couldn't possibly begin to understand, but that he will when he is ready. He does not force Luke. He leaves him with the freedom to deny the path placed before him, to do what he feels is right instead. He only plants the seeds that he hopes will sprout into the inspiration Luke needs to begin discovering himself. A mentor opens their apprentice's eyes to a larger world and inspires them to become brave enough to enter it.

Tragically, it's only because Luke's aunt and uncle die at the hands of stormtroopers looking for C-3PO and R2-D2 that he can overcome his fear and leave the obligations of his past behind. They become the latest parental figures to suddenly exit their role in a young hero's life, through either death or separation, enabling him to begin to live his life on his own terms instead of theirs. If Owen and Beru had lived, the pressure to stay in the life he knew would have been too strong. He would never have undergone the initial catalysis that would eventually transform him into the adult version of himself. For most people, fear will be stronger than curiosity or ambition until a situation becomes intolerable. Luke was able to finally answer the call to adventure because he had no comfort waiting back home anymore. The only direction left to travel in was forward. He processes the trauma of the loss of what was holding him back extremely quickly compared to Anakin's response to losing his mother.

When Luke finally tells Ben that he wants to come with him to Alderaan, it's his way of saying he is free from the guilt that prevented him from discovering what else he could become beyond what he already knew, what his parental figures insisted he was. He has a new mythic image in his mind to follow as his guiding star, that of his father, the legendary Jedi Anakin Skywalker. That image is what will finally lead him out of childhood and into belated adolescence, where he will be forced to confront the opposite of everything he believed to be true about the world and himself in the following film.

For seasoned travelers and adventurers like Ben and the soon-to-join pilot Han Solo, the chaos of the alien cantina at Mos Eisley spaceport is just another day out in the universe. But someone like Luke, who has never even left Tatooine, has the same reaction that theater audiences in 1977 must have had when first witnessing the absurd scene of upbeat jazz and all manner of strange alien creatures. The cantina represents a microcosm of the unknown and uncomfortable new world Luke is stepping into by leaving the comfort of home, and he is utterly unprepared for what he will encounter out there. Sensing Luke's vulnerability, like that of an out-of-place tourist in a bad part of town, two alien thugs approach to harass him. Ben, remaining calm, has learned not to escalate a fight if it need not be escalated. It is only when one of them shoves Luke that he, as acting father figure, steps in to defend the hapless child. Luke is not ready for this wild new world of antagonizers and uncertainty he is entering. Ben, the unassuming old man, is prepared to kill to defend himself and those he cares about without breaking a sweat, but he does not need to feel enraged to do so. He is entirely dispassionate, in accordance with the Jedi code, activating his lightsaber only when necessary and deactivating it immediately afterward. Luke, like Anakin in *The Phantom Menace*, might not even have survived his first steps outside the comfort of home without his mentor there to protect him, which will make it all the more perilous for him when he loses that mentor.

Han Solo's role in Luke's life will come to be that of the jaded older brother figure. He has, through his experiences, come to believe that he understands how the universe works, and he has carved out a niche for himself to thrive within that understanding. He is not as open-minded as his little brother anymore, and he wants to guide him to adopt the same cynical outlook. When he sees Luke training with his lightsaber against a remote and trying to feel the Force for the first time, he can't help but mock him for it. Han trusts in only what he can see, what his experience tells him is true and practical, like the reliability of a blaster. Han, the eternal rogue, is characterized by his refusal to accept anyone's or anything's mandates about how his life is supposed to go, rejecting any concept of <u>anything that controls his destiny</u>.

Luke is the opposite. He is learning to trust that there is more to reality than what he has directly experienced of it and the narrow way he has learned to categorize it. And if he relies too heavily on what his mind and senses tell him or the limits of the tools and technology available to him, he will not grow to become everything he is capable of, and he will not learn to access those parts of the world that are still undiscovered. Ben insists to his protégé that a Jedi can feel the Force flowing through him, encouraging him to tap into a subtler kind of sensing and knowing that precedes interaction with the physical world outside the body. Ben is indirectly referencing the high concentration of midi-chlorians in Luke's blood, a trait passed down from his father that will enable him to feel his own biological processes in ways that others overlook when they speak of the Force as some mystical and ethereal energy field that is distinct from their own physical existence. From sensitivity to that feeling, his power in the Force will start to grow. When Luke successfully deflects the blasts from a training remote with his helmet's blast shield down, without the use of his sight, it's a small drop of foreshadowing of the power of his intuition that will come when he switches off his X-wing's targeting computer to let the Force guide his proton torpedoes during the Death Star trench run.

Ben calls it his first step into a larger world. This "larger world" does not just include everything external to young Luke. He's uncovering more of the truth of who *he* is and his vast, unrealized potential. Ben is telling Luke that he is more than he has known himself to be so far in his limited young life. He's not a simple farm boy. He's the son of the Chosen One, who is learning to tap into his profound, innate connection to the Force. He's the only pilot in the Rebellion who can make the impossible shot required to destroy the Death Star. He's the man whose optimism and unwavering hope will one day redeem the devil. He's the man destined to help his father bring balance to the Force and topple the evil Empire that enslaves the whole galaxy. He's a pure soul who will restore the Jedi Order and lead it into a bright new future when he is ready to.

Luke already begins to display his newfound agency after the gang is taken aboard the Death Star when they arrive at the destroyed remains of Alderaan, first planetary victim of its laser superweapon, and Ben goes off on his own to deactivate its tractor beam. Ben tells Luke to stay and watch over the droids instead of joining him, stressing that <u>his destiny lies along a different path</u>. Ben is wise enough to know his role in the story and that it is not his job anymore to be the lone heroic warrior who saves the universe. He's getting too old for that sort of thing. His role is to ensure that the heroes of the next generation are set up to do that in his place.

Luke's first chance to prove himself worthy of the heroic path comes when he learns that Princess Leia is aboard the Death Star and scheduled for termination. Here, in the worst possible place he could be, surrounded by legions of stormtroopers and in the heart of the machinery of death commanded by the Empire, Luke will have to begin thinking for himself. Will he hide away and seek to minimize the risk? Or will he take heroic initiative and overcome impossible odds to do something that matters to him? Will he approach the dangerous task with childlike enthusiasm, as his father did before he ever knew the pain of loss? Upon entering Leia's cell, he declares that he is Luke Skywalker, and his purpose is to rescue her. He speaks with confidence that he did not have until he chose what was important enough to him to risk his life on.

At this point in the story, Han has no emotional investment in anything beyond completing the job he was hired for: transporting his passengers from Tatooine to Alderaan, which, technically, he has already accomplished despite Alderaan having been destroyed. His only priority is self-preservation, which means staying put and minimizing risk until Ben deactivates the tractor beam and they can leave. But Luke, the younger brother in this dynamic, has a childlike sense of heroism, of wanting to rush into danger to do the right thing, which, in this case, means rescuing the princess for no other reason than because she's a beautiful girl and she needs their help. Somewhere in the course of his bonding experiences with Luke and Leia aboard the Death Star, in which they creatively overcome problems by working together and narrowly survive death and capture, Han's own sense of heroism and authentic values will awaken, and he will choose to start doing the right thing simply because he knows it's the right thing. And Han's unexpected contributions will be one of the critical factors setting up the impossible shot that allows Luke to destroy the Death Star and save the Rebellion.

Darth Vader is gravely concerned when he feels the presence of his old master, Obi-Wan Kenobi, aboard the Death Star. He knows what a threat this single old wizard poses, with the Force at his disposal, to the entire station. He has the power to insert a wrench into the gears of the Empire's war machine. The Death Star is considered the ultimate power in the universe by the Empire because of <u>the fear it commands to keep the populace in line</u> as the largest source of offensive power in existence due to its ability to destroy entire planets. In conventional terms, there is nothing the Rebels could ever do to overpower it. So long as the people of the galaxy fear the Death Star and believe there is no way to counter it, they will submit to a state of total obedience, meaning no choice or will, negating even the need for the Senate and bureaucracy to keep them in control any longer. But so long as there is the smallest chance its overwhelming might can be brought down, the Force is the tenacious tendency that will find it.

The Force, creative conscious self-expression, is the reason individuals have the power to change the course of history. Obi-Wan won the duel he should have lost against Anakin on Mustafar because he retained his composure and ability to think for himself when Anakin relied on overwhelming might, just like the Death Star. The man Vader is today has learned from Anakin's mistakes. He once told Obi-Wan that he underestimated *his* power. It is now, ironically, Vader who knows not to underestimate the unassuming Obi-Wan.

This new dynamic is reflected in the awkward fight choreography of their duel. Vader's entire fighting style has had to change to accommodate the restrictions of his suit and cybernetic limbs. While Anakin fought with speed and complex footwork and acrobatics, Vader is slower, methodical, and (at last) patient in his approach. He is normally fearless, but he moves in cautiously against Obi-Wan, the one exception to his impervious demeanor, because Obi-Wan is the only living man to have ever beaten him in a fight. The Chosen One's incredible power is compromised when facing his old master due to the complex and conflicted emotions he still feels about him. Rather than coming at him full force like an attack dog let off its chain, a la Darth Maul, they dance around each other, sparing like expert fencers, more in line with Count Dooku's refined dueling style. They even take time to trade dialogue, sizing each other up and posturing themselves to gain the emotional advantage over one another, a feature that was notably absent during their fast-paced duel on Mustafar.

Both men are unsure exactly what they are facing now, as they cannot know how much has changed since the last time. Is Vader weak now because of his injuries and suit? Or does he have extra strength and power he didn't have when it was just his organic body doing the fighting? Has Obi-Wan grown weak in the Force by hiding away in exile all these years? Or has he been studying and concentrating his power into a form Vader is unprepared for? Ben has known for a long time that this day, this conflict, would come. Vader almost seems to be in disbelief that his long-awaited chance for revenge against the man who humiliated and maimed him is finally happening, right there, on an unassuming day, in the most unlikely of places, aboard the Death Star.

Broken people like Vader hate those who remember the truth they have distanced themselves from and who hold them accountable to a past they prefer to forget. The people who played the biggest roles in helping them form the old identities they rebel against are the biggest threat to the new identities they have adopted. Obi-Wan is the biggest threat in the galaxy to Vader because he was there with Anakin from the beginning. Vader cannot fully block out his past so long as Obi-Wan is around to serve as a living reminder.

After all these years, Vader is still so insecure, still so frustrated at the perception of his own inadequacies and lack of development that he feels the need to assert that he has, finally, grown up and should be treated as such by the father figure he resents so much. He confidently asserts that the circle is complete, that he is not a learner anymore but the master. In his own twisted way, Anakin is saying, "I don't need you anymore, Obi-Wan. Look how much I've accomplished without you." By countering with the fact that Vader is only a master of evil, Ben is diminishing all of what Vader considers to be his greatest accomplishments. His old apprentice has developed in the wrong direction and become only a progressively worse version of himself.

When he sees the twin children of Anakin suddenly reunited, Ben knows he must do anything necessary to ensure their escape and to keep Vader's focus off of them. He knows the only thing Vader would care about more than preventing the intruders on the Death Star from escaping with the princess is killing his old master. He allows Vader to strike him down, transforming his consciousness into a Force spirit that will continue to guide Anakin's son from beyond the grave in a form more powerful than his living body. Luke witnesses his mentor, his new father figure, get martyred by Vader, the monster he believes killed his actual father, and screams out "<u>Noooo</u>!" in blind emotional reaction. The disembodied voice of Ben, though, quickly appears in Luke's head to urge him to run while he has the opportunity. Ben has achieved the immortality that Anakin was so obsessed with, and the disappearance of his physical body upon death shocks Vader long enough for the Millennium Falcon to escape.

To become immortalized as a mentoring spirit in others' minds requires one to look beyond the limits of their own experience and life, to commit themselves to a cause greater than themselves. The Sith, being so consumed by greed and immediate satisfaction, could never reach or even envision such a state.[67] When Anakin returns as a Force spirit in the final scene of the saga, it will be the result of finally having learned the lesson that there is something bigger than himself to care about, something that extends beyond his own direct experience and lifespan.

At the Rebel base on Yavin 4, a Rebellion general details the Death Star's critical design flaw that will make destroying it possible with a targeted strike force: a thermal exhaust port at the end of a long, narrow trench. One pilot remarks that what they are trying to accomplish <u>is impossible, even for a computer</u>. Luke, drawing on his experience with his T-16 Skyhopper, naively compares the task to bullseyeing womp rats on Tatooine. He is showing both his inexperience and his optimism. The closest thing he has to real military experience is shooting large rodents for sport in a recreational vehicle. He believes that because the animals he's hit before are roughly the same size as the Death Star's thermal exhaust port, shooting proton torpedoes at it while flying at high speeds in a trench full of enemy fighters and defense guns, should be just as easy.

Luke is about to have a very rude awakening about the realities of space combat. Yet, the fact that he is the only one who never doubts the impossible task can be done plays a major role in why he is the only one able to do it. He will lose some of this childlike optimism by the time he runs into Yoda in Episode 5 and is suddenly skeptical that it is possible to lift his X-wing out of the Dagobah swamp with the Force.

Before embarking, Luke makes one last attempt to uncover the fundamental values residing deep within Han, insisting that there must be more to him than money and superficial reward. Han, for his part, attempts the inverse with Luke. He invites him to abandon the Rebellion and its suicidal assault on the Death Star to join him in a life defined by shallow pleasures. Neither brother gets the reaction they want out of the other. Leia reminds Luke that Han must follow his own path, not have it chosen for him, just as Ben did not force the hero path upon Luke, despite knowing everything he did about his lineage and potential. Luke wishes Ben were still there with him, not yet realizing that Ben *is* still there with him in a spiritual sense, living on in his memories and working cognition, guiding his development.

Despite everything that has happened since he grew brave enough to leave home, Luke is not battle-ready. He's overwhelmed in his X-wing when the Rebels begin their assault on the Death Star, first by turbolaser gun towers and then by Imperial TIE fighters. It's nothing like the minor skirmish of a few TIE fighters he had to shoot down earlier from the turret of the Millennium Falcon, which was actually a fun exercise for him. It's like entering Mos Eisley Cantina all over again, only his father figure is not there to protect him, and retreat is not an option. Luke will either have to master the situation he has been thrust into or die, and the Rebel Alliance along with him. The voice of Obi-Wan appears in his head to remind him that the Force will be with him and to <u>trust his feelings</u>, which is an example of the type of advice Anakin needed to receive, but which Obi-Wan was not ready to give back then.

Even the best pilots of Gold Squadron, pilots far more experienced than Luke, using the best available technology in their targeting computers, cannot make the impossible shot. If Luke is going to succeed where they failed, he's going to have to try something they never did, something they never could. With one minute remaining until the Death Star is in firing range of the Rebel base on Yavin 4, Red Squadron prepares to take their attack run. Luke hopes that it will be just like Beggar's Canyon back home, the deep and winding gorge on Tatooine where Anakin raced his pod in Episode 1 and Luke practiced bullseyeing womp rats. Both of the Skywalker boys learned to be pilots in the very same gorge, and now Luke's race in his X-wing down the Death Star trench will mimic the tension of Anakin's high-speed pod through the trenches of the Boonta Eve Classic on Tatooine.

As Luke turns on his targeting computer and prepares to take the shot, he finally calms himself enough to begin to tap into the influence of the Force, and its musical theme peeks through the action score, complemented by Ben's voice telling him to use the Force and let go. Even Vader, in hot pursuit in his TIE Advanced, can sense Luke's connection to the Force now, and he knows he has reason to be worried about what this lone Rebel pilot in an X-wing might actually be capable of. After all, the only other pilot who might have been able to make the impossible shot would have, ironically, been Anakin himself.

What is the memory and Force spirit of Ben instructing Luke to "let go" of here? His acceptance of and emotional attachment to the way he thinks things are supposed to be done. By telling him to turn off his targeting computer, he is telling him to trust his own intuition, the one thing every other trained pilot in the Rebel attack fleet would have failed to do. In his very first space battle, young Anakin had to disengage the autopilot on his Naboo Starfighter in order to accomplish something none of the trained pilots fighting alongside him would have thought to or been able to do. He had to stop following their way of seeing and doing things. Luke, like his father before him, has to take control of the machinery built to serve his goals instead of letting it make his choices for him. He must be the master of his mind and emotions without letting them master him. He has to demonstrate the *patience* to wait for the right moment to shoot according to his own analysis.

Luke is not a pilot or a soldier. He's just an idealistic kid recklessly following his own newfound heroic ideals. For the first time in his life, thanks to the loss of his family, mentorship from Ben, and his success at rescuing Princess Leia, he has the confidence to do something unprecedented and achieve an impossible victory. It is hard to believe that this is the same boy who, just days earlier, whined that he would be stuck on the farm for another season. He has taken his first step into a much larger world: the world of adulthood responsibility and self-determination.

This is the most important moment in *A New Hope*, the moment Luke begins to truly believe in his abilities as a Jedi. But his natural abilities, impressive as they are, are not enough to secure victory for the Rebel Alliance. Luke relies on one more miracle, set up through his earlier interactions with Han, which have inspired him to heroism. The Millennium Falcon appears just as Vader is about to shoot down Luke, clearing him to make the one-in-a-million shot. He closes his eyes, patiently waiting for just the right moment, no longer relying on the targeting computer to tell him when it will be but now trusting his own judgment of exactly when to pull the trigger. Luke audibly gasps in a quasi-orgasmic moment as he releases his building emotional tension along with his torpedoes, which precisely enter the narrow chute of the exhaust port, ending the threat of the Death Star in a magnificent spectacle, just as it was about to fire the laser that would have ended the Rebel Alliance.

It is important for Luke's characterization that his victory does not come from raw ability alone, as it might have from his father before him, but from the peace and optimism he has already begun to spread in his society, and which allowed him to forge the social bonds that saved him when he needed them. Han could only save Luke because Luke had, in a way, already saved Han by getting him to feel and to care again. The same type of awakening and reciprocal salvation will happen on a grander spiritual scale with his father two movies from now. Saving Han is practice for saving Vader. Luke's victory is built on love and a strong sense of emotional attachment to others, the very qualities the Jedi Order tried to bury in Anakin.

How did a simple farm boy from Tatooine, with limited piloting and combat experience, reduce the biggest and most powerful battle station ever built, <u>the ultimate power in the universe</u>, to smithereens with one shot? The Empire's technological terror had a fatal weakness that they were too invested in their own propaganda to notice or do anything about, even when it was brought to the attention of Grand Moff Tarkin during the attack. Luke won because he was able to overcome the story he had been conditioned to believe about himself as a nobody from a backwater planet farthest from the bright center of the universe. Aunt Beru was right; he had too much of his father in him.

A ceremony is held on Yavin 4 to commemorate the Rebel victory. The musical track *The Throne Room* plays, featuring a ceremonial fanfare reminiscent of the celebratory music that played after the apparent victory on Naboo in Episode 1. The Force theme returns in triumphant form, replacing the Emperor's theme as the melody that played back then. It foreshadows the more spiritual victory celebration that will end the whole story in the final scene of Episode 6 on Endor.

Both Luke and Han receive medals not just as recognition for their role in destroying the Death Star but in acknowledgment of their spiritual growth. Both are completely different people from what they were at the start of this story. They made choices and accomplished feats that would have been impossible for the people they started as. Luke is not the hapless, frustrated farm boy he was a few days ago, and Han is not the selfish mercenary he was when he refused to help rescue Princess Leia. They did this by fully embracing what they cared about and fearlessly pursuing it. Their medals act as recognition of the expansion of consciousness that is the result of discovering more of who they authentically are. Other heroic characters, such as Chewbacca or Leia, did not have to undergo fundamental changes in the course of this film, which is not to say that there is anything wrong with them or that they won't be seriously challenged later on. Han and Luke have both grown up, just a little, as a result of their role in the plot of *A New Hope*. Both, however, will continue to be tested in larger ways in the films to follow.

NOTES

63. "When you're a kid, you know, it's he's the pinnacle of all evil, there is that mystery there, you know. He is a man behind a mask, and up until now, we didn't know who that man was. So it allows, you know, the audience to really instill their own imagination into that character and make that evil whatever they wanted it to be." George Lucas, interview in *The Chosen One*, featurette on *Star Wars: Episode III – Revenge of the Sith* (DVD, Lucasfilm Ltd., 2005).

64. Concept art from Episode 3 depicts Anakin wearing a cloak similar to Dooku's, possibly indicating the original intention was to have him take Dooku's garment as a trophy after killing him, clearly demonstrating the influence Dooku had on the manufactured personality he would adopt as Vader.

65. Deleted scenes from *Revenge of the Sith* showed Padmé forming the Alliance to Restore the Republic along with other key loyalists like Bail Organa and Mon Mothma, which became the Rebel Alliance in *A New Hope*. Anakin became suspicious of her, and Palpatine stoked that suspicion by suggesting that she was hiding something.

66. The 2022 Disney+ series, *Obi-Wan Kenobi*, provides a canon origin of how Ben adopted this mythic version of Anakin's death in season 1, episode 6: *Part VI*. Ten years after the events of *Revenge of the Sith*, Obi-Wan faces off against Darth Vader once again, damaging his mask and revealing part of the scarred, familiar face underneath. Obi-Wan stops fighting and addresses Vader as Anakin… only for him to reject the name, insisting that Anakin was gone and that he killed him. Obi-Wan reluctantly accepts this new version of events and that Vader is a distinct identity from Anakin, at last dismissively calling him "Darth," just as he will when they meet again aboard the Death Star in *A New Hope*. There are also other instances in expanded canon and Legends material where Vader references "killing" or "destroying" Anakin Skywalker, such as when facing off against Ahsoka Tano in season 2, episode 20 (*Twilight of the Apprentice – Part 2*) of the animated series *Star Wars: Rebels*.

67. "There are no Sith ghosts. They cannot conceive of anything beyond death." George Lucas, quoted by Sam Witwer (@SamWitwer), "Tweet," X, 15 September 2023.

LUKE'S ADOLESCENCE

After his impossible victory against the Empire, Luke Skywalker believes in his abilities as a Jedi. But like all adolescents, having reached this first developmental milestone, he accepts prematurely that there will be no significant challenges ahead. Anything that comes next in his journey couldn't possibly compare to what he has already done, so he naively thinks. The evil Empire is conquerable. Darth Vader, the monster who killed his father, is defeatable if he continues training with the Force. He believes the path ahead is linear now, from a low state of ability to a higher one through straightforward effort and action. He does not know there is more to being a man than being a boy with greater size and strength.

Growing up requires the undoing of childish assumptions about the nature of the world and even the nature of oneself. Just as Episode 2 represented Anakin's passage through adolescence, so too will Episode 5 represent Luke's. And just like puberty, it will, at times, be chaotic, frustrating, and disorienting for the one going through it and those he entrusts to lead him through it. Should Luke fail to find appropriate guidance during this sensitive time in his life, he will not arrive at a stable platform of identity, built upon authentic values, for his adult self. He will repeat the same mistakes his father did and, no matter how physically powerful he might become, forget who he really is inside.

Since their victory against the Death Star, the Rebel Alliance has been chased by the Empire across the galaxy and forced to move their secret base to the ice world of Hoth. Hoth is cold, in contrast to the lush environment of Yavin 4. Everyone there is afraid of the Empire's revenge. Their terror will be made manifest by the slow march of towering AT-AT walkers that will manage to destroy their shield generator and force them to flee. And while the Empire pursues the rebels in an impersonal, militaristic way, Vader is more concerned with Luke as an individual. Audiences in 1980 were meant to believe it was only Luke's potential with the Force that captured Vader's interest, but we know it is the parental relationship between the two that matters to him. Vader sees himself in Luke and a last chance to accomplish what he wanted to do with Padmé all those years ago.

Early in the movie, we find Luke trapped in the physiological embodiment of disorientation as he awakens hanging upside down in a wampa's frozen cave. Everything is the opposite of how it should be from his point of view. Everything he thinks he knows will be challenged as he moves away from the fairy tale version of reality from his childhood. Everything he thought he was fighting for and fighting to become, everything he thought defined him, will be torn away by the events that follow. In this first of three dangerous caves guarded by three beasts that he will encounter, Luke finds the presence to calm his mind, remember his teachings, and concentrate. He uses the Force to call his father's lightsaber to him from the nearby ice and free himself in his first display of Force telekinesis—a common feat for Republic Jedi who had been trained to use the Force since birth, but a major accomplishment for someone just starting without anyone to teach him. He panics, though, due to how afraid he is after cutting off the wampa's arm, and runs out of the wampa's cave into the blizzards of Hoth instead of taking the time to assess the situation and to realize that taking shelter in the cave would have been his best chance for survival. Trauma causes him to act on impulse, and it will nearly cost him his life as he collapses into the snow, unable to do any more on his own. Once more, he will depend on his older brother figure, Han Solo, coming to his rescue as he did during the attack on the Death Star because of the awakening influence Luke has had on him. Han repeatedly saving his baby brother is how he shows his gratitude for what he has done for him.

Luke arrives with R2-D2 on Dagobah in search of Yoda and immediately crashes into the misty swamp, disabling his X-wing. Everything is going wrong, and Luke is once again reminded that he is utterly unprepared for a new, dreamlike environment of strange beasts and hidden dangers that his journey has taken him into. A small goblin-like creature appears behind Luke, watching him. It's Yoda, but not the Yoda we knew as the Grandmaster of the Jedi Order who trained Jedi for 800 years and dueled with the devil for the fate of the galaxy in the Senate chamber 22 years ago. Here, he presents himself in the guise of a whimsical imp in order to test the character of the son of Darth Vader, to see if he's actually ready to be trained as a Jedi and become the hero they have been waiting for him to become.[68] Luke's prejudgment and senses are being tested. All is not as it appears to be. Ben was not a strange old desert hermit. Yoda is not the funny little creature he pretends to be. And Darth Vader, he will soon learn, is not merely the embodiment of evil who betrayed and murdered his heroic father.

Vader, on a call with the one man in the galaxy he is still subservient to, learns that Emperor Palpatine has determined that the Rebel pilot who destroyed the Death Star is the offspring of Anakin Skywalker, a fact Vader already learned on his own but had kept hidden from his master.[69] Vader was already determined to turn Luke to the dark side independently and overthrow the Emperor with him.[70] Palpatine describes the revelation as a great disturbance in the Force, the same phrasing Ben Kenobi used upon sensing the destruction of Alderaan in Episode 4. Both men have had their worldview and sense of order upheaved by a change they could not have predicted and cannot control. Palpatine now fears that Luke could grow to be as strong in the Force as the Chosen One he sprang from, and that if he becomes a Jedi, he could even destroy the Sith Empire he and Vader have built. Vader, showing his first hints of paternal instinct, describes his son as just a boy who has lost his mentor, who he incorrectly believes Obi-Wan can no longer help. He quells Palpatine's desire to kill his son before he can become a threat by suggesting that they work together to turn him to the dark side and recruit him into their Sith lineage. Vader must now act as though he had not already been planning on doing this without Palpatine, as though he is pursuing Luke only with the blessing of his master. That is the Sith way: lies, deceit, and creating mistrust to subvert one another.

On Dagobah, Yoda's jester antics are calculated to annoy Luke and reveal his character and immaturity. Once he has seen enough, he drops the act and decides he cannot teach him because he <u>has no patience</u> and too much anger, like his father. The Force spirit of Ben, though, holds out hope for Luke to outgrow these juvenile character flaws, being wise enough to recall that he was once the same, just as all mature adults were once immature adolescents. Yoda berates Luke for having an unserious mind and being incapable of deep commitment, mocking him for the childish longing for excitement and adventure we saw in Episode 4. Unlike Anakin, who could not take his mind off his traumatic past, Luke has always been looking away to the future and the horizon, displayed literally as he stared off into the binary sunset of Tatooine and dreamed of excitement and adventure. Neither Skywalker has been able to focus on what he does in the present, which calls back to Qui-Gon's first lesson about keeping concentration here and now, where it belongs. The qualities that served Luke in his previous stage of development, by prompting him to leave Tatooine and begin his heroic journey, will now work against him as he prepares for adulthood.

Yoda, now running out of excuses for not training the last best hope for the Jedi and the Rebellion, falls back on the same shallow dogma that once stopped him from accepting Anakin as a student. If Anakin was too old to begin the training at nine, Luke is *certainly* too old at 22. However, the *way* in which Luke is too old is different than his father. Anakin was too old because he had already progressed out of a state of infancy and into childhood. He had strong emotional attachments that he was not ready to abandon. But Luke spent the first 19 years of his life, until his adventure in *A New Hope,* in a state of extended childhood, with Uncle Owen and Aunt Beru exerting a dampening effect on his development. Even now, at the same age his father was at the peak of his accomplishments as a Jedi, Luke has tapped into only a fraction of his inherent power. Anakin was afraid of being powerless; Luke is afraid of being powerful because he has spent too long thinking of himself as an ordinary, helpless person. He has too much to unlearn about himself.

Luke only starts to sway Yoda with the sincerity he shows about how much he has already learned and how badly he does not want to go back to being the old, limited version of himself. He <u>promises to finish what he begins</u> and not fail Yoda. He's <u>not afraid</u>, he says, but Yoda knows it is only a matter of time before he will have to confront what he fears most.

Training under Yoda begins with a grim warning about the nature of the dark side, just as it did with Anakin 35 years ago when he first stepped into the Council chambers. Yoda says Luke will recognize the dark side as the <u>fear, anger, and aggression</u> that join him in a fight, or, in reality, any tense situation where he feels threatened, upset, or offended. The Jedi trained from infancy to suppress or avoid these emotions so that they did not have the opportunity to take root in their minds. They believed that once a Jedi started down the dark path, it would consume them and <u>dominate their destiny</u>. That this happened to Anakin Skywalker, the supposed Chosen One who was meant to be the greatest of all the Jedi, is the final confirmation of this fact in Yoda's mind. Yoda was much quicker than Obi-Wan to accept that Anakin was gone and consumed by Darth Vader when they first saw security holograms of what he had done in *Revenge of the Sith* during Order 66. Yoda has probably seen good Jedi turn bad many times throughout his long career, including even his most recent padawan, Count Dooku. Never has he seen anyone recover once they have fallen;

none have ever had the emotional tools they would need to do so. The Jedi Order was incapable of providing them.

All this talking up of the dark side leads Luke to wonder if it might actually be stronger than the light, for how else could it corrupt great Jedi? Yoda insists the dark side is not stronger, only quicker, easier, and more seductive. The dark side prevails because it feels stronger than the weakness that drew someone to it. It grants a superficial illusion of security and power, but the illusion must be constantly reinforced. It's like a drug addiction that requires higher and higher doses of the same poison to receive the same high, or else the whole thing threatens to collapse into an even lower point than someone was at when they aligned themselves with a false reality. Vader is self-soothing and reaffirming the validity of his path every time he kills someone or commands respect through intimidation. It's the only way he can continue to believe that he has made the right choice by doing all the terrible things he has done and avoid the devastation that would come from honest self-reflection.

According to Yoda, the difference between good and bad is easy to see when the mind is calm, at peace, and passive. The emphasis on patience that has underscored the entire saga until now is beginning to make sense to Luke. Yoda is warning him to remain conscious and in control of himself. He must not let stress or trauma rob him of his deeper values. He must never slip into unconsciousness and autopilot simply because it is easier than consciously dealing with everything he feels. Yoda rebukes Luke's desire to ask why he has to do things the way he has been instructed instead of just accepting Jedi dogma at face value, just as Obi-Wan once did with an adolescent Anakin who couldn't help but question the mandate he had been given about protecting Padmé instead of investigating her attacker. Headstrong Luke, like his father in Episode 2, does not blindly accept instructions from even the former Grandmaster of the Jedi Order and the only being in the galaxy left to instruct him in the ways of the Force. Yoda grows frustrated that his final padawan pushes back against his authority, something his padawans in the Republic never did.

Luke <u>feels cold</u> when he senses the death and evil emanating from a mysterious cave, a physical manifestation of the fear and insecurity he will confront within. Despite the instruction that he will not need his weapons, Luke brings his lightsaber and blaster, eager to fight whatever he finds within. Inside, he is met by the image of Darth Vader, whose power is so strong that he slows the camera's frame rate with his presence on-screen. We are not seeing the actual, flesh-and-circuitry Vader, only Luke's fearful projection of him, the beast Luke has made Vader out to be in his mind. Vader commands respect through fear, and that fear magnifies in the minds of those who mythologize him as an agent of evil instead of the pathetic man he really is. Vader's musical theme, used abundantly in the film thus far, is absent in this scene, suggesting this is not the real deal. It has been replaced by an eerie and dissonant whining that emphasizes the psychedelic quality of what Luke is experiencing right now: the scariest thing that he can imagine. Luke is the first to draw and ignite his lightsaber, eager to fight the monster before him instead of being patient and assessing the situation. Pseudo-Vader's defeat is not a victorious moment. His decapitated head rolls onto the ground, revealing Luke's own face beneath the mask. What Luke fears most is not actually Vader; it is the looming threat that he will become like Vader in his quest to avenge his father.

When Luke's X-wing begins sinking into the Dagobah swamp, the characteristic hope and optimism in the face of impossible tasks that defined him during the last film are gone. He immediately concedes defeat to the swamp, whining that he'll never get his ship out without even attempting to. He believes that moving stones around with the Force is incomparable to trying to lift an entire X-wing because the latter is so much bigger and heavier. This same boy was undaunted by the impossible task of destroying a moon-sized battle station because he believed in the Rebels and his own abilities. He has to unlearn and recategorize many of the basic truths he has accepted all his life about how the world really works. To grow up, Luke needs a paradigm shift, but it will not come without an emotionally resonant demonstration of something he believes to be impossible, according to the limits of his point of view. We will see this same principle apply to sudden shifts in worldview and values when Darth Vader is confronted with something he considers impossible, forcing him to re-assess the lies he has been living by at the end of the final film in the story.

Sheepishly, Luke says he <u>will try to lift the X-wing out of the swamp.</u> Yoda tells Luke to <u>either do it or not do it</u>, that trying is not an option. The difference between doing and trying is the difference between reality and illusion. To *try* is to project your own ideas onto reality and hope it reacts in accordance. To *do* is to humble yourself before reality and play the game according to its rules. The Jedi *tried* to raise Anakin as the Chosen One. They missed that they were failing to because they did not look closer at what they were actually doing. Obi-Wan *tried* to kill Anakin on Mustafar, despite his indication at the start of their duel that he would *do* what he must. Promises, which so many characters in *Star Wars* have made at critical moments, are the equivalent of trying. They are based in projection and preference, not reality as it is.

Luke makes a valiant effort with the Force, even beginning to move the ship. For a moment, Yoda seems surprised that this unserious boy might actually pull it off. But Luke quickly gives up, needing to sit down and catch his breath when the X-wing does not lift the way he hoped it would, berating his master for <u>wanting the impossible from him</u>. He has adopted a defeatist attitude, accepting things as they appear rather than applying his mind and effort to uncover what possibilities might lie beneath the surface. If Luke had had this attitude during the Death Star trench run, he would not have been able to make the impossible shot. He would not have even attempted the attack because his consciousness effort would immediately have been nullified by the giant battle station's terror-inducing appearance, just as the Empire designed it for.

Yoda then performs a miracle by closing his eyes and effortlessly lifting the X-wing out of the swamp. Luke has to make a choice now: either accept that the premises he has been operating under are wrong, to unlearn what he has learned, or consciously deny what he has witnessed. For now, Luke does not believe what he has just experienced, which is why he failed. He could not do it because he did not believe it could be done. His optimism and ambition, characteristic of children, have been replaced with the cynicism characteristic of adolescents.

Echoing his father's premonitions about his mother and Padmé, Luke senses the coming suffering of Han and Leia on Cloud City. Vader has captured them with the intention of torturing them in order to draw Luke out of hiding and into a trap. He knows that if Luke is anything like he was at that age, he will sense the people he loves in danger and prioritize their well-being above all else, just as Anakin did in a panic. Yoda insists that Luke consider that the best way to serve his friends is not by rushing off to save them, but by honoring the values they fight for, that they would be willing to give up their lives for, and completing his Jedi training to end the Sith and the Empire once and for all. It is a similar choice that was offered to Anakin many times as he matured: the obligation to duty and principle versus people and emotional attachment, or, in other terms, the mind versus the heart. The two were never in harmony or balance for Anakin, and they are not for Luke now. Luke is in no condition to consider the wisdom of Yoda's words and reflect on the choice presented before him. The Force spirit of Ben Kenobi appears to remind Luke that his anxieties are not guarantees of what will occur, that even someone as powerful as Yoda cannot know the fate of his friends.

Luke is adamant that he can help Han and Leia because he now feels the Force flowing through him. However, all that power makes Luke all the more dangerous because he lacks the maturity and wisdom to control it. He is like an explosion waiting to happen, just like his father was in his adolescence. Obi-Wan calls it a dangerous time for Luke because of the crucial stage of maturation he has entered. Luke already failed this test once when he was baited into attacking his projection of Darth Vader in the Dagobah cave, and Yoda fears the same thing will happen again, with far more drastic consequences, if Luke faces the real Vader now before he is ready. He will too easily lose control of himself when provoked. Luke <u>promises to return and complete the training</u>, but like so many promises already made in *Star Wars*, it is not a promise he will be able to keep in the way he intended.

Yoda's final warning is that only a fully trained Jedi Knight, with the Force as his ally, will be able to succeed against Vader, the Emperor, and the dark side. If Luke chooses the quick and easy path by ending his training now, he will not be able to face the challenges those two masters of evil place before him in their attempts to turn him to the dark side. A fully trained Jedi, one who has completed the transition into stable adult maturity, one who knows for sure what kind of person they are, will be immune to such temptation. Such a person knows their fundamental values and what defines them. As long as Luke remains internally conflicted, he does not truly know who he is, making him susceptible to emotional coercion. The quick and easy path that Yoda refers to is the path of impatience, of following immediate emotional impulses because they gratify us and ease our discomfort, without stopping to reflect on whether they will actually accomplish our goals or if they are in line with our authentic values. We must be willing to suffer for what we believe in, maybe even die for it, or allow others to, if we are to remain good. Luke will only learn that lesson at the climax of the whole story when he throws away his lightsaber and leaves himself defenseless in the name of what he believes in.

Ben reminds Luke that if he chooses to face Vader now, he will do it without his guidance or protection. As a spirit, a memory, Ben cannot physically fight the battle ahead for Luke. More importantly, by Luke abandoning Obi-Wan's wisdom, he will venture into dark territory that he has not developed a moral roadmap for. He will have to think in the moment and make his own choices with woefully insufficient understanding. He will not be able to rely on his parental figures' experience garnered over previous generations. He is cutting himself off from everything gained by having lived through the prequel era, which mirrors the state of consciousness moviegoers were in the first time they saw this film upon release, with no idea about the plot twist and character reveal they were heading for with the upcoming revelation of Vader's identity.

Ben and Yoda are at a crossroads as mentors now. By not telling Luke the full truth about Vader being his father, the great Jedi Anakin Skywalker who turned to evil despite everything good about him, they are risking Luke finding it out himself in a less controlled way, which will damage his relationship with his mentors. If he discovers that they lied to him, and he doesn't trust that they had a valid reason for doing so, a reason he would ultimately agree with once he is fully mature and informed of the situation, he might abandon their path and stop learning from them altogether. Trust in adolescence is a fragile thing because children have begun to grow out of their simplified understanding of how the world works, which was primarily shaped by their parental figures who imposed a certain way of seeing upon them. If Luke does not remain willing to listen to Ben and Yoda's guidance, he will be far more susceptible to turning to the dark side and joining his father, especially once Vader demonstrates he is willing to share the whole truth they are not. Luke chooses to trust his own feelings here and disobey his mentors, but he operating from fear and insecurity, which are leading him astray.

Since they left Hoth together, romantic tension has been brewing between Han and Leia in a fashion related to that of Anakin and Padmé in Episode 2. Padmé rejected Anakin's advances because he was too young for her, too much of a child who had not yet grown up. She was five years *older* than him. Leia, however, is 22 in Episode 5, and Han is 32. She is ten years *younger* than him. She rejects his advances because she perceives him as too much of a rogue or scoundrel for her, someone who, despite his advanced years, is not taking life seriously. Like her mother before her, Leia is too mature, too experienced for her age. Padmé became the source of motivation for Anakin to grow up too fast and catch up with her. Leia becomes the motivation for Han to start acting his age, as he finally has a reason to take life seriously.

Leia overcomes her aversion to Han by being forced to spend time in close proximity to him, just as Padmé was with Anakin. She witnesses how resourceful and heroic he can be, coming up with unexpected solutions to overwhelming problems, such as flying into an asteroid field or hiding on the back of an Imperial Star Destroyer to avoid detection. She realizes he has been doing all this to protect her. She finally sees him as someone who will always protect her in ways no one else could, just as Padmé once started to see that same trait in young Anakin. She drops the defensive personality she has been wearing to keep him at bay, becoming softer, more feminine, and more loving by the end of this film and well into the next one.[71]

On the planet Bespin, Lando Calrissian provides yet another example of how fear causes people to betray their values and become their worst selves when he makes a deal with Darth Vader to keep the Empire from shutting down his mining operation. He betrays Han, claiming he <u>had no choice</u> and that it was the only way to <u>ensure security for Cloud City</u>. By Vader torturing Han to lure Luke out of hiding, he weaponizes his own trauma and becomes obsessed with inflicting the same pain he once felt on someone just like him. In this way, he gains a superficial sense of control over that which he could not control before, that which left him vulnerable. The boy who once wished nothing more than to stop people from dying has become a master of making others die. The victim of fear now inflicts it upon his own son to manipulate him, just as he was once manipulated by it.

As Han is prepared to be frozen in carbonite to be delivered to Jabba the Hutt, he shows more restraint than we've ever seen from him when he orders Chewbacca not to fight back, insisting that there will be another time in the future when they can make a more effective heroic stand. Han, unlike some other characters in this story, has learned the value of patience and reflection, rather than rushing into battle with guns blazing. One movie ago, Han was chasing down an entire squadron of stormtroopers alone and nearly getting himself killed during the escape from the Death Star. Earlier in this one, he was rushing out into the blizzard of Hoth on a tauntaun to save Luke, ignoring a warning that he would surely die out there. Leia's influence has forced him to grow up because he values her more than victory. Leia, suddenly being made to confront how much she cares for this roguish man she may never see alive again, blurts out, to her own surprise, that she <u>loves him</u>. Unlike the desperate declarations of love we saw given to Anakin by the people closest to him, this one is confidently received instead of falling short, being rejected in anger, or coming too late. Han doesn't even need to say it back. He simply says, in stoic confidence, that *he knows* she does. She never even needed to say it at all for him to receive it. The duo will repeat this exchange with the roles reversed on Endor in Episode 6, this time Leia maturing to the position of confidently embracing Han's love without it ever needing to have been said at all.

Luke enters the third and final cave of the film, this time in the form of the dark and steamy carbon freezing room. The beast in the cave this time is the real Vader, waiting patiently for him. The first thing he tells his unknowing son is that the Force is with him, but that he is not yet a Jedi. Luke has grown in his self-awareness and abilities. But he has not yet reached the point of stability where he can reliably choose who he is going to be in all circumstances. Luke, as before, during his trial run in the cave on Dagobah, makes the mistake of drawing his lightsaber first, which ignites quickly, signaling his readiness to fight. Vader responds by drawing his, which ignites slowly, the crimson blade taking a few seconds to extend to its full length. Vader is the calm, calculating, and patient one in this encounter, mirroring the dynamic of when a reckless teenage Anakin rushed in to fight an older and more reserved Count Dooku.

Luke attacks first, showing how little he has learned from Yoda's wisdom about the importance of using the Force for defense. Vader parries with one hand, knocking Luke back and to the ground. Vader's fighting style has changed dramatically since his days as a young Jedi and his unfortunate duel on Mustafar. Instead of fighting with overwhelming speed and forward momentum, his lightsaber strokes are precise and controlled. He fights more like Count Dooku[72] now, the man who first bested him in a duel, than like Anakin Skywalker, elegant and surgical instead of overpowering, partially due to the limitations of his suit and partially due to the lessons he has learned from his past.

Luke's next strikes are somewhat more coordinated, managing to clash blades several times in succession, even dodging one of Vader's strikes and causing him to hit the surrounding machinery in a shower of sparks. Luke fights with more focus than we've seen from him because he believes he is facing down the man who killed his father. He's fighting Vader with the intent to kill. Vader, meanwhile, is merely toying with Luke, or else this imbalanced fight would already be over. It's the first time he has ever interacted with his son. He's testing him, even bonding with him in a twisted way, using the opportunity to coach and mentor the boy he believes is lacking mentorship. He insists to Luke that <u>his destiny lies with him</u>, revealing his intentions, his vision for what Luke should become as heir in the family's dark side lineage, even lying about, perhaps wishfully projecting, that Obi-Wan also knew this to be true.

Vader backs Luke into the carbon-freezing chamber, thinking prematurely that the fight is over—a common mistake among Star Wars villains. Luke surprises him by leaping with the Force out of the chamber before it can be activated, which serves to impress Vader. He praises Luke for <u>having controlled his fear</u> of facing him, but commands him to <u>release the anger</u> he has been holding back because <u>only his hatred</u> can destroy him, echoing the taunt that Dooku once spoke to Anakin in the heat of conflict.

The second stage of their fight sees Vader unleashing more of his still barely tapped power as they move deeper into the facility, now that he has seen what Luke is capable of. Vader's onslaught eventually forces Luke to the ground on a narrow catwalk, the blade of a red lightsaber pointed at him, with Vader behind it, telling him to admit defeat. Luke fights back anyway, recklessly knocking Vader's lightsaber blade to the side and getting back to his feet. Tapping into the dark side now and fighting with an intensity that almost matches Vader's, he lands a glancing blow against his shoulder armor, causing him to yell out in pain and surprise. It is at that moment that Vader decides this bonding exercise has gone on long enough. In one moment, he knocks Luke's blade away and cuts off his now unprotected hand, as Dooku once did to teach young Anakin a lesson about overconfidence and pride. Luke has just paid his pound of flesh for making the same mistake his reckless father once did: rushing into a fight he was not ready for.

Luke is in the worst possible position he can be in now, backed into a narrow corner, injured, physically and emotionally exhausted, and without even his weapon to defend himself anymore. Vader asks Luke for a second time not to make him destroy him, as Anakin once asked Obi-Wan not to make him kill him on Mustafar. Luke can neither fight nor run now, so he has no choice but to listen to the words that are about to change his world forever.

When Vader asks his son to join him so that he can complete his training, he's saying, "Trust in me to teach you how to become a man. Let me guide you the rest of the way into adulthood, to cement what kind of person you will be for the rest of your life." Vader is desperate to play this role for Luke because he still feels the loss of never having had someone to properly play it for him. Vader wishes to end the conflict that has engulfed the galaxy and bring order, by which he means eliminating all resistance and ensuring that everyone in the galaxy falls in line with his vision. Anakin's desire to rule the galaxy with Padmé, so the two of them could make things the way they wanted them to be through force, is echoed here.

Luke, having no reason to want to join with the monster who killed his father and who has now maimed him, aggressively refuses his offer. However, he is about to learn the context under which Vader is making the offer. It's not enough to tempt Luke by telling him about the power of the dark side in a general way. Luke does not lust for power like Anakin did. Vader has to connect it to something deeply personal for him, like the image he holds, in mythical reverence, of his father. Vader tells Luke the single most devastating truth he could, one that violently removes the illusions around which he has based his identity and structured his development. His mentor lied to him. Vader didn't *kill* Luke's father. He *is* Luke's father. Luke cannot accept this revelation, repeating the word "no" before declaring it to be impossible, at last crying out in anguish at something so terrible he cannot accept it when Vader confidently insists it to be true: "Nooooooooo!"

Vader's view of Luke's destiny is to rule the galaxy with him, as it once was with Padmé, and he insists that his only option is to come

<u>with him</u> and join him. But Luke does not accept this externally forced destiny. He chooses to fall into the endless pit below him, knowing not what he will meet at the bottom or what will become of him. The endless unknown below is more tolerable than facing the terrible truth waiting for him in Vader's outstretched hand. He would rather die or face whatever else comes next in the abyss than live in the reality this monster is presenting to him.

Heroic Luke has lost all his bearings for navigating the world he thought he was starting to understand. It is useless to make a stand about anything when potentially everything he has ever believed is wrong. His look of acceptance as he chooses to let go and fall is punctuated by a quick, triumphant horn blast in the score, indicating that ignoring fear and surrendering to the fall is the most heroic thing he can do in that moment. Luke appears to shrink before our eyes on the screen as he falls, disappearing almost into nothingness before he is blown into a hatchway that opens onto a hanging weather vane over the planet's atmosphere. Luke desperately holds on with his remaining hand before being flipped upside down, mirroring how he began this episode in the wampa's cave. The clouds that were below him, the opposite of where they ought to be naturally, are now above him again, relatively speaking, somewhat righting his warped perspective.

This is the moment in *Star Wars* that most derails Luke's path because it reframes his sense of identity and the person he chose as his role model. In the year between *The Empire Strikes Back* and *Return of the Jedi*, he will have to reflect upon what he has learned, what it means for his identity, and what he will do and become with the weight of this revelation hanging over him. He already felt the pain of the loss of a mythic structure when he lost his first mentor. Even then, he was still able to hold onto the ideas Ben had placed into him about the nature of the Force, his place in the lineage of a great and powerful Jedi warrior who was his father, and, therefore, what the future of his path would hold for him. But the revelation that Vader *is* his father turns that entire structure against him.

Luke now has to wonder about the truth of *everything* Ben and Yoda have taught him. If his father, Anakin, can fall to the dark side and superficially prosper as Darth Vader because of it, it validates the idea that the dark side really *is* stronger. If his father was such a great hero and chose darkness over the alternative, maybe it means *he* will make the same choice too. Luke feels betrayed by the Jedi he trusted to give him the parental guidance he needed, just like Anakin once did. If he has enough maturity, he will reflect upon the events that led to his mentors misleading him and ultimately come to agree with their decision. If not, he will only grow in his resentment for them before running into Vader's arms, the alternate mentor who has shown up in his life and offered his guidance along a different path.

Luke calls out to Ben because he needs his guidance desperately now, needs the structure his mentorship once brought into his life that has now all fallen with him. True to his word, the Force spirit of Ben Kenobi does *not* interfere. He cannot, so long as Luke has abandoned the path his mentorship set out for him. He will not show up until Luke comes to terms with what has happened and seeks his wisdom and understanding again on the terms he has laid out to offer them. Like the last time he was hanging precariously upside down, Luke regains enough composure to remember his training. He closes his eyes and reaches out through the Force, not to his lightsaber this time, but to Leia, who he intuitively understands will be the only one capable of hearing him due to their secret connection in the Force. The Millennium Falcon arrives just in time to rescue him with TIE fighters and Vader's Star Destroyer hot on their trail.

In a very subtle way, Episode 5 has begun to show the re-awakening of Anakin within Vader. When Vader confessed his paternal relationship to Luke, it was the first time he had spoken of himself as Anakin

Skywalker again instead of as a separate entity. For the first time since Padmé died, there is a strong emotional reason to remain connected to the life he shut out from his memories and autobiographical identity. Vader allows himself to become defined by his relationship to Luke, just as he was once defined by his relationship to Luke's mother. It is the first step in the journey to reclaiming his authentic self through a familial connection that reminds him who he really is and of the love he has always been searching for.

In the absence of Ben's guiding spirit to fill the role, Vader reaches out to Luke with the Force in an attempt at long-distance father-son bonding, asking Luke once again to <u>come with him</u> and insisting <u>it is his destiny</u>. Luke perks up from his bed as he hears Vader's voice in his head, unthinkingly calling him father before calling out to an absent Ben once again to ask, in anger and betrayal, why his mentor didn't tell him the terrible truth he just learned.

When R2-D2 employs his creative abilities to fix the hyperdrive aboard the Millennium Falcon, and it disappears into the stars, we expect Vader to be furious. The beginning of a renewed capacity for self-reflection in Vader's heart can be seen as the shot lingers, without dialogue, on Vader watching his son escape into hyperspace. He is so caught up in his thoughts and emotions that he ignores the officer responsible for letting them get away. Two times in this film, we have seen Vader mercilessly choke the life out of Imperial officers who failed him with simple but important tasks: first, Admiral Ozzel when he came out of lightspeed too close to Hoth, and second, Captain Needa when he lost track of the Millennium Falcon in the asteroid field. Now, despite Admiral Piett being directly responsible for losing Vader's son, he shows no anger. He is lost in deep reflection on what has just occurred with the one remaining emotional connection in his life. That newfound capacity for self-reflection will be key to his return to the light soon enough.

Aboard the Rebel medical frigate, Luke receives a new robotic arm to replace the one he lost, just as his father did at the midpoint of his journey. And though he has just lived through the most traumatic experience of his life, where everything he valued was torn away from him, his dark night of the soul, he is visibly happy to be among his closest friends and family unit again. Anakin had to hide his trauma from those closest to him, with the exception of Padmé, when he lost his mother. Luke's position is different because he is safe to express his pain among those who will help him heal from it and move on in the healthiest way possible, so that it does not fester inside him like it did for years with his father.

Anyway, Luke does not have time to rest on the devastation of what has occurred because Han still needs to be rescued from Jabba the Hutt on Tatooine. And Luke, even at his lowest, will never let the people he loves down.

NOTES

68. "I wanted Yoda to be the traditional kind of character you find in fairy tales and mythology. And that character is usually a frog or a wizened old man on the side of the road. The hero is going down the road and meets this poor and insignificant person. The goal or the lesson is for the hero to learn to respect everybody and to pay attention to the poorest person because that's where the key to his success will be." George Lucas, quoted by Laurent Bouzereau, ed., *Star Wars: The Annotated Screenplays* (New York: Del Rey, 1997), 167–168.

69. In canon, Vader discovers Luke's identity on his own after the destruction of the Death Star through Imperial intelligence, bounty hunters, and his own investigations. In Marvel's 2015 *Darth Vader #6* comic, he hires bounty hunters to identify the pilot who made the impossible shot. Boba Fett reveals his name is Skywalker, allowing Vader to make the connection that he is his son, meaning that Palpatine lied to him about the circumstances of Padmé's death and that Obi-Wan has been hiding Luke from him all along. He then begins formulating a secret plan to recruit Luke and, with him, overthrow the Emperor.

70. "When [Vader] finds out Luke is his son, his first impulse is to figure out a way of getting him to join him to kill the Emperor. That's what Siths do! He tries it with anybody he thinks might be more powerful, which is what the Emperor was looking for in the first place: somebody who would be more powerful than he was and could help him rule the universe." George Lucas, interviewed by Gavin Edwards in "*George Lucas and the Cult of Darth Vader*," *Rolling Stone*, June 2, 2005.

71. In my book *The Romantic Ideal—The Highest Standard of Romance for a Man*, I reference Han and Leia as an essential example in film of a woman in a restricted social position and a rogue independent man who are attracted to each other due to their opposite strengths in an unconventional and socially unapproved pairing: "In the *Star Wars* original trilogy, Princess Leia is not confined by societal restrictions in the same way as conventional princesses. She's a headstrong leader in a rebellion against an evil empire. Still, she has to learn to open her heart and embrace her femininity by accepting her attraction to scoundrel smuggler with a heart of gold Han Solo, despite initially butting heads with him. Her demeanor is notably softer and more at peace by the final film as a result of loving him." Gregory V. Diehl, *The Romantic Ideal—The Highest Standard of Romance for*

a *Man: A Hopeless Romantic's Exploration of Masculine Intimacy, Sex, and Love* (Identity Publications, 2024), 143–144.

72. Dooku's lightsaber form, Makashi, emphasized economy of motion and clear tactical intention in one-on-one duels by redirecting attacks from less-refined opponents. His distinct curved-hilt saber reflected this by allowing a finer degree of wrist articulation for one-handed precision and control.

LUKE'S ADULTHOOD

eturn of the Jedi has the most solemn and reflective tone of all films in the hexalogy because it serves as the culmination of a long cycle of human development. It feels like witnessing things from the end of an old life, which is the opposite of the childlike and warm qualities we started with so long ago in *The Phantom Menace*. The lens through which we watch this story has been growing up alongside us and the characters. The story knows that it is coming to a close, or, as Yoda would say, that twilight is upon it and that soon night will fall, ending our window onto this world.

Within the storyworld, Yoda will entrust Luke with the responsibility of carrying on the information, experiences, and wisdom accrued across his long and storied life. On a meta level, the film is entrusting us, as witnesses to all that has occurred, to do the same thing outside the storyworld.[73] To pass on what you have learned does not mean merely to spread the gospel of *Star Wars,* but to deliberately inculcate its values in *your* life and society. Learn what you can from the simulation so that you do not repeat the same mistakes in real life. Inoculate yourself against its characters' failures and emulate their successes.

Luke's adulthood begins with him returning to the place where he grew up, the desert of Tatooine, to rescue Han Solo from vile gangster Jabba the Hutt. Anakin returned to Tatooine in a similar rescue attempt for his captive mother. Where Anakin failed in saving his mother, Luke will succeed in saving his elder brother. Jabba's palace is a practice run for the strength he will need to later save another familial figure, whose consciousness, not body, needs rescuing.

The return home gives Luke the opportunity to reflect on how much he has grown since *A New Hope*. Back then, Tatooine represented the limits to his worldview and development, what he described as the planet farthest from the bright center of the universe that he was never getting out of. It was an unconquerable obstacle preventing him from getting to know the world and himself. Now, just four years later, he has lived through so much, reflected so much, and accomplished so much that Tatooine seems trivial to him. He will dismiss it entirely, reflecting to Han that there's virtually nothing to see there. His spiritual concerns have grown so great in scope that what once had the power to overwhelm his child consciousness is powerless over him now. He will waste no time reminiscing once his mission of rescuing Han is accomplished. He will depart his childhood home for the last time in his life to return to Dagobah and fulfill his promise to Yoda to complete his Jedi training.

Luke strolls into Jabba's palace full of false confidence and composure, hoping to bluff and intimidate his way as a prematurely self-appointed Jedi into getting what he wants from his enemies. He is still a teenage boy pretending to be a man, based on his limited exposure to what a man, such as his recently realized dark father, is supposed to be. Luke, donning a black cloak to command respect through intimidation, is unconsciously employing Darth Vader as a role model. His deception works on Jabba's Gamorrean guards, who flee in fear at a simple demonstration of Luke's Force choke, a show of power he picked up from his father. Jabba's majordomo, Bib Fortuna, is also easily mind-tricked into believing what Luke wants him to, a tactic he picked up from his light father figure, Ben Kenobi, but twisted for a dark purpose.

The setting in Jabba's palace reflects the novelty, strangeness, and overindulgence Luke faced in Episode 4 when he left home and entered Mos Eisley Cantina with Ben as his protector. Back then, he was overwhelmed by novel stimulation and social conflicts. Jabba himself represents grotesque animal impulses, not unlike those of the Gungans from Episode 1, but totally isolated from awareness and responsibility. Jabba is a proud tyrant, a greedy gangster, a wrathful captor, a lazy sloth, an overweight glutton, and a lustful sex slaver. He is everything we should be ashamed of about our sinful lower nature. He is an animalistic force of nature that cannot be bargained with.

When Jabba does not fall for Luke's charade, Luke is forced to double down on the act before panicking and improvising. He's hoping to use Jabba's greed as his ally, like Qui-Gon once did with Watto on Tatooine, while warning him <u>not to underestimate his power</u>. Luke is overcompensating for his lack of control over the situation. Realizing the jig is up, he desperately Force pulls a blaster into his hand and attempts to fire on Jabba. His sudden assassination attempt with a common blaster instead of the new green lightsaber he built for himself, his appointed weapon as a Jedi Knight, is, in the words of Ben Kenobi, clumsy and random, just as it was when Obi-Wan was forced to use one against General Grievous' exposed heart in *Revenge of the Sith*. Obi-Wan was forced into that situation by circumstance, but Luke was reckless and failed to think ahead. Similarly, Luke will only barely manage to defeat the rancor by throwing a rock at a switch that brings a heavy door down upon the beast's head, notably forgoing use of the Force because he is too panicked to concentrate and maintain his focus. Throughout this awkward sequence, we see Luke at his lowest and most human while posturing himself as the opposite.

Aboard Jabba's sail barge over the Sarlacc pit, Luke becomes composed enough to stay calm and take control of a situation where he is at the mercy of his captors. Now, he demonstrates his attunement with the Force through carefully coordinated acrobatics, unexpected fighting techniques with his lightsaber, and coordination with hidden allies. There is a Luke that is utterly incapable when he struggles to win alone, and there is a Luke that accomplishes the impossible when he grounds himself in who he really is and the strength of others. Even an enslaved Leia finds the strength to choke the life out of her captor, Jabba, with her own chains, unknowingly carrying out some of the abandoned Skywalker legacy of fighting slavery on Tatooine.[74]

When Luke returns to Dagobah, one year after he rushed off to face Darth Vader, he looks upon Yoda differently. In the time that he has known him, he has gone from seeing him as an annoying little goblin to a mysterious and powerful wizard. But Yoda hobbles slowly around his hut and coughs now. Luke looks at him with surprise, like he is realizing for the first time how fragile this 900-year-old man actually is. Luke lost his first mentor, Ben, during a valiant duel against a monster. Now, he is losing Yoda to a force not even he can resist. Famously long-lived Yoda has become visibly older in appearance and behavior. Luke, the grown child, must confront the nature of mortality and that even the most powerful beings we look up to most to guide us eventually wither. Yoda can now barely even crawl into bed and pull his blanket over himself without Luke's assistance. Is this the legendary Grandmaster of the Jedi Order that so many heroes and villains have aspired to surpass in power? Yoda knows that he will die soon, and he is at peace with it. It seems that he has only been hanging on this long to have one last conversation with Luke so that he will feel complete before allowing himself to pass on, mirroring Shmi Skywalker's passing after seeing her son one last time after he fulfilled his promise to return to her on Tatooine.

Luke is not so ready to lose another mentor, and he rejects the possibility of Yoda dying. Yoda reminds the young man that, strong as he is in the Force, even he is <u>not strong enough</u> to stave off death forever. Yoda is the gold standard that various characters have been comparing themselves to across the saga, each in their own way seeking to become more powerful than him. Here now, this most powerful of all Jedi, whom others strive to become like, is calmly accepting his limitations. Yoda tells Luke that he no longer requires any training from him, as he already knows everything he needs to. Nothing else will prepare him more than he has already been prepared by facing Vader once, and not only surviving, but resisting the temptation to turn to the dark side. Luke chose to maintain his values, as evidenced by his return to Dagobah as he had promised to. The only thing left to do now is confront Vader again with the confidence he has attained in the strength of his morals and authentic identity. Then, at last, he will be a real Jedi and a real adult. Yoda is saying, "You need to prove that you have completely mastered your own darkness, the same darkness that consumed your father before you. Only then will you be immune to corruption."

Luke then surprises Yoda by asking a question he was not prepared to answer. He needs to know if Darth Vader is really his father. Yoda, until this moment, did not know that Vader had revealed this information. He calls this revelation unfortunate for Luke, not because he knows the truth but because he rushed to face it before he was ready, before his training would have prepared him to deal with the burden of knowing such an emotionally difficult fact. Luke demonstrates his growth by reflecting on his impulsive actions in the previous film and apologizing for not listening to his mentors when they warned him not to leave Dagobah. Yoda repeats his warning from Episode 5 that if Luke even starts down the dark path, it will <u>dominate his destiny</u> forever. So certain is he of the irredeemability of those who are lost.

Yoda is *wrong* here. For all his wisdom and experience, he has not yet figured out one truth that young Luke already has: the power of loving attachment expressed in a healthy way. It is not impossible to return once someone starts down the dark path, only exceedingly difficult. The end of Anakin Skywalker's story is meant to demonstrate this overlooked fact. It's like drowning. The longer you stay underwater, the less strength you have to try to swim back up to the surface again. Sink far enough, and you might no longer even be able to see the light from which you descended. You're trapped in complete darkness, almost out of oxygen, and metaphorically on death's door. You need someone you love, trust, and feel completely connected to to be there for you, to throw you a lifesaver, pull you up, and show you that the light is still there and within your reach.

Luke's newly appointed role from Yoda is to carry on the wisdom and responsibilities of the generations that preceded him. This sacred act began in *A New Hope* when he first learned about his father's past as a Jedi and received his lightsaber, a weapon symbolic of his father's responsibilities. With Yoda's passing, Luke is about to be the last of the Jedi, the only one to keep their fire burning in the universe. He must pass their values on to others who are ready to receive the wisdom of the past, modified through his unique perspective. Naturally, this will start with his secret twin sister, who carries the same sense of heroism and potential with the Force as him.

Luke's burden as a vessel from past to future has gone from small and personal (carrying on his father's legacy) to grand and impersonal (carrying on the legacy of the entire Jedi Order). Nineteen-year-old Luke initially rejected that minor burden, insisting he couldn't get involved. Twenty-three-year-old Luke accepts his new, much larger responsibilities. This time, he does not reject the call. He is ready to save the world and its soul.

Yoda dies, and his body disappears into the Force, cementing for Luke that he is the last one left to do what must be done. By witnessing death in this enlightened manner, rather than the chaotic, traumatic one Anakin did, Luke is learning the vital lessons about impermanence and letting go that his father never did. Like Ben Kenobi's before him, Yoda's imprint will continue to carry on in Luke's memory for the rest of his life, immortally guiding him. He will always be asking himself what wisdom Yoda would share with him or what he would do in a given situation.

Luke initially seems somewhat offended to see the spirit of Ben again, addressing him as Obi-Wan, his old name, for the first time in his life in an accusatory tone, as if to indicate that he's not sure he knows who he is anymore. Luke feels betrayed by his first mentor for lying to him about Darth Vader, manipulating him onto a path he otherwise might not have chosen. He needs to know why Ben told him that Vader betrayed and murdered his father when the literal truth was so far from that. Ben's justification for the bent truth he shared is that the good man, Anakin Skywalker, was destroyed when he betrayed his values and became Darth Vader.

Ben has come to believe that a person is defined not by the continuity of their body but of their mind, values, and worldview from which their behavior emerges. Ben ceased to see Vader as Anakin once he knew the terrible things he had done, like murdering children and assaulting the woman he loved. He ceased trying to pull him back to the light once he saw how distorted his point of view had become by calling his own family, the Jedi, evil. It was a simplified and metaphorical truth that, from a certain point of view, communicated the most relevant facts to Luke in a way he would interpret appropriately. He was like a parent talking to a child. Parents tell their children as much as they believe they can understand, as much as will be useful, and won't harm or overwhelm them. If Ben had refused to answer Luke's questions about his father or admitted to him that he was only telling him a partial truth, it could have led Luke to try to find out the truth on his own, which would be dangerous for the additional reason that it would risk Darth Vader discovering he had children. By *Return of the Jedi*, Luke is more mature and wiser than he was in *A New Hope*. He is ready for the full truth now.

Ben was once blinded because he had clung to a version of the truth that depended on the interpretation of the prophecy passed on to him by Qui-Gon that Anakin was the Chosen One who would destroy the Sith and bring balance to the Force. His interpretation of Anakin's behavior depended greatly upon the point of view he had at the time. He has since had more than two decades to reflect upon his inadequacy as a mentor to Anakin. And now it is time for Luke's point of view to evolve too, to become large enough to embrace the literal truth of what happened to his father and accept why Ben and Yoda felt the need to conceal it from him.

Luke displays both his optimism and his remaining naivety. Knowing what a good man his father used to be, he cannot accept that goodness is gone. His optimism reflects his mother's final thoughts about the goodness in the man she loved. But Ben has long since moved on from that position, insisting that Vader is now twisted and evil, more machine than man, speaking both literally of his reconstructed cyborg body and metaphorically of his unfeeling mentality that has made him a slave of automatic processes. Luke must now do what Ben failed to do so long ago on Mustafar: kill Darth Vader, ending the threat he poses to the galaxy. He <u>cannot escape this destiny,</u> Ben claims, before giving Luke the hint he needs to intuit that Leia is his secret twin sister and a fellow offspring of the man he is trying to save from Hell.

Spiritual patricide is a common theme in heroic stories because it's a necessary part of a young man maturing to the point where he can live beyond his father's image and influence as his own man. Luke has had the heroic image of his father, Anakin Skywalker, destroyed and replaced by the dark and villainous one of Darth Vader. He has no internal compass for who to become, only what he fears becoming. When Ben tells him that he must face Darth Vader again, he is telling him to destroy not just the physical body of his father, but also the positive image of him in his psyche. Confront everything you fear and everything that holds you back from embodying yourself. Luke refuses this call, like the first call to leave Tatooine when he was young, but this time for reasons related to his internal values instead of external ones thrust upon him by his aunt and uncle. He cannot kill his own father because he cannot divorce himself from the aspirational image of the great man Anakin was, and therefore the great man he, himself, is supposed to become. He must hold onto the hope that that image was real and possible, or else he will not know who he is anymore. Luke does not yet realize that he is not only making it possible for himself to live up to the ideal image of his father, but also for his father to finally do so, too.

Luke is now the living vessel for the Jedi to carry on into the future, equal to his mentors in this regard, as he has absorbed the distilled wisdom of generations prior. He must become the seed of a new generation that improves upon what came before, or else the galaxy is doomed to a stagnant and self-destructive cycle. The rest of Luke's story will be about going where neither of his mentors could have taken him with their wisdom. Where Luke arrives will be an undiscovered place that is the result of his commitment to the values he has discovered within himself. He will accomplish what the wisest Jedi of the Republic considered to be impossible by trusting his own feelings and disobeying his mentors once again, this time out of love instead of fear.

In *A New Hope*, Han had to be convinced by Luke and Leia to join the heroic effort against the first Death Star. Now, he recruits a strike team to deactivate the shield generator on Endor that protects the partially constructed second Death Star. He has completed his developmental arc from a loner and self-absorbed hedonist into someone willing to sacrifice everything superficial for a cause he believes in and the people he loves.

On Endor, the Rebels making peace with the Ewoks mirrors the unity between the Naboo and Gungans that began the story in Episode 1. Luke, now playing the role of peacemaker and spiritual guide that Qui-Gon did then, employs his mystical powers and invokes the Ewok's conception of their gods to help secure the partnership. Qui-Gon pulled a similar trick by appealing to the demands of the Gungan gods about a life debt to secure their help. They unite under a common mythology for a common cause. C-3PO takes this one step further by co-creating a new myth with the Ewoks by relating the story of *Star Wars* to the children of the Ewok tribe, retelling the events that brought them there. Their culture will be shaped by the power of this story and their participation in the heroic battle to come. Luke, too, by hearing his life choices narrated in this way, will have the opportunity to reflect on the mistakes he has made until now and choose better in the trials still to come.

Before the final battle, Luke pulls Leia aside to tell her Ben's revelation that she is his sister and why he must leave Endor to face Darth Vader. He demonstrates his maturity by choosing to face Vader now, not because Ben and Yoda told him to or because Vader will force him to, but because he knows it is the right thing to do. It is an expression of his authentic values, not merely a circumstance he has been forced into. When Luke faces Vader and Emperor Palpatine in the Death Star throne room a few scenes from now, they will both speak of destiny in the same way so many other characters have throughout Star Wars: as a fated path that cannot be avoided, so it might as well be surrendered to. Destiny is like entropy to them. Luke has rejected this narrow view in favor of one that empowers him to change the course of his destiny to align with his highest possible self-expression. He will not become part of the machine running on autopilot as they have.

When Luke surrenders himself to Vader, it's the first opportunity the two have for father/son bonding since their unfortunate encounter on Bespin, the true nature of their relationship fully revealed now. In the year that has passed since then, Luke has had to come to terms with the new world he is living in, and he has done it largely without the help of his mentors. This prolonged state of reflection has forced him to mature, making him into a different person than he was before, now virtually an equal to his father,[75] demonstrated in part by the symbolic act of having constructed his own lightsaber after losing his father's (and the hand wielding it) in their last duel. The burden of living up to that symbol of Anakin's greatness and duty is gone. The adult son has outgrown his childish image of what his father was supposed to be and addresses him now not as either the avatar of absolute good or evil but as simply a flawed and broken man.

This is the first critical scene in *Return of the Jedi* that showcases Anakin beginning to emerge, as evidenced by the capacity for self-reflection in Vader. There is no aggression or antagonism when he addresses his son. He is surprisingly patient, thoughtful, and inquiring—until Luke addresses him by the name Anakin Skywalker, an accusation which triggers his insecurities. Vader immediately deflects the reminder as a personal attack, <u>insisting the name Anakin no longer has any meaning for him</u>. Despite his protests, Vader inadvertently refers to himself and Anakin as the same entity again. He is progressing toward a reintegration of his split psyche as a result of the connective power of Luke's familial influence. Luke hopefully insists that Anakin is the name of his true self, that he's only forgotten the man he used to be and what he cares about, the authentic values of the slave boy on Tatooine who knew nothing of greed, thought the biggest problem in the galaxy was that nobody helped each other, wanted nothing more than to fulfill his heroic image of the Jedi and free all the slaves in the galaxy, and wished to save the ones he loved from dying.[76]

Luke asks his father to <u>come away with him</u> and abandon the life and identity he has built within the Empire. Padmé attempted the same thing with Anakin on Mustafar, but Anakin did not think there was anything wrong with what he was doing then. Vader recounts that Obi-Wan once thought the same as Luke does, when he tried to talk sense into Anakin during the forced pause in their duel over the lava on Mustafar. Anakin shot down his attempts because he was too enraged to reflect on anything Obi-Wan had to say. That's the power of the dark side that Vader insists Luke does not know. It is too difficult to interrupt that process within a mind once it has begun... to reflect, to take accountability, reverse course, and backtrack once someone has started acting drastically in a state of passion. The fallen will only fall further into delusion and separation from reality the longer time goes on. Vader believes that he must continue to obey his master, referring both to the trauma that initially corrupted him and its personification, Darth Sidious.

Luke wants to believe that his father is incapable of turning him over to the Emperor or even killing him if he refuses to turn to the dark side. But Vader accepts this as a possible outcome of what he <u>identifies as Luke's destiny</u>, which is quite different than what he claimed only one movie ago about his destiny of joining him to rule the galaxy. Vader has killed thousands of people. He can justify slaughtering anyone he has convinced himself is his enemy. Luke is banking on the hope of a familial connection and on the belief that he cannot do the same to him once he has taken ownership of him as his son. Anakin's influence grows stronger the more Luke urges him to <u>let go of the hate</u> that has fueled him for 23 years. But Vader insists it is too late for him, in a way acknowledging that he has gone down the wrong path in life but is nevertheless powerless to change it now. Vader is more self-reflective now than we have ever seen, but it is not enough to stop him from delivering Luke to the Emperor.

Only upon hearing this admission of close-mindedness to a new future does a previously optimistic Luke appear to accept that it's impossible to save his father. Luke, the most hopeful of the hopeful, considers now that Anakin Skywalker may actually be dead if he can proceed with the abominable thing he is about to do to his own son. He speaks of death in the same sense as Ben. Anakin's consciousness is no longer capable of enacting its values in the world so long as Vader is suppressing it. The shot lingers on Vader walking over to a railing and silently leaning on it in reflection, the third time we have seen him framed in such a way throughout his story. Even though we cannot see his facial expressions beneath the mask, the change in his posture conveys the hidden truth. Anakin is somewhere inside there considering what his son has told him—if it really is too late for him. This forced state of self-reflection will come again, one more time, in a moment of crisis just before Anakin returns to life.

The Emperor's Theme plays as Luke and Vader enter the Death Star throne room, a spire, which, from the outside, resembles the tower of the Jedi Council chambers Anakin first turned to the dark side in. A low, subdued choir returns to the score for the first time since we heard the music of the prequel era, when choral singers were prominent in pieces like *Duel of the Fates*, *Anakin's Betrayal*, and *Battle of the Heroes* to highlight each piece's mythic and sacred properties. Now, the presence of choir represents the return of the sacred in an ominous way, as though the demonic figure of Darth Sidious has enacted a cult-like authority over the Force under the rule of the Empire. The Sith of all generations past seem to be chanting his praises from beyond the netherworld of the Force.

Vader and Palpatine have both expressed a desire for paternal rights to Luke, each positioning themselves as the superior option to guide him into adulthood, pass their values onto him, and shape his destiny. But neither is in a position to earn this status in Luke's life authentically, like Ben and Yoda did. They must compel and coerce their way into his life. Palpatine knows that Luke has come with the intention of returning Anakin to the light. Like Yoda, he believes this to be so fundamentally impossible that he does not consider it a threat to take seriously, that bad people cannot change and the unconscious cannot become conscious again. He believes that Luke's compassion for his father is a critical weakness that will be his undoing.

Luke adopts a new mask of arrogance and false bravado as he faces the man responsible for his father's downfall. He seems like a completely different person from the caring and compassionate man he was just moments ago on Endor, pleading with his father to come with him and return to the light. He's back to how he was when facing a threat he was underprepared for in Jabba's palace, postering himself before his enemy because he lacks the confidence that he will win. He didn't actually expect to have to face the Emperor when he surrendered himself to his father. He's out of his element and completely unprepared for what may come next. Luke's strength with the Force is insignificant compared to the combined might of Palpatine and Vader. And Palpatine, it turns out, knows all about the secret Rebel strike team on Endor.

This information pushes Luke into a state of panic, making him more susceptible to the dark side. Palpatine is weaponizing Luke's anxiety to manipulate him into making a fatal moral mistake he will not be able to recover from, like when Anakin panicked and attacked Mace Windu. Luke has an urgent dilemma to deal with now. With the news that troops are waiting to ambush his friends, he believes all they have worked for will be lost. Han and Leia will die. The Rebel fleet will be destroyed, and the Alliance along with it. Anakin will not be saved. Nothing lies ahead but failure on every front. Luke looks to his lightsaber, now in Palpatine's possession. The only move he has left is to kill the Emperor himself.

Killing Palpatine is *not* wrong. If any man in the galaxy deserves death, surely it is him. But Luke's emotional state has been compromised, and he is not fit to carry out the act without corrupting himself in the process. Palpatine urges him to take his lightsaber and strike him down <u>with all of his hatred</u> as a seemingly defenseless target for slaughter, framing himself the same way he did when Windu was his attacker. This is the escalating and uncontrollable state he needs him to be in for Luke to surrender conscious judgment. The more aggression grows, the more hatred flows, and the more control he sacrifices to Palpatine.

Over the years, Palpatine has grown so confident in his ability to turn good people bad that he no longer even conceals his intentions. When he seduced Anakin, he did so under the guise of helping him.

He was patient and cautious, planting seeds in the mind of his target for years before acting on them. He reframed evil as good so that Anakin could ideologically justify the change in his behavior. He does not conceal evil now; he only presents it as superior. Vader seems to have abandoned all pretense about his own corruption, too, telling Luke that it is pointless to resist the temptation before him, that he will inevitably make the same type of mistake he did because he is not convicted enough for anything else. Palpatine is also so accustomed to winning that he no longer considers that anything could happen other than in the manner he has designed, that everything will transpire as he has foreseen, both within his throne room and stretching out into the galaxy all around them, like a god.

Luke correctly identifies this overconfidence as Palpatine's weakness. Like so many villains before him in *Star Wars*, Palpatine is celebrating a victory too early because he is too sure of himself to allow for emergent events that change the trajectory of destiny, such as authentic human choice. Anything outside the scope of what we consider possible is a miracle, and Emperor Palpatine cannot foresee the one that is about to occur with the resurrection of Anakin Skywalker.

Palpatine's fatal flaw is overconfidence, believing too much in himself, the extreme embodiment of greed. Luke's is having too much faith in others, the extreme embodiment of compassion. Luke's role has always been that of a communal integrator. His purity, his optimistic outlook, and his unwillingness to give up on others are traits that have brought out the best in everyone around him, turning ordinary people into heroes in their own right. Attempting to do the same with Darth Vader is the ultimate challenge for his values. Not giving up on his father, when everyone else has, will test the strength of his conviction more than anything else could. If Luke <u>gives in to hate</u> here, as Ben once direly warned him not to, the battle of his hope and optimism will be lost. Spiritual corruption will continue unabated throughout the galaxy. But if he can remain conscious and compassionate when it is nearly impossible to do so, good will finally overcome evil, and his en*light*ening influence will spread forth onto the rest of the galaxy.

Luke, for now, surrenders to his aggression, summoning his lightsaber, igniting its green blade, and attempting to strike down Emperor Palpatine in anger and panic. Only Vader's suddenly ignited red blade prevents it from making contact. Vader has simultaneously defended his master and his son here by saving the life of one and preventing the moral downfall of the other. Vader redirects Luke's aggression away from Palpatine and toward himself in another bout of twisted father/son bonding. Vader, who should be a master in the domain of hatred compared to Luke, is out of his element. He does not really want to hurt Luke here, but he is locked into awkward combat due to the demands of the man he has subordinated his consciousness to.

Luke deactivates his lightsaber in an effort to de-escalate the situation, refusing to fight his father any longer. He allows Vader to slowly approach, his robotic limbs carrying more weight than they did before, but he cautiously backs away in fear because he cannot be sure what to expect from his father now, as Padmé once backed away from Anakin on Mustafar when she realized she didn't know him anymore. Vader yells that Luke is unwise to lower his defenses, meaning both his lightsaber and the emotional barriers he has removed by choosing to be open and vulnerable, as he suddenly strikes, trying to force the conflict to continue. Vader is intent on keeping his own emotional defenses in place, for now, because he is still afraid of what will happen if he allows himself to be vulnerable with his son. But Luke sees the difference in the man beneath Vader's mask. He knows he is getting through to him, that the conflict between the person Palpatine has coerced him into being and the person he really wants to be is growing.

Luke flips onto an overhead catwalk, and the music briefly turns triumphant as he attempts to elevate himself above the conflict he has been coerced into while insisting that he feels the good in his father. Vader takes offense at his son's attempts at taking the high road, defending the dark side by insisting to Luke that he underestimates its power, echoing the words Anakin spoke to Obi-Wan on the lava bank of Mustafar. Vader has learned from Anakin's mistake. He no longer haphazardly throws himself at Luke in his elevated position as before on Mustafar. Instead, he hurls his lightsaber at the catwalk supports to force Luke down into the shadows with him. This, he refers to as Luke meeting his destiny, a path down into the darkness with him that he is forcing his son onto.

Vader stalks Luke in the dark beneath the platforms, probing his mind and taunting him to give himself to the dark side and save his friends. Luke's anxieties resurface now because of how vulnerable he feels, his inner state reflecting the shadows he is hiding in. This gives Vader the opportunity to home in on a critical feeling Luke had been suppressing, just as Ben warned him might happen. Luke's greatest fear lies with the safety of not just his friends, but his recently discovered sister. Vader's voice turns shades of maniacal, like Palpatine's, when he unlocks this missing ingredient to corrupting Luke. In this moment, Vader temporarily ascends to the status of Master in the Sith domain because he is no longer an underling relying on Palpatine to tell him what to do in service to the dark side. Luke has refused to fight his father because of his love for and familial connection to him, but that very same heroic value can be turned against him by someone who knows how to exploit it. All Vader has to do is threaten to find Leia, his other familial connection, and turn her to the dark side instead of him to awaken the rage within Luke and get him to finally abandon his conscious principles and start acting animalistically.[77] Vader has succeeded in baiting Luke into abandoning his conscious principles and letting his fear take over as a precursor to surrendering completely to the dark side.

A Jedi's Fury plays as an incensed Luke fights with fury we have never seen from him. A low male choir sounds simultaneously heroic and haunting, as we are unsure whether we should actually be rooting for Luke to win this encounter and for Vader be beaten by his own son in this manner. Luke attacks Vader with a new type of hatred, not as before, when he hated him in a fantastical sense as the monster he believed killed his father. He *hates* him now, fully aware of who he is, his father, the man who intends to capture and corrupt his sister and, most monstrously of all, the daughter of the woman he loved. It's an echo of the disgust Obi-Wan felt upon witnessing Anakin assault Padmé on Mustafar, taking it as confirmation of how monstrous he had really become to turn so violently against what was once so important to him.

Vader undergoes a sudden personality shift, too. He has just learned that he has a second offspring, a girl who came from Padmé and who, in all likelihood, carries all her positive qualities, just as Luke carries his. It is conceivable that in this critical moment, Vader has begun to put the pieces together, just as Luke did, and to realize that his secret daughter is, in fact, Princess Leia, the woman he interrogated and destroyed the home planet of. All the guilt he has accumulated over the years about hurting Padmé is compounding for him, and he is weak and uncoordinated because of it.

Luke wins this duel, bashing his lightsaber against his father's until he gets him on the ground and severs his artificial hand in a reversal of the position they were in when Vader severed his on a Cloud City catwalk over an abyss. Luke embodies an echo of his father's state on Mustafar in Episode 3. *The Emperor's Theme* returns as Palpatine laughs to underscore that he is the one in control of their conflict. He is the only one actually winning this battle. Vader is resigned to a physical and emotional state we have not seen him in since he first submitted himself to Palpatine. He is on his back and holding his remaining hand up in a defensive position, struggling to breathe, wordless but pleading with his body language for his son to show him mercy. Gone is all the false bravado we've come to associate with the fearsome Vader suit and his ability to command respect through intimidation as he begs his own son not to kill him. Luke is now in the same position his father was in with a disarmed Count Dooku at the start of Episode 3, with Palpatine encouraging him to kill the man lying helplessly before him, to strike his father down and take his place at his side.

Suddenly, we, the audience, have become upset with watching what has become of the young hero we were rooting for. We are happy that he beat Darth Vader, but we are also extremely uncomfortable with *how* he did it. In any conventional hero story, this scene would have been the moment where the underdog hero finally mustered the missing strength to overcome and defeat the villain, and it would have been framed as heroic and celebratory. Instead, we are filled with dread as these events unfold. The framing of Luke's victory as a dreadful event forces the viewer to realize it was wrong for Luke to beat Vader in this manner. We suddenly don't want to cheer our hero on anymore. We want to tell him to stop, to help him realize he is going too far. With that comes the realization that evil is not just about the actions we take, but what motivates us to take them, and the emotional state we are in when we do. Luke has won the physical battle against the physical Vader outside of him but is losing the emotional battle against the emotional Vader rising up within him. Luke's sudden aggression gave him a momentary advantage in the fight, but then it almost cost him everything, mirroring what happened in Obi-Wan's fight against Darth Maul in Episode 1.

Despite everything that has occurred, Luke still has a choice to change the path he is on and not act like a machine operating on autopilot, as his father did.[78] He sees the damage he has caused to

Vader's hand and compares it with his own. Now he feels compassion for his father, the monster, because he is able to empathize by having been put into a similar position, which prevents him from fulfilling his duty to kill Darth Vader. He casts away his lightsaber and declares that the Emperor has failed. He will never turn to the dark side. He firmly knows this now and feels ready to appoint himself a Jedi, not by Ben's and Yoda's standard of the title but by his own. This sudden reversal has happened because the psychic context has shifted. Luke's awareness has been broadened by the sight of Vader's machine arm, compared with his own, forcing him into a deeper state of self-reflection. He sees his father's path reflected in him now, and that he is making the same mistakes he made in the last film.

Luke's refusal to join the dark side here is calm, in contrast to when he screamed in desperation in Cloud City that he would never join Vader. It was an animalistic response to an overwhelming threat. Now, it is a conscious choice, born of self-reflection. Luke, as a stable individual atop a pillar of permanent values and master of his own destiny, did not truly exist until this moment. He has grown immune to fear and insecurity. He extends that same standard onto his father by comparing himself to him, saying that he is like his father before him, inspiring Anakin to be like the son he sees standing against the dark side, an image of the Chosen One he should have been. The image of the father once inspired the son to heroism, and now the son returns the favor. If Anakin's son can accomplish the impossible, maybe he can too.

Because Luke has the perspective of his father's failure in front of him, he realizes how machine-like he is becoming by allowing himself to be driven by fear and anger. He sees exactly what he *shouldn't* allow himself to do and become in a way Anakin never did. Vader is now a mythic image of the dark for him to stand against and learn from, just as it is for us watching at home. And because of this reversal, only moments later, Anakin himself will return to win the emotional battle against Vader because he will have an example of what he *should* do and become in his son. Luke conquers the dark side by witnessing Anakin's failure, and Anakin only beats the dark side by witnessing Luke's success. Both extremes are necessary. The final victory over evil in *Star Wars* is a symbiotic one, forming a complete circle between dark and light, master and apprentice, father and son, and past and future generations.

Palpatine interpreted Luke's fury against his father as foregone proof that the battle was already won and his fall to the dark side was already complete. He believed conscious redirection from that state was impossible and that Luke would never be able to recover from killing his father in anger. This is what Yoda warned Luke about when he told him that the dark path would dominate his destiny if ever he started down it. Luke does something unprecedented by defying the destiny thrust upon him. He has achieved the standard of Jedi by his own analysis and confidently proclaims it so, even defying Ben and Yoda by not killing Vader but saving him.

Luke has just survived the strongest possible temptation and consciously confirmed the stance he only started to take in the last film. He knows that he would rather die and lose everything than betray his values. Luke is immune to emotional corruption and coercion now. He demonstrates what a new breed of Jedi should be by showing compassion for his enemy instead of seeking revenge against the man who cut off his arm, the lesson Anakin never learned. He has experienced turning to the dark side vicariously through his father, who spared him the trouble of going through hell himself to garner its lessons and wisdom.

At last, Palpatine's unbreakable demeanor changes. He sees that Luke is no longer a desperate boy he can manipulate. He is a man now with his own self-determined values. Any further efforts to turn him will be a waste, so he must be destroyed. He begrudgingly accepts Luke's new designation, calling him "Jedi" with a bitterness that did not exist before when he mocked him with the title.

A blaring horn version of *The Emperor's Theme* plays as Luke pleads for his father to save him from Palpatine's sudden electrical attack. This is the end. Another apocalypse is upon us and the world of *Star Wars*. The Sith spirits singing out in the choir know that evil has won. It is agonizing for us to watch, just as it must be for the presence of Anakin within Darth Vader. Vader's mask moves from his son in agony on the floor to his master gleefully torturing him. We are meant to imagine the conflict in the facial expressions of the man within that he cannot express until the mask is removed. He is reflecting on the mistake he made 23 years ago between the Sith path and the Jedi path in Palpatine's office in Episode 3, unsure of whether to help Palpatine or Windu as electricity flew around him, and how he would choose differently if he could do it all again.

Palpatine pauses his assault to announce that Luke will die. Deep within Vader, Anakin hears this and realizes what is occurring. He is *watching someone he loves die*. He is about to let it happen again, the one thing he was so determined to stop, which he failed at twice before and which led to everything terrible that has become of him and the world. He speaks the word "no" softly to himself, and then yells it out in heroic defiance of his master, breaking through the limits to his consciousness with sheer force of will.[79] Every melodramatic "noooooo" that has appeared in each episode of the saga until now has been a reaction to something awful that a hero was powerless to stop, especially Anakin's at the end of Episode 3, when he learned that he was responsible for Padmé's death. This "no" is different because it pre-empts the terrible thing and comes just in time to stop it from occurring. This is Anakin defying the destiny Palpatine chose for him and pushing back against spiritual entropy with the conscious might of the Chosen One.

The Force musical theme takes over the Emperor's in triumphant fashion as the villain miraculously transforms into the hero. The rising ghostly choir that plays now sounds like all the evil of Anakin's past being exorcised out of him. Their echoes fade into oblivion as Anakin grabs Palpatine, absorbing his lightning, and throws him down a reactor shaft, where he explodes, taking all the evil in the galaxy with him. Palpatine, who should have had time to react to his apprentice suddenly turning against him, instead was so shocked by that which he considered to be impossible suddenly happening to him that he could only remain consumed by the rage from which his lightning flowed. He remained powerless to defend himself, just as Maul once was in the climax of the saga's first Jedi vs. Sith duel, and was, in the end, rather easily defeated once he lost the illusory grip of control he held over Anakin's fragile psyche.

Vader has spent the last 20 years killing out of hatred, but Anakin performs his final execution out of defense for what he loves, his passion, at last, responsibly embodied. He has become the hero of legend again, and the prophecy of the Chosen One is, at last, fulfilled, though not in a way the Jedi could ever have predicted. He has completed the attempt at spiritual patricide he began on Mustafar, when he tried to prove he could live beyond Obi-Wan's influence by striking him down in a duel. He wasn't ready to stand on his own then, and Obi-Wan was immediately replaced by Palpatine. This time, he has freed himself from the dark, restrictive father figure who prevented him from fully becoming himself. Luke is left to watch over a terminally injured and newly redeemed Anakin, struggling to breathe beneath the mask of Vader.

All his life, Anakin has been obsessed with acquiring more power, which he believed would be the key to finally achieving what he valued. In the end, it was not an overwhelming display of physical strength or even power in the Force that enabled him to save Luke. Throwing an old man into a pit is not the grand heroic kind of final battle we expect from great warriors. Instead, it is the greatest display of *emotional* strength shown anywhere in *Star Wars*. Anakin's journey was never about becoming physically powerful. His mistake was to concentrate his attention on that domain of his life until it consumed everything else. He needed to grow emotionally in order to stop a stronger pain he could not ignore, embodied in a pure parental bond of unconditional love for the son he finally takes paternal responsibility for.[80] He had become the father figure he needed all along.

Anakin asks Luke to help him take the Vader mask off so he can look upon him with his own eyes before he dies, interfering with his son's attempts to get him off the Death Star before it is destroyed. He's asking him to relieve him of the burden of Vader, of living out this angry false identity for the last 23 years instead of being himself. To look with his own eyes is to see his son without the bias of Vader's values and agenda, to remember how clearly he saw the world before he was corrupted. Let me look at you as my son, who I love, instead of as a tool for me to gain more power.

Luke hesitates because he knows that Anakin will die without the medical support of his suit to keep him alive. Anakin accepts that <u>nothing can stop him from dying now</u>. He has finally adopted the same wisdom as Yoda about humility and the acceptance of natural limitations. He will die not just because of the injuries he sustained from Palpatine's lightning. He is dying because he has finally let go of the hatred that sustained him in active rebellion against death since he should have died on Mustafar. He doesn't desperately cling to life anymore. He knows now that his influence, the good he managed to do before he died, will live on in his son, that he has earned a degree of immortality as the proper father figure he both needed and should have been.

Vader's theme plays one last time as we see Anakin unmasked, and we see peace and joy in the pained smile on his face[81] for the first time since *Revenge of the Sith*, except it does not sound terrifying or militaristic anymore. It has taken on the tone of a delicate and dissonant funeral march, as it did at the end of Episode 3, this time commemorating the death of both Anakin and Vader. The return to the light is not as clear-cut and easy as we might prefer, and even Luke is unsure of how to feel about the man lying before him. Anakin urges his son to leave him, but Luke refuses. It's not in his character to give up on the people he loves, ever, so he won't leave him there in his moment of weakness, contrasting with Obi-Wan's mistake on Mustafar, when he abandoned a dying Anakin in Hell. He must save his father, but Anakin absolves him of that responsibility by telling him he already has saved him.

Anakin, unmasked, seems somehow very young and very old at the same time, with a pale, bald face that resembles that of a newborn baby, as if he has not been able to develop his own personality and signature characteristics. His real appearance evokes diametrically opposite emotions from his manufactured appearance in the suit.[82] He has played an appointed role for so long that his authentic personality, his soul, has atrophied. Yet, he also seems very old, withered, exhausted, and scarred, as if his body has just barely been holding on for years. Anakin is canonically only 45 years old when he dies, but the actor who portrays him in the unmasking scene was 73 in 1983 at the time of filming. We are seeing the life-consuming toll the dark side has taken on him, well beyond the effects of his injuries. The whiteness of his face against the black void of the Vader armor conjures the image of the spot of white within the swirling black half of the yin-yang, as does the exposed white inside flap of Luke's black clothing that hangs on his chest now. The darkness consumed Anakin for 23 years, and Luke very nearly joined him in it during the events of this film. Both, somehow, held onto the little bit of light always present within the dark.

Anakin uses his dying breaths to ask Luke to make sure his sister knows he was right about there still being good in him. He sees Luke as a proxy for himself, which is why he was so intent on making him follow the same path to the dark side, so that it wouldn't seem like a mistake. When Luke succeeded where Anakin failed, Anakin began to realize there always had been another path available to him.[83] If his proxy could do it, so could he. And even though he has only just learned of her existence, Anakin sees his daughter as a proxy for Padmé, too. There is another one of her in the world now, and he has the chance to fix his biggest regret, which was that the last thing Padmé saw of him was the monster he had become. Padmé's last words were that there is still good in him. He knew, on some level, that her final conscious thoughts were the hope that he might return to the light one day. Anakin redeemed himself as a combination of seeing the proxy of himself (Luke) make the right choice in a situation where he had made the wrong one, and the inspiration to have the proxy of Padmé (Leia) see that there was still good in him. He needed his daughter to know he died a good man. Only such a strong familial connection could have saved Anakin. Padmé once accused Anakin of having been blinded by his possessive love for her, leading to his fall into the dark, but now it is that same love extended to Luke and Leia in a compassionate way that opens his eyes and allows him to see the light again.

The longer someone goes on living within the worldview of a false identity, the harder it is to ever remove it. The distance between reality and the adopted self-justifying narrative only widens so long as self-reflection remains absent. And as long as the fallen no longer cares about what is true, only what is narratively convenient, there is no hope for reaching through to them. To emotionally mature, a person must be able to self-reflect and consider that there may be something wrong with the way they're seeing things or acting. If you've spent your life living with one narrative, it's unlikely you're suddenly going to generate the ability to question it. The exception is a sudden shift in life circumstances that renders your current beliefs intolerable, compelling you into a heightened state of self-reflection. This is what causes those miraculous reversals of suddenly expanded awareness of what's really going on. If you stand to lose something even more important to you than your worldview, because of your unwillingness to change it, you just may be shocked into epiphany. That's what brought Anakin back in a moment of exceptional confluence, many powerful realizations hitting him at once and propelling him to break free of his false identity.

On Endor, Luke burns Anakin's body in the Vader suit in an open funeral pyre, like that of Anakin's original father figure, Qui-Gon Jinn, which will likewise be followed by a celebration after letting go of the one who was lost. The weight of all that has occurred is resting on Luke's face, as are the implications of what the future holds for him and the galaxy with everything he has experienced. But Luke does not look longingly off into the future now, as he did with Tatooine's sunset when he was still living as a child. He has the temperament of a man now, and his face shows that he is reflecting on the past, on the lessons that have brought him to the wisdom he now holds. This is not the same boy who began his story in *A New Hope*.

The theme of the necessity and inevitability of death is so prominent in *Star Wars* to help us accept that nothing is perfect enough to last forever without change, and trying to hold onto it longer than is natural, healthy, or appropriate corrupts one's soul by tying it to a fixed state.[84] We do the best we can with the life we have and pass on the best of ourselves to those who come after, instead of exalting ourselves above the natural cycle. We progress from one milestone to the next, with periods of chaos and disorder in between, like a child becoming an adult through the disorienting years of adolescence. In total chaos, structure itself is impossible. The alternative is to spend our lives trying in vain to maintain a state of rigid order that could never adapt or grow.[85]

Victory Celebration, the last of three celebratory musical pieces from across the films, plays over the final scene of the saga as our heroes celebrate with the Ewoks on Endor, and familiar locations across the galaxy welcome the end of the Galactic Empire with fireworks and cheers.[86] The tone, this time, is both spiritual and grounded, representing not just the victory over the Empire, but the moral victory over the weakness that leads to evil in the hearts of good people. The tune begins with child voices singing out in celebration but progresses into adult voices singing the same melody, capturing the theme of growing up and reminding us how far we have come from the childish origins we began with in *The Phantom Menace,* and reconnecting us to the childish spirit of the Ewoks we now celebrate with as we prepare for the rise of future generations. Episode 1's ending victory was premature, the beginning of a false path that inevitably led to the apocalyptic devastation that concluded Episode 3, with Padmé's somber funeral procession on Naboo in place of celebration. Episode 4's was partial; it set the groundwork for the real and complete victory we are experiencing now. The ending of Episode 6 releases the tension of the whole saga by giving us the full and complete victory we have been waiting for.

What, exactly, is the victory our heroes are celebrating? And by proxy, what should we, as the consumers of this story, feel has been accomplished at the end of two generations and six films' worth of lessons unfolding before our eyes? The overt and impersonal answer is the destruction of the second Death Star, the death of the Emperor, and the end of the Empire through a strategic military effort from the Rebel Alliance. The subtle and personal answer lies in Anakin's victory over the dark side as he returned to the light and his highest state of being, supported by the people who love him. The external social victory is a reflection of the internal spiritual one. The very title of the movie, *Return of the Jedi,* is ambiguous enough to refer to the macro and micro storylines contained within, with the word "Jedi" being either plural or singular. The collective Jedi Order is coming back into existence after its extinction. At the same time, a singular Jedi, Anakin, is pulling himself back up from the depths of Hell. Without Luke's spiritual revolution, the military victory would ultimately be in vain. Similarly, had Anakin made the right choice by remaining loyal to the Jedi and ending the incidental threat of Darth Sidious back in Episode 3, technically fulfilling that aspect of the prophecy of the Chosen One by destroying the Sith, no evolution from their stuck state would have occurred. He would not have brought balance to the Force. The emotional character of the galaxy must change to prevent a resurgence of the same cycle, and Luke is the vessel through which that will happen. Because of Luke, the Sith can never return again because their return was the result of flaws and imbalance within the Jedi Order and the spiritual state of the galaxy. Bringing balance to the Force means wiping away the sins of the past and creating new hope for the future to grow from.

Star Wars, in its final moments, shows us what our response to someone returning from the dark side should be: victory, joy, and glee, like a wedding instead of a funeral. It should be as though someone we love and have lost has miraculously returned from the dead. Our heroes stand and rejoice that Anakin has transformed into the Force, aligning with the advice Yoda once gave to someone who feared confronting death. Should we immediately forget and forgive the crimes they committed while they were under the influence of the dark side? All the ways they betrayed us and the harm they caused? All good people, all who are repentant, should be held accountable for the truth of their actions. They should be willing to carry the weight of the wrong they have done. If he had survived the events of *Return of the Jedi*, the redeemed Anakin would certainly have been willing to stand trial before the New Republic for his crimes as Darth Vader. But part of the reason he allowed death to overtake him was because he knew he could never make up for the evil he had committed, and the guilt would have destroyed him.

The Force spirit of Anakin appears to Luke alongside that of Ben and Yoda, watching over the new heroes and feeling good about whose hands they have left the future of the galaxy in. While Ben still looks old, Anakin looks young again, resembling his 22-year-old self from *Revenge of the Sith*.[87] Identity is a self-reflective mechanism; it's how you conceive of yourself, your operating system for interacting with the world. Anakin died when he became Darth Vader because he no longer reflected upon himself in that capacity. He identified only with his pain, his rage, and his righteous indignation for every wrong he perceived had been committed against him. When Luke brought Anakin back, he inspired him to tap into the repressed memory of who he used to be, how he used to think of himself, and the values he used to identify with. The memory he carries of himself from that time, of being that person, is the visage of the young Jedi Knight in his prime. Anakin identified as a young man, one about the same age as the son he sees as a proxy for himself.

Episode 3, the midpoint of the story, ended with our heroes and the story itself descending into Hell, captured musically in the apocalyptic battle hymn, *Battle of the Heroes*, as Obi-Wan dueled on Mustafar for the sake of Anakin's soul. Episode 6 inverts this by ascending the state of things up into Heaven, now represented by the musical opposite, *Victory Celebration*, as Anakin's soul is restored before us. Hell was the end of the world, the loss of everything good that the heroes believed they were working to build. Heaven is the opposite: the restoration of all that is good in the world, the recovery of lost order. Anakin's redemption does not suggest that he, in some way, *deserves* forgiveness or to enter "Jedi Heaven" with Ben and Yoda. Luke forgave his father and held out hope for him when no one else would, *despite that he did not deserve it*. He extended love that Anakin did not earn. Anakin's redemption is about the restoration of his consciousness from a state of unconsciousness. His choice to give up his own life was his first true choice in decades in accordance with his authentic values.

To the galaxy at large, Darth Vader died a monster. No one will honor the memory of Anakin and his heroic sacrifice after he is gone except the one person who matters. By saving his son in such an emotionally resonant way, Anakin will live on forever as a positive influence in Luke's eyes. That singular good deed could never make up for all the evil, but it can create a lasting positive impression for the one it was done for. Anakin's sacrificial death only means something because its lessons are passed on to Luke, who will go on to propagate them in the new culture of the New Republic and new Jedi Order. Anakin, in the end, became his son's greatest mentor. The true identity of the Chosen One was affirmed, and in the end, he managed to fulfill the prophecy and be the father his son needed him to be and pass on the lessons of his errors.

The Skywalkers are a crucial nexus or vergence of change in the storyworld of *Star Wars*. Anakin and Luke embody destructive and creative aspects of evolution. Anakin's role was to eliminate all the unsustainable traits accumulated over a thousand years of Jedi doctrine in a near-extinction event known as the Jedi Purge or Order 66. This culling process pushed for the proliferation of more resilient traits that eventually spread to become the new norm before the errors could compound any longer. The galaxy had to fall into darkness before it could restructure itself and fix its institutional problems. The Jedi Order had to be wiped out before it could be rebuilt without its dogma. For the Chosen One to destroy the Sith, he had to first allow himself to become corrupted and then overcome it. What destroyed Anakin was his attachment to his mother and his wife expressed in an unhealthy way. What saved him was his attachment to his children expressed in a healthy way that the Jedi of old could never have been capable of.

Luke, like all heroic young people emerging out of their societies, exists in the intergenerational chain of influence to preserve what worked from previous generations and carry it into future ones, including even the good bits of Anakin that survived within Darth Vader. He is the bridge between the past and the future. Together, father and son form an intergenerational yin and yang as destroyer and rebuilder. Each is needed to play his part in order to bring the galaxy to the next stage of evolution. Vader had to purge what *was* before Luke could build what *will be* upon the bones of the best of the past.

Now, having surpassed the trials placed before him and ascended beyond what his father and the Jedi were capable of, Luke's hero journey is over. He has graduated to a new state of existence: the originator of a higher state of social order and a paragon in his own right. He is the only one who can rebuild the Jedi Order and pass on the lessons he has learned over the last three films, and indirectly the events of the three that preceded them by absorbing the lessons of his father's tragic life. He will restore the world without the weaknesses that left it susceptible to corruption. Culture and understanding will evolve, and revolutionary new traits will proliferate in society when it once seemed inhospitable to them.

Luke's path is an emergent one, born out of his conscious need to do what he feels is right, as Ben once told him to, at all costs. He is the first of a new breed of Jedi with the emotional capacity to destroy evil in the galaxy, not by fighting it but by integrating, forgiving, and healing it.[88] That is the attitude that the Jedi guardians of peace and justice throughout the galaxy need to have when they confront the spirit of Vader in all its future forms.

While we have been watching each of the Skywalker boys undergo their own developmental journey, the galaxy has been doing the same thing on a cosmic scale. The prequel era of the Old Republic was its childhood, the thesis of denial and restriction of the human soul upon which its developmental journey was started. The Empire's reign in the original trilogy was its chaotic adolescence, the antithesis of over-indulgence that challenged everything it stood for. What naturally follows next will be its adulthood, the stable state that will be instigated by Luke and those he influences to join him in a synthesis of the two[89] in the form of responsible indulgence. His sister, Leia, will play a similar role in the formation of a New Republic that has been cleansed of its baggage and retained what it needed from before it grew up. The son carries on in the image of the best of his father, and the daughter does the same with her mother.

If *Star Wars* has a singular point in its six-movie arc, it's this: Love, responsibly applied, wins out in the end. This is what it means to embody balance in the Force with your thoughts and emotions, fully feeling and expressing everything going on within you but never allowing it to take you over. Anakin Skywalker only finally learned this in the final moments of his tragic and dramatic life, but in doing so, he made it possible for his son to learn it much sooner and without as much trauma. *Star Wars* itself is a bridge carrying the most useful and relevant bits of myths of the past into the future, fighting against the entropic descent of human culture into autopilot, a world in which people only live out their anxieties and cultural conditioning instead of thinking creatively and introducing emergent forms of conscious self-expression.

NOTES

73. "I feel good when I have kids and people come up and, you know, are shaking and want to say, you know, you've changed my life, you feel good about that. No matter, no matter how many sort of intellectuals or whatever say you're, you know, an idiot, you know that you've had an effect. And when I sit in a movie and I watch people react, I know it works. And that's all I need to know, is I know I've taken somebody on a trip that is going to make them a more interesting person. And that's all I do." George Lucas, interviewed by Bill Bradley for *American Voices*, November 15, 2015.

74. The Hutts were actually the original owners of the Skywalkers. In Episode 1, Anakin mentions that he and his mother were once owned by Gardulla the Hutt. She lost them in a podracing bet to Watto.

75. "[Luke] is his own man now. He is not a son anymore. He is an equal." George Lucas, quoted by Dale Pollock, *Skywalking: The Life and Films of George Lucas* (New York: Da Capo Press, 1999), 36.

76. "The issue of how do we get Darth Vader back is really the central issue. How do we get him back to that little boy that he was in the first movie? That good person who loved and was generous and kind?" George Lucas, interviewed by Bill Moyers, "Of Myth and Men," *Time*, April 18, 1999.

77. "We didn't have that actual moment that we needed where you got the sense that Luke is hiding, he's not gonna fight him, he refuses to fight, he'd rather die first, and then something turns him around and makes him fight. And I'd never really come up with a satisfactory answer to that, what he could possibly say that would set Luke off. In the process of evolving the importance of Leia as the sister, it became obvious that turning her to the dark side would be the thing that would set Luke off again." George Lucas, interviewed in *From Star Wars to Jedi: The Making of a Saga*, directed by LeVar Burton (Los Angeles, Calif.: Lucasfilm Ltd., 1983), documentary film.

78. "Luke is faced with the same issues and practically the same scenes that Anakin is faced with. Anakin says yes and Luke says no." George Lucas, quoted by Jim Windolf, "*Star Wars: The Last Battle*," *Vanity Fair*, February 1, 2005, 117.

79. Prior to the 2011 re-release of *Return of the Jedi*, Vader's dialogue was absent in this scene. He made the choice to save Luke and kill the Emperor silently. Lucas

added his repeated and then exclaimed "no" to make Anakin's re-emergence more emotionally explicit and to mirror his similar exclamation upon learning of Padmé's death at the end of *Revenge of the Sith*. Prior to this addition, Episode 6 was the only film in the hexalogy without a "noooooooo" from some character, though Luke's shouting of "Never!" when Vader threatens to turn Leia to the dark side serves the same purpose.

80. "Children teach you compassion. They teach you to love unconditionally. Anakin can't be redeemed for all the pain and suffering he's caused. He doesn't right the wrongs, but he stops the horror. The end of the saga is simply Anakin saying, I care about this person, regardless of what it means to me. I will throw away everything that I have, everything that I've grown to love—primarily the Emperor—and throw away my life, to save this person. And I'm doing it because he has faith in me; he loves me despite all the horrible things I've done. I broke his mother's heart, but he still cares about me, and I can't let that die." George Lucas, quoted by J. W. Rinzler, *The Making of Star Wars: Revenge of the Sith* (New York: Del Rey, 2005), 221.

81. "Joy lasts forever. Pleasure is purely self-centered. It's all about your pleasure. It's about you. It's about... It's a selfish, self-centered emotion. That's created by a self-centered motive of greed. Joy is compassion. Joy is giving yourself to somebody else or something else. And it's a kind of thing that is, in its subtlety and lowness, much more powerful than pleasure. If you get hung up on pleasure, you're doomed. If you pursue joy, you will find everlasting happiness." George Lucas, in his speech at the Academy of Achievement, 2013.

82. "Do I still take the mask off and have [Darth Vader] be this funny little man? Well, again, I sort of came to the decision that that was the original story, that's the way it should be, and if the public can't deal with it, then what can I do about it? A lot of people have objected to the fact there's a human in there at all. But the film is about human frailty, it's not about monsters." George Lucas, interviewed in *From Star Wars to Jedi: The Making of a Saga*, directed by LeVar Burton (Los Angeles, Calif.: Lucasfilm Ltd., 1983), documentary film.

83. "All of my movies are about one thing, which is the fact that the only prison you're in is the prison of your mind. And if you decide to open the door and get out, you can. There's nothing stopping you." George Lucas, interviewed by Bill Bradley for *American Voices*, November 15, 2015.

84. "Holding on is in the same category and a precursor to greed. And that's what a Sith is. A Sith is somebody that is absolutely obsessed with gaining more and more

power — but for what? Nothing, except that it becomes an obsession to get more." George Lucas, quoted by J. W. Rinzler, *The Making of Star Wars: Revenge of the Sith* (New York: Del Rey, 2005), 213.

85. "What all these movies are about is: greed. Greed is a source of pain and suffering for everybody. And the ultimate state of greed is the desire to cheat death." George Lucas, quoted by J. W. Rinzler, *The Making of Star Wars: Revenge of the Sith* (New York: Del Rey, 2005), 213.

86. Prior to the 1997 re-release of *Return of the Jedi*, a different piece of music, featuring Ewoks diegetically singing and playing tribal instruments, titled *Ewok Celebration—Yub Nub*, played over this scene instead. The tone and title of the original music implied a more toned-down and localized celebration that was replaced with a grand and sweeping orchestration of *Victory Celebration* over shots of the whole galaxy celebrating. Now it comes across more as a meta-celebration of the whole saga and all its people instead of just our small band of heroes on Endor.

87. Prior to the 2004 re-release of *Return of the Jedi*, Anakin's Force spirit in this scene was depicted by Sebastian Shaw, the same actor who plays him in his unmasking scene on the Death Star, instead of Hayden Christensen, the actor who played the younger version of the character from the prequel era. This change implies several important aspects of identity, death, and resurrection in *Star Wars*. It also serves to create a more explicit visual link between the original and prequel trilogies, making them feel a bit less like two separate stories.

88. Facing monsters or challenges rather than resisting or escaping them leads to integration into a more coherent internal structure in the Jungian and Campbellian model. The boon the hero receives at the end of the Hero's Journey is clarity over themselves and the world. Each new challenge reveals another layer of emotions that must be acknowledged and organized, then spread what they've learned to the rest of society, such as by Luke going on to remake the Jedi Order and the galaxy in a better image that is prepared to deal with the dark side of the Force.

89. J.G. Scammell (josh_from_xboxlive)'s YouTube video essays *Does Anakin Skywalker Have an Arc?* (https://youtu.be/NEjHoiwzl7g) and *Does Luke Skywalker Have an Arc?* (https://youtu.be/i_M84USrRtQ) discuss *Star Wars* through the filter of dialectics, a form of argumentation that seeks to take opposing points of view and combine them into a new synthesis of both, retaining the best and eliminating the worst (thereby breaking the cycle of two opposing forces permanently fighting

each other for dominance or control). Depending on how you look at it and in which order you watch the Lucas trilogies, either Luke's character arc in the original trilogy represents the thesis and Anakin's in the prequel trilogy its opposing antithesis, or the societal structure of the Republic and Jedi in the prequel trilogy represents the thesis and that of the Empire and Sith in the original trilogy its opposing antithesis. Both interpretations result in a synthesis that elevates the story to a new state of operation implied to be Lucas' original plans for a sequel trilogy with Episodes 7, 8, and 9.

ON RETURNING TO AND REMAINING IN THE LIGHT

On my study wall hangs a portrait of our protagonists from the end of the Mustafar duel in *Revenge of the Sith*. In the picture, Obi-Wan holds Anakin, who has been dismembered but not yet burned, in his arms. He seeks now to comfort his corrupted and dying friend. The scene didn't happen this way in the film. My portrait is a lie, an artistic revision. Obi-Wan never embraced Anakin like this after defeating him. Instead of showing him love and understanding after rendering him no longer a threat, he lectured and threw the pain of his disappointed expectations at him. Then he left his friend-turned-enemy for dead and sealed his fate on the dark side under the identity of Darth Vader.

This revisionist image represents what we can imagine as Obi-Wan's final regret. Should he have taken this opportunity to try to save Anakin's life? Should he have shown pity on him and comforted him as he slid into death from his injuries? Might it have prevented all that followed? Perhaps in solitude on Tatooine, Obi-Wan dreamed of holding Anakin on Mustafar, weak and dying, and letting him know one last time that he was still there for him, that he would never leave or give up on him, no matter how far he had fallen.

There are lines from Obi-Wan's speech that were omitted from the final cut of Episode 3, between Anakin's dismemberment and burning. Anakin was supposed to call out, "Help me, master," finally displaying self-reflection about what had become of him. Obi-Wan would have responded, "I can't help you, Anakin. I loved you, but I couldn't help you." Only then, upon his master's final rejection, would Anakin's eyes have turned Sith yellow as he screamed out in fury, "I hate you!" before immolation. Obi-Wan surely would have hated himself even more if that had indeed been his final interaction with a pleading Anakin, thinking for the rest of his life that he could have saved him if he had not given up hope.

I have seen many people I loved throughout my life descend into their Hells, forgetting the bond we held and even, from the limits of my point of view, the truth of who they are. Hell looks different for everyone. The Jedi shaped Anakin into a living weapon, so it manifested as indignation, rage, and murder. But sometimes it just looks like terror and avoidance because you are so insecure about expressing a part of yourself. Sometimes it shows up as petty vindictiveness, simply wanting to hurt someone because it makes you feel better. Sometimes it's chronic neurosis, being worried about everything that can ever go wrong, because you do not believe it is in your power to create a stable and secure state of existence. The result is always a lowering of conscious awareness, the ability to reflect, and the ability to choose. It creates a pathological feedback loop wherein negative emotions feed into more negative emotions, keeping a mind trapped in a state of suffering it does not know how to climb out of, like demons dragging one's soul into the depths of the inferno.

The fall can be just as sudden as it was with Anakin. And just like with Anakin, it's always long built up to if you know what to look for in hindsight. In all such cases, there is a sudden reversal from one set of values to its opposite. And in each case in my personal life, someone who thought very highly of me, perhaps even loved me, suddenly saw me as their mortal enemy. And when it happens, you have no assurance that it will get better, that the person you love will recover to the state you knew them in.

The first response is to feel bitter toward the person who has betrayed you, as Obi-Wan did toward Anakin, maybe even to hate them as much as they now hate you. It's a reaction based on the assumption that you are still dealing with the person you know. What is *wrong* with them for suddenly acting this way? How can they do this to me after everything we've been through together?! We must always inquire whether the fallen is self-aware enough to recognize that something is wrong with the way they are acting. Are they taking delight in the ugly way they treat you? Or is it a desperate defense mechanism? Do they display signs of inner conflict about their path, as Anakin did even as he murdered the innocent? What happens when you confront someone with how their behavior is affecting you? Does the truth prompt them to reflect on their actions and strive to improve themselves? Or does it send them into a self-defensive panic, as it did with Anakin when confronted by Padmé on Mustafar?

When you accept that you are no longer dealing with the same person, the most appropriate reaction is to mourn a great loss. Mourning frees you from expectations and gives you space to adapt to the new reality and move on in a healthy way, while still holding onto the memory of the good person you knew to honor them.

Below my fan-fiction portrait of Obi-Wan holding Anakin on Mustafar is another portrait, framed on a similar shot, but this time one that actually occurred on film: Luke facing his unmasked father at the end of *Return of the Jedi*. This scene at the end of Episode 6 is the counterpoint to what occurred at the end of Episode 3. Luke refused to leave his father for dead, physically or spiritually, after Obi-Wan, in heartbreak, did. My first portrait is what *should* have occurred to set things right for Anakin and the galaxy; my second portrait is what finally *did*. It is the resonant image we are meant to take away from the story about how we are to act with those in the dark we still love.

My wife, Ruzan,[90] is the only person I have ever known to complete the circle, going from loving me in an immature and unhealthy way, to hating me, and then loving me again in a mature and healthy way, from the light to the dark and the light again. I refer to the two-year period where she hated me and we didn't talk as the Dark Times in our relationship, a la Ben Kenobi. Even now, I can't be 100% sure that things are always going to stay good between us because sometimes I still see that side of her that's hijacked by upset. It happens in short bursts during which she's not fully conscious, not aware of what's really going on. But she always comes out of it eventually. There's a wavering back and forth.[91] I grow suspicious, unsure of who I am dealing with on a given day, the good Ruzan or the bad, the real Ruzan or the fake one, the identities I have taken to calling Ruzanakin Skywalker and Darth Ruzader, respectively. But I believe in her so much, despite everything we've been through (and in many ways, *because* of everything we've been through), that I chose to marry her.

I knew Ruzan for nine years before I married her, and I am nine years older than her. We met when she was 18 and I was 27. I've seen her grow from an adolescent to an adult in the time I've known her. It would not be until after the maturing effects she had to go through in her fall and recovery, some eight years later, that I would begin to see her as an equal, and it would be possible for us to be mature partners to each other.

I always saw Ruzan's passion and temperamental nature, and therefore her potential for darkness. Like Anakin, she had a good heart and was quite sensitive to the world, but when she was upset, she could justify almost any kind of self-indulgent or manipulative behavior. I took it upon myself to show her *Star Wars* to expose her to Anakin's story because I saw how similar she was to him. She saw it too. My forewarning did not stop her from turning to the dark side when her frustration became too great to bear, but I like to believe that it eventually played a role in helping her understand what happened to her and bring her back into the light two years later. She has since then gained a greater awareness of the same thing happening in others and recognizes the suddenly shifted behavior when it occurs, which I believe has also played a role in rehabilitating her. She remembers what it was like to be in their place and how far she has come since then.

Ruzan's fall was a product of how possessive of our bond she became as we grew closer together, first as friends and later as romantic partners. And it was at least partially my fault for not being careful enough with her as the older and more experienced person in our dynamic. She often confessed how afraid she was of losing me someday. I told her then that that would only ever happen under two conditions: if she chose to leave me, or if she became an unrepentantly bad person I could not safely associate with anymore. It was unexpectedly prophetic of me, because both those things happened during her fall.

When she was 23, Ruzan switched from seeing me as the object of her affection and the most valuable person in her life, a familial connection unlike any other, to seeing me as a monster and hating me because she couldn't have me in the way she wanted. She wanted to possess me romantically just as Anakin did with Padmé. I went from being an angel from her point of view to being the devil. In moments, she rewrote our entire history as having been fake from the start, telling herself that I had manipulated her for years to take advantage of her. She discounted our entire five-year history all too quickly, just as Anakin did once he began to believe the Jedi were manipulating him and keeping things from him. He needed to convince and condition himself that the Jedi and Obi-Wan deserved death because he could not get what he wanted from them.[92]

People feel something very strongly, and they need a story that supports feeling that way. If you suddenly feel like you hate me, there needs to be a reason in your mind that justifies your hatred. Without that, you'd have to engage in deep reflection about why you feel the way you do and, if necessary, consciously redirect yourself away from the state based on what you rationally know to be true. But self-reflection is impossible when attention is always pointed outward at some source of offense that someone imagines is causing their upset.

I became so angry at Ruzan for the chaotic way she was treating me. I made the mistake of meeting her fire with more fire because I felt betrayed on many levels because it was as though she had instantly forgotten who I was and everything positive we had shared together. Ruzan was defined by passion, and now that passion was spilling over into a volcanic eruption, from which I saw the ugliest and most shocking parts of someone I thought I knew emerge.

I did not handle her fall the way I should have. I tried to reason with her, talk sense into her, and even lecture her like Obi-Wan did to Anakin on Mustafar. I told her sternly then that I believed there was still some part of her that understood that what she was doing was wrong. Ruzan is one of the smartest people I've ever known. She should have been able to reason through it, I thought. I made the mistake of thinking she had the capacity to act as her best self under all possible conditions. I was too harsh with her, too judgmental, overly critical, and too disciplinarian. I deeply regret it now. I was trying to talk to her like an adult, like someone reasonable, because that was how I thought her to be. But in that state of mind, someone is operating more like a child or a force of nature who can't be reasoned or bargained with. They're not thinking clearly. They're just being led by powerful emotions that have to be resolved one way or another. Every stern word said by Obi-Wan to Anakin on Mustafar only pushed him further into the dark.

My approach could never have yielded the results I was seeking. Fire cannot fight fire. All forms of pushback only strengthen the fallen's conviction and make you more of an enemy. Vader feeds on conflict and aggression. When Obi-Wan confronted Anakin on Mustafar in

Revenge of the Sith, he made the critical mistake of addressing his padawan with scorn and disapproval. He came there prepared to fight. He could not look upon Anakin with love anymore. He escalated the situation when it was possible it need not have been escalated. Luke made the same mistake against Vader on Bespin in *The Empire Strikes Back,* only learning his lesson in their second encounter, when he finally grew mature enough to meet Vader's hate with love. Only by the end of *Return of the Jedi* did Luke finally realize that throwing his weapon and his aggression away was the key to his and his father's salvation.

I know now that it's not about being reasonable or analytical with someone in such a state. It's just about enabling them to fully feel the emotions they are going through, and not to provide any kind of resistance. And if you resist it and fight it and try to argue with it, you just perpetuate it. My response should have been to give her the space and time she needed, and to let go of the idea that there's necessarily something I could have done to jump in and fix this problem myself. So long as she saw me as her enemy, even just my presence might have triggered her and made the situation worse.

Ruzan's return to the light began with forced empathy and reflection under apocalyptic conditions in my life. Something so awful happened that it forced her to start considering me as a human being she cared about again, not the cartoonish villain she created in her mind. A year before her fall, Ruzan had brought a blind calico kitten named Matit into my life. Matit became my cat soulmate, the single greatest source of joy in my life, and I realized I had never known before that it was even possible for a person to love a cat as much as I loved this one.

And one day, three years after Matit came into my life and two years after Ruzan went out of it, a large dog killed Matit in front of me. That morning, I held her body in my arms, feeling a bit like an overwhelmed Anakin in the Tusken camp with his mother, unable to process the intensity of what I was feeling at the sudden loss of something so beautiful. But I felt no anger then. That came later. The sadness at what I lost overshadowed all the hatred I felt toward the dog that did it and its irresponsible owners. It was more important to me in that moment to sit in mourning and reflection upon everything Matit meant to me and integrate the truth of what I had just experienced, overcoming even the instant desire for revenge against the mindless animal that could not have known the suffering it caused me.[93]

My thoughts took me to a place where I urged myself to accept that I was now living in a new world, one where that cat would exist only as a memory. I did not want to miss an iota of what I was going through. I forced myself to experience the pain of it as deeply as possible. That was the only way I could honor Matit and everything she meant to me: to refuse to wince from the unbearable pain of losing her so suddenly and integrate it into my consciousness.

Weeks after the loss, I published a public eulogy for Matit.[94] Ruzan eventually found out that the cat she brought me, who she knew better than anyone how much I loved, was dead. This finally allowed her to start seeing the truth again through the cracks in the wall she had built between us. And that's when she contacted me for the first time in two years, telling me she knew how important that cat was to me and what I must be going through.

Ruzan broke through her shield of hate because she realized the suffering I was enduring at the loss of something so important to me, something she had a personal connection to, without anyone to be there for me. She had recently lost a family member, too, so she was sensitive to the pain of loss in those moments, which forced her to begin to empathize with the devastation she knew I must be going through. That unpredictable confluence of conditions overpowered her overwhelming resentment toward me. She couldn't keep blocking out her memories of the good man she knew me to be, of the caring and empathetic person who had bonded so deeply with an innocent living creature.

This took superhuman humility. No one can enter that state so long as their pride and sense of identity are attached to an alternative narrative about who they are and what has occurred. Change will only come when they submit themselves to a less flattering reality because the pain of not doing so is greater. The good in Ruzan, wherever she had hidden it away beneath the part of her that tried to impose a more empowering narrative over reality, could not allow me to suffer without reaching out in a genuine act of humanity. This person, who knew me better than any other human alive, and who had been there from the beginning to understand the unique circumstances of my connection to the cat I had lost, now had to reconcile a truth that conflicted with the narrative she had adopted because it served her emotional insecurities. In her prior paranoid state, she could not fairly assess that I never betrayed her; I simply didn't give her everything she wanted, needed, or demanded of me. From her warped point of view, that was the equivalent of betrayal. Now, she had to reconsider that either *I* was a monster for failing to give her what she needed from me, or *she* was a monster for abandoning me when I needed her most.

I didn't know what to make of Ruzan's sudden extending of the olive branch. I thought that even if her sympathy was sincere in that moment, there was no way I could trust she would continue to act that way the following day, week, or month. I no longer knew who she was. But in my pain, I found the space to continue observing, continue reflecting on what was true instead of assuming I already knew everything. I had to be open to the possibility of genuine change in her, no matter what she had done to me, because I remembered how much I valued the person I knew her to be. So long as there was any hope of recovery, I had to keep looking for it. That took humility from me, too, as continuing to see her as the woman who betrayed and abandoned me would have been so much simpler.

Then, when I began to think things were good between us once more, she'd do something to make me doubt my optimistic assessment, spontaneous moments of disregard or disrespect. And I'd take that as proof that she was still a kid, still not in control of her emotions or actions. And I'd wonder if I'd made a mistake thinking we could repair the damage, if it was inevitable that we'd descend back into Hell. That way of being, indulged in too long, becomes habitual, like a form of whole-body muscle memory. It becomes instinct to default to anger when you've spent so long in it as a chronic state.

For almost two more years, I wondered if things could ever be the same as they once were between us, if I could ever see her as my family again. What began to cement in my mind that she might be back in more than a partial or momentary way was when I would see her sad for extended periods. All these emotions that she normally repressed came out again. Sadness is pain pointed inward, which means the capacity for self-reflection. Anger always pushes it outward, away from the self, thinking that only the outside world (the perceived source of the pain) needs to change. In sadness, it becomes possible to consider that you are, at least partially, responsible for your own suffering. This is the genesis of recovery and the earnest desire to improve yourself. It was the doorway to reenabling the full spectrum of healthy emotional expression for Ruzan.

I know Ruzan still harbors an enormous amount of anger, though it's not usually pointed at me anymore. She still has the capacity to lose her sanity sometimes in moments of emotional intensity. For a few minutes, an hour, or a day, she stops seeing things clearly, and I feel like I am dealing with a different person than the woman I love. I do not know how long it will take for that scar to heal, if it ever even can fully. She still does not feel completely safe with me or in general. Every time I see that immature, angsty, unconscious, out-of-control version of the woman I love, I get concerned. I don't think of it as the real Ruzan, but a fake persona that has temporarily taken over. Stress brings out her worst impulsive traits. And in those moments, I worry that she might relapse into being the worst version of herself again, like a drug addict falling back into an old habit. But I also see how she has evolved when she pauses, reflects, and regains self-control in a difficult situation, when previously she would not have.

When she's operating from her dark side, I remind myself that it's not really her. It's a mask she's wearing, just like Vader's. I know it's not a product of consciousness and choice, but a defense mechanism caused by the insecurity she still carries. It's compensation for feelings of inadequacy and frustration. Sometimes, it is the hardest thing in the world to keep seeing the Ruzan I love when she is acting like the opposite of that person, but doing so is the strongest display of love that I can show her: Despite everything you are capable of, I still love you. The focus now is always on how I can help bring her out of that state and back into consciousness. It strikes me that, at various points in our evolving relationship, I have played the archetypal roles toward Ruzan that three critical figures (Padmé, Obi-Wan, and Luke) played toward Anakin in his story, first as object of romantic possession, then as overly critical mentor and object of resentment, and finally as familial figure who refuses to give up and makes healthy love possible. These were the lessons I had to learn from the challenges she brought into my life.

It is too easy to stop loving those who betray us, to treat them no longer as the person we once loved but as some demonic force that has replaced them. And it is even cathartic to do so, for it helps us process the trauma of losing someone we love. But to do so is also to deny everything real about the person you love and all you have shared. It takes maturity to hold onto everything good about your experience, together with the bad that has now overtaken it all. Ben Kenobi found the strength, after many years, to reflect to Luke that his father, Anakin, was a great Jedi and good friend, because he kept in mind those parts of the truth of him even after he became Vader.[95] Remember why you love them. Remember what was real, or else you have accepted that your experience was entirely delusion. Now is when they need you most, not to forget what good they are capable of when they have forgotten it themselves.

I have only ever attempted to remain connected to and hopeful about the people I unconditionally loved. There was a parental aspect to the relationship, like Shmi or Qui-Gon toward young Anakin, embodied in love that persists even without being reciprocated, or even when it is scorned. It is the asymmetrical role a caretaker takes on for the one they are watching over. To help someone recover from the dark side is to play a quasi-parental role in their life. What parent has never felt the pain of their child lashing out in disproportionate anger, swearing they will never speak to them again, that they will run away from home... or even that they *hate them* despite everything shared between them and done for them?

To love someone is to love the principle of who they are. Within the scope of that principle exists the potential for their best and worst, their highest virtues and lowest vices. When you love the principle, you see what else they could and ought to become, even when they are showing you their worst parts. Likewise, you remain intimately aware of the worst they could be even when they are treating you well. The universal human struggle lies in trying to embody the best of ourselves in circumstances that don't always make it easy.

My marriage to Ruzan marks the start of a new state of operation for us both: a well-deserved victory celebration that is not confined to a single day or joyful ceremony but extends indefinitely from that point onward as we work together to maintain it with what we have learned from the trials that brought us here. To love your partner "in sickness and in health" means more than being there to take care of them when they can't get out of bed. When either partner is not being their best self, the self their partner knows they should be capable of being, it is their duty not to abandon them. Tending to the one you love when they are in a state of emotional disintegration is no different than tending to them in a state of physical disintegration, when they have a fever or a broken leg, to be there for them under the worst possible conditions, even when no one else will, to love them even when it is most difficult.

If you'd asked me during the Dark Times if it was possible that Ruzan and I would be married someday, I would have said absolutely not. I would have considered it unlikely that we would ever even be on speaking terms again. I did not know that the *impossible* could occur, that someone could recover from a prolonged fall into unconsciousness. Once Ruzan extricated herself from my life, I was prepared to never see her again. I believed that all hope was lost between us. I will wonder for the rest of my life how things would have turned out for us had an unpredictable tragedy of a highly particular nature not befallen me at a time when she happened to begin opening her heart again. Perhaps it was only a matter of time for Ruzan to pull herself out of Hell, and Matit's death was simply one of many possible catalysts for that resurrection.

I don't know that Ruzan and I could have grown closer if we hadn't made it through our Dark Times. Indulging in darkness for a time might be a necessary intermediate step toward total self-actualization for a certain type of person. Because of her fall, we got to experience life without each other for two years. That gave us a valuable perspective on what it's like to have and lose each other. We can both decide now, fully informed, that we are better together than we are apart. Her being with me now is the bravest possible thing she could do. She could spend the rest of her life surrounded by people who would tell her whatever she wanted to hear and play along with whatever narrative she wanted to live by. She should be terrified of me because I'm the only one who will hold her accountable to the light instead of validating the darkness. That she has remained honest with herself about her part in what occurred between us instead of flying into a self-defensive panic when confronted, to the extent that she is even willing to let me share our story and its lessons, is proof of her growth and her willingness to reflect upon the truth because she recognizes how important it is.

The path back from darkness begins with a willingness to see clearly what we've worked so hard to avoid seeing. If we have not explored all parts of ourselves, we are unaware of the uncontrolled darkness within us. Only those willing to confront their fear directly, to integrate it rather than suppress it, can break the cycle. Abstractified fear over the scarcity of what we perceive we need to be happy is what drives us into prolonged panic and autopilot, as it did with Ruzan's fear of losing me and what I represented to her. The most abstract horror denies your capacity to deal with it entirely because it convinces you that it is unbeatable. You have to be absolutely immune to abstract fears to remain true to yourself and your principles so that you cannot be controlled. We must remain willing to feel everything, however wonderful or terrible, but not let it rob us of ourselves. This is the only way to make the Force your permanent ally and become immune to the pull to the dark side. Immunity means the ability to maintain consciousness under pressure. To be incorruptible, for the Force to always be with you, total self-embodiment must be the highest priority.

Just as the fall is different for each person, so is the re-awakening of self-awareness. The fallen must begin to question their ability to distinguish right from wrong, good from evil, and recognize that there *is* right and wrong in the universe.[96] But more importantly, the insecure must be made to feel secure again. Hope for recovery is evident in someone who is in deep pain as a result of their actions. If it pains them to act as they do, some level of consciousness and self-reflection is still operating beneath the facade. But if someone revels in the power the darkness brings, there is no hope of reaching them until that changes.

Anakin could be saved because there was still some conflict and doubt within him during his worst acts,[97] still something he wanted more than everything he gained by becoming Vader, and he realized at the last possible moment how close he was to losing it. There were never any such signs of a chance for redirection in Maul, Dooku, or Sidious; each one lacked any deeper value that could have caused them to reflect and realize what a mistake they had made (at least in the context of what we are shown on screen).

If the sacrifice of the authentic self can be seen as spiritual death, those who remain true to themselves indefinitely are the world's only immortals. No matter what you do, it should be you who is consciously doing it, which means that, like Anakin, every person has to reach a state where they can take responsibility and shoulder the burden of being who they are. The greatest sin is to abdicate control of your own mind to unconscious processes. *Patience* is essential to remaining in the light, as it counters the urge to act on strong emotions immediately. Through reflection, one can consciously rewire oneself to take a different path than what one is accustomed to doing on autopilot. Mentors are a way to become introduced to better self-organizing principles to follow, but they still have to be reflected upon and consciously chosen. Good mentors like Ben and Yoda know to help cultivate the conditions that allow someone to see the path out of the clouds and into the light. Someone who is constantly afraid, ashamed, worried, or otherwise suppressed cannot make their own choices. Dark mentors, like Palpatine, keep others in this state for the purpose of slavery or subservience.

I suffer no idealistic illusions about my wife. I know exactly what kind of monster or Sith Lord she's capable of being. Ironically, I believe that I can trust her more than any other woman because I have seen the worst that she can become, and I have seen her choose not to be that anymore. She and I have seen the worst of each other and been through the Hell of repairing our relationship. She's the only person in the world who knows what it means to marry me. But I cannot ever have complete confidence that she will never relapse and let her dark side come out again permanently. It's a lifelong battle that requires eternal vigilance. I can only promise to be there along the way, to give her what she needs to defend herself against the weakness inside her. And to help her come back to the light again if she should ever need it. Terrible things happened to Anakin when he forgot that the people in his life loved him. Ruzan should never again be capable of forgetting that.

Ruzan's progress gives me a living reminder of the possibility of resurrection when all hope seems lost. I believed during the Dark Times that I had lost my friend forever. I accepted that outcome. I have to keep the same perspective I have about Ruzan now with everyone I love who seems lost on the dark side beyond all hope. Sometimes, all we can do is disappear and wait for them to be ready, until the time is right.

NOTES

90. Ruzan is a common Armenian name similar to Roseanne, but with the "oo" sound in the first syllable, as in "you'll rue the day you betrayed me," which happens to be a fitting phrase for my wife's personality.

91. The 2023 Disney+ show *Ahsoka* (season one, episode five, *Shadow Warrior*) features the return of Anakin's spirit five years after his redemption and death in *Return of the Jedi*, when he visits his former padawan, Ahsoka Tano, in a vision. Anakin's spirit is depicted as wavering back and forth between the light and the dark, sometimes calm and loving, sometimes furious and hostile. His appearance briefly flickers into the Vader armor, his eyes turn Sith yellow, and his blue lightsaber blade turns red as he fights her before he finally regains composure. Everything he went through during his time as Darth Vader persists in his consciousness, even after his return to the light. It suggests that recovering from a prolonged fall to the dark side is not a simple and complete reversal from bad to good or unconsciousness to consciousness again. There are lingering destructive effects that must be managed.

92. "When you become greedy, then you do bad things to get stuff from other people. Once you get that stuff, then you become afraid. Once you become afraid that somebody's going to take it from you, then you start striking out at people. And you start, you get angry at things, you get worried, and that puts you in a whole psychological mindset that makes you turns you ultimately into an evil person, where you're doing horrible things to people, thinking that you're doing the right thing, but you're doing it because you're afraid they're going to hurt you before you hurt them." George Lucas, interviewed by Bill Bradley for *American Voices*, November 15, 2015.

93. I was not totally immune to the influence of the dark side after the trauma of losing my cat soulmate. Months later, a different dog broke into the shelter where my ducks nested and ate all their eggs. I was immediately furious, even ready to kill that dog because I perceived, once again, that my animals, my family, were under attack by a malevolent actor who would kill more of my cats at the first chance it got. But by being patient, humbling myself, observing, and thinking the situation through, I realized that the canine culprit had had every opportunity to harm my defenseless ducks while in their territory and only ate their eggs. Once I caught that dog in the act, I saw how skinny and friendly he was, and I realized I had made a critical error in my assessment. This was not an *aggressive* dog, but

a *desperate* one whose owners did not feed him. He had been forced to seek out food wherever he could find it. And in that moment, I, someone whose deepest values include animal welfare, *hated* myself for defaulting to anger and violence against a creature who was a victim like me because of how hurt I was from losing something so valuable. I nearly allowed myself to begin to embody the opposite of my values. I ended up feeding the dog (with proper dog food) for a while before finding a new home for him.

94. That eulogy, titled *Matit Deserved to Exist*, is available online on my personal blog at www.gregorydiehl.net/l/matit-deserved-to-exist.

95. Along the same lines, the final episode, *Part VI*, of season one of the 2022 Disney+ series *Obi-Wan Kenobi* features a scene of Ben talking about Anakin in a positive light to a ten-year-old Leia, describing him as passionate, fearless, and forthright (without revealing his identity). Despite seeing everything awful that has become of Darth Vader since *Revenge of the Sith*, Ben maintains the positive image of the man Anakin once was, which he passes along to both Anakin's children for their benefit.

96. "The conflict between good and evil is the basic conflict. The universal question is: Am I a good person? … And it's something you have to ponder because you're doing it every day. You're saying, should I do this or shouldn't I do this? … Is this really good? Am I really doing the right thing here? Am I really being a kind, compassionate person?" George Lucas, interviewed by Bill Bradley for *American Voices*, November 15, 2015.

97. "You've made a decision – but you don't know if it's the right decision… There's always this good in you, and this little part is always asking, *What am I doing?* Even at the very end. That's what makes you turn and kill the Emperor." George Lucas addressing Hayden Christensen, quoted by J. W. Rinzler, *The Making of Star Wars: Revenge of the Sith* (New York: Del Rey, 2005).

AN UNEXPECTED FIRST-TIME
STAR WARS VIEWING ORDER

tar Wars, as a six-movie viewing experience, is defined by the central identity plot twist along Anakin Skywalker's path. Depending on the order in which they watch the movies, first-time viewers will experience this twist quite differently. Until now, there have been two widely endorsed, and in their own ways valid, approaches:

Release Order (4 5 6 – 1 2 3): This was the order experienced by anyone who saw *Star Wars* for the 22 years after the release of the original film and before the release of the first prequel, from 1977 (when Episode 4 came out) to 1999 (when Episode 1 came out). The central plot twist comes two movies in, at the end of Episode 5, when the viewer learns that Darth Vader is Luke Skywalker's father at the same time as Luke. Everyone who grew up with the original trilogy remembers the shock of hearing that famous line coming from the villain of the story: "No, *I* am your father."

Then, there's a secondary twist, just one movie later, at the end of Episode 6, when Vader redeems himself and Anakin returns to the light by saving Luke. Everything that follows after that, as the viewer experiences the events that led up to *A New Hope* in the prequel trilogy, is just filling in the details of what we already know, waiting for the inevitable to unfold: Anakin turning to the dark side and becoming the villain from the original trilogy. One of the weaknesses with this approach, in my opinion, is that Anakin is defined in this context as

Luke's father instead of being a character in his own right and the central figure of the story.

Chronological Order (1 2 3 4 5 6): This is the order George Lucas intended the films to be viewed in once he created the prequel trilogy, from its start to its end. The central plot twist now comes almost halfway through the story, midway into Episode 3, when we see Anakin betray his principles, turn evil, adopt the name Darth Vader, and abandon his heroic destiny. The story you were expecting to follow suddenly turns against you. The hero, as it turns out, is not actually the hero, but his son may be. You spend the following three movies thinking this is the case until Anakin's surprise redemption at the end of Episode 6.

Seeing Anakin fall to the dark side this way, without any forewarning, is tragic and heartbreaking. Still, hearing him be called Vader for the first time and seeing him put on the suit doesn't carry quite the same weight as it would if you had already grown invested in Darth Vader as his own iconic and villainous character before seeing his backstory, which is one of the strengths afforded by seeing the original trilogy first in release order.

I agree with George Lucas that chronological order is generally the best way to watch *Star Wars*, particularly on repeat viewings. However, somewhere in the process of introducing *Star Wars* to new audiences who had no idea what to expect, I realized there was a better way to prepare them for the shock and eventual resolution ahead. In the West, we tend to take for granted that virtually everyone knows what *Star Wars* is and is familiar with its plot, themes, and characters, including the identity of Darth Vader and his relationship to Luke Skywalker. This remains true even among people who have never seen the movies. It makes it difficult to experience the story without having its most crucial themes and character revelations spoiled in some regard.

For over ten years, I conducted an informal social experiment, introducing new people from all over the world to the *Star Wars* films. Because I have traveled to many countries where *Star Wars* is relatively unknown, I have witnessed how people who have no idea what to expect from it react to the events as they unfold. This led me to reflect more deeply on what the optimal viewing order of the trilogies might be in the modern day, as the order in which you learn certain crucial information biases your interpretation of the events that follow. The solution I came up with for first-time viewers is what I now call the **Combined Order (4 – 1 2 3 – 5 6)**: starting with Episode 4, going back to the prequels, then finishing the story with Episodes 5 and 6.

For the shock of the twist to reach maximum impact, it is important that the viewer is first introduced to Darth Vader as the irredeemable villain of the story, the challenge Luke will have to overcome. They cannot, at first, see him as the story's sympathetic victim because that's not how Luke sees him. The magic of the journey lies in how our and Luke's interpretations of Darth Vader change with more information.

Lucas himself states, in *The Chosen One* featurette included in the DVD release of *Revenge of the Sith*, that the perception of Darth Vader changes depending on whether you first meet him as Vader (as viewers of Release Order do) or as Anakin (as viewers of Chronological Order do):

"Darth Vader became such an icon in Episode 4, that icon of evil sort of took over everything, much more than for what I intended. If it had been one movie, that wouldn't have happened. He would have been to be revealed as this pathetic character at the end of the movie. But now, by adding Episodes 1, 2, and 3, people began to see the tragedy of Darth Vader as what it was originally intended to be. I liked the idea of the person you thought was the villain, is really the victim, and that the story is really about the villain trying to regain his humanity because it's really the story of Darth Vader's redemption."

J.W. Rinzler, in *The Making of Star Wars: Revenge of the Sith*, quotes Lucas explaining with a high level of meta-awareness about his own art how much the emotional experience of *Star Wars* changes by doing nothing more than "moving the blocks" around:

> "If you see them in order, it completely twists things about. A lot of the tricks of IV, V, and VI no longer exist. The real struggle of the twins to save their father becomes very apparent, whereas it didn't exist at all the first time [audiences saw Episodes IV, V, and VI]. Now Darth Vader is a tragic character who's lost everything. He's basically a bitter old man in a suit. 'I am your father' was a real shock. Now it's a real reward. Finally, the son knows what we already know. It's a very different suspense structure. Part of the fun for me was completely flipping upside down the dramatic track of the original movies. If you watch it the way it was originally released, IV, V, VI, I, II, III — you get one kind of movie. If you watch I through VI, you get a completely different movie. One or two generations have seen it one way, and the next generations will see it a completely different way. It's extremely modern, almost interactive moviemaking. You take blocks and move them around, and you come out with different emotional states."[98]

If you watch the original trilogy first, the big twist is that Darth Vader is actually Luke's father, not the man who *killed* Luke's father. This is powerful because you know how awful Darth Vader is, and the idea that our hero Luke is descended from him offends all our expectations of his origins and character progression. If you watch the prequels first, the big twist is that Anakin turns to the dark side instead of being the hero of prophecy. Since we have not already been introduced to Darth Vader, the viewer will, at most, have only a general culture awareness of Darth Vader as "the bad guy" in *Star Wars*. Making that connection in their brain to the character of Anakin that they've been watching for two and a half movies will be a shock, but it will not carry the necessary weight of actually having seen Darth Vader in action, including the expectation set by Ben Kenobi in Episode 4 about who Vader is and what he has done to the Jedi and Luke's father.

We must not overlook the narrative value of the shock that comes from experiencing that the character you accepted as an icon of evil was once a pure-hearted little boy and heroic young man.[99] By watching Episode 4 first, then Episodes 1, 2, and 3, as suggested in my Combined Order approach, the viewer will get the best elements of both twists combined into one soul-shattering super-reveal. Halfway through *Revenge of the Sith*, the viewer is forced to reconcile that:

1. Anakin is turning evil (response: heartbreak).

2. Anakin is Darth Vader, the villain we saw in Episode 4 (response: shock).

3. Luke's father is actually the evilest man in the galaxy, and he's going to have to kill him, and he doesn't even know it yet (response: dread).

Some considerations set *A New Hope* apart in the saga and prevent it from ruining the experience of watching the prequels afterward.

The six *Star Wars* films can be parsed into three distinct segments according to how the films were planned and produced:

1. Episode 4, planned and produced on its own.

2. Episodes 5 and 6, planned and produced as the conclusion to the story that Episode 4 set up.

3. Episodes 1, 2, and 3, planned and produced as the first half of the whole story.

If the viewer is going to break up the original trilogy into parts, separating Episode 4 from Episodes 5 and 6 is the only interruption that makes sense. *A New Hope* is the only film in the saga that works as a standalone because it's the only one produced that way, without any guarantee that more would come after. It's the smallest *Star Wars* movie by design, which is a huge contrast to Episode 3 that precedes it chronologically. *Revenge of the Sith* is the biggest and most impactful episode of the whole story. Beginning the story with its smallest segment makes it seem deceptively simple to first-time viewers. They don't yet see the scope of the epic tale they are embarking on. It provides an effective point-of-view character for the rules of the *Star Wars* universe through the eyes of young Luke at the beginning of his journey, as first experienced by the public in 1977, before anyone knew what *Star Wars* was or would become.

Without knowledge of Vader's backstory as Anakin Skywalker, all we see is the imposing villain he intentionally portrays himself as in Episode 4. And that is exactly how we need to perceive Vader, at first, for the startling revelation of his identity to have a bigger impact. What do we actually see Vader do in *A New Hope*? He chokes an Imperial officer, interrogates Princess Leia, blows up a planet, fights and defeats Obi-Wan Kenobi in a lightsaber duel, and expertly shoots down some of the Rebel ships attacking the Death Star. He also nearly shoots down Luke, the hero of the story. It's an excellent one-dimensional villain setup, and we are meant to believe that the story will revolve around Luke becoming strong enough to avenge his father and defeat this evil and awesome character.

After *A New Hope*, *The Empire Strikes Back* and *Return of the Jedi* were planned together to complete the story as a trilogy, with the most obvious result being the cliffhanger of Vader's identity revelation at the end of Episode 5 that creates urgency to complete the story with the final remaining episode. It does not make narrative sense to interrupt the continuity between Episodes 5 and 6 with so much left unresolved.[100] Episode 4 is the only film in the saga that ends almost wholly resolved with its own stakes. It's a complete story on its own.

In Episode 4, the Emperor is only mentioned, not shown, and without the name Palpatine. First-time viewers won't know that Senator Palpatine becomes the Emperor when they meet him in *The Phantom Menace* and will have to figure out on their own that he's the villain pulling all the strings as they proceed through the prequels. This aspect enhances the reveal of Anakin's downfall because viewers' attention will be so focused on figuring out the suspicious truth about Palpatine that they will be less likely to notice what's subtly going on with the supposed hero of the story until the rug is pulled out from under them in *Revenge of the Sith*.

A New Hope is also the only film in the saga that does not contain any musical cues from Darth Vader's theme. Because in Episode 4 we do not associate that music with Vader, it will not give away the twist that Anakin becomes Vader when viewers hear those familiar notes on screen throughout the prequels.

There is an obvious difference in production quality between the original and prequel trilogies, owing to the roughly 20-year gap in their production and respective budgets. This is nowhere more evident than in the transition from the last and most expensive movie made (*Revenge of the Sith* in 2005, at $113 million) to the first and least expensive movie made (*A New Hope* in 1977, at $11 million, which is less than one-third as much when adjusted for inflation). I have seen how jarring it can be for first-time modern viewers who grew accustomed to the digital effects of the prequel trilogy to suddenly drop down in quality to the grimy, practical effects of the film that started it all, even when taking into account its remastered and digitally updated releases. Starting with Episode 4 lessens this effect.

When the viewer goes back in time to view the prequel trilogy, the juxtaposition of foreknowledge from having seen Episode 4 forces them to reconcile two seemingly incompatible characters with one another: Darth Vader and Anakin Skywalker, just as Luke has to when he comes to terms with the truth. And well before they've had a chance to come to terms with it, they are already watching Anakin slaughter Jedi and younglings. Without the foreknowledge of how awful Darth Vader is and the story Ben primed Luke with of Vader being his father's killer, the full weight of the revelation won't land. Even seeing Anakin put into the suit and use his iconic new voice and breath at the end of Episode 3 won't mean much unless you have seen the fear these features will command in the future.

By watching Episode 4 first, you experience the story from Luke's perspective throughout, as presented to him by Ben. You believe you are seeing the story of Anakin becoming a legendary Jedi and being terminated prematurely in what will certainly be a heroic death at the hands of the villainous Darth Vader. You think the rest of the story after that will naturally be about Luke avenging his father. Thus, when the hammer drops, you feel shocked and betrayed by what you were told and how your expectations were manipulated, exactly how Luke feels toward Ben upon finding out the truth about his father. *"Why didn't you tell me?"*

Episode 3 now becomes crucial for connecting the two halves of the story and removing the viewer's illusions about what they thought they were watching. It is the part of the story where the reality of the situation hits us, forcing us to reconcile our expectations and beliefs. Only then do we start to see all the obvious foreshadowing in Episodes 1 and 2 of what was going to happen to Anakin. Now that we've removed the narrative bias of who we *wanted* Anakin to be, who we and the Jedi *projected* him to be, his drastic turn of face seems depressingly realistic.

After the prequels, the expectation becomes that Luke needs to kill his evil father to bring down the Empire. As a result, the final twist of Anakin's redemption in Episode 6 is as effective as the initial twist of his downfall. Going into *The Empire Strikes Back* knowing that Vader is Luke's father, transforms the "I am your father" reveal from one of surprise to one of suspense. You've had one movie to process this information and come to terms with it, but seeing Luke receive the worst possible news in the world is a stark reminder of the terrible truth you already learned. You are waiting for Hitchcock's "bomb under the table" to go off, which the viewer can see ticking down, but which Luke is unaware is about to blow up in his face.

In order to experience the crushing blow of Vader's identity revelation, we have to have previously accepted Anakin as the hero of the story. We have to have once thought of him the way Luke did when Ben told him the revisionist version of the story. We still remember and care about Anakin, just as Luke remembers the heroic image he had of his father. It's now a tragedy for us because we have seen the change. We know the potential Anakin had and the hero he was supposed to be—the enormous difference between good and bad, and everything that was lost when Anakin died and was replaced by Darth Vader. The viewer should be just as disillusioned as Luke, just as lost in the dark night of their soul. It's the only way to set them up for the triumph that will follow with Anakin's glorious return.

Experiencing the story this way, we view Vader through a different lens in each episode of the original trilogy. In Episode 4, before we know the backstory, Vader is just an exciting and intimidating villain to us. In Episode 5, after learning the tragic truth in the prequels that Vader is actually Anakin, we experience a sense of betrayal by both Vader and the story. But by Episode 6, the shock of betrayal has worn off. Now, we feel sadness, sympathy at remembering how much we loved him before he fell, and we secretly hope he'll redeem himself and run away with Luke. This reflects how Luke sees him in each episode. In the end, it is unbelievably satisfying to see young Anakin greeting Luke next to Yoda and old Ben Kenobi as a Force spirit. It solidifies the continuation and conclusion of this lengthy, elaborate story told in the wrong order across decades, generations, and technological eras. I imagine that when I introduce my children to *Star Wars* one day, I will start by showing them *A New Hope* when they are young, to familiarize them with the simple worldview into which Luke is introduced. I will show them the prequels when I believe they are old enough and ready for the weight of what they will realize by the end of *Revenge of the Sith*, and their perspective on the storyworld is turned upside down, to be followed by the resolution of the story in *The Empire Strikes Back* and *Return of the Jedi*.

A final note on spoilers: It's important that you inform the person you are introducing to *Star Wars* not to look up any information about any of the characters or the story until they have completed all six movies. Tell them that they will spoil major plot points and hurt their experience of the story. Someone who has never seen the films may have already been exposed, through cultural osmosis, to the idea that Anakin is Darth Vader and/or that Darth Vader is Luke's father. To avoid making the impact of the spoiler worse, stick to Ben's version of the story until Anakin's fall to the dark side in Episode 3. Tell them that Darth Vader was a student of Obi-Wan who betrayed the Jedi and killed Luke's father. Even if someone has already learned through cultural references that Vader is Luke's father, they still don't know for sure that it's Anakin who becomes him. It's just as easy to assume that Anakin is not actually Luke's father and Vader is some other character who comes along to father him. Be aware that some versions of Episode 3 box art and promotional descriptions even reveal that Anakin turns to the dark side or becomes Darth Vader during the film, as the publishers obviously assumed everyone knew this crucial bit of lore going in.

NOTES

98. George Lucas, quoted by J. W. Rinzler, *The Making of Star Wars: Revenge of the Sith* (New York: Del Rey, 2005), 85.

99. In the Legends novel *Star Wars: Tatooine Ghost* by Troy Denning (New York: Del Rey, 2003), which takes place after the events of *Return of the Jedi*, Leia is not quick to forgive Anakin for his crimes. It doesn't matter to her that Luke tells her about his return to the light and how he sacrificed himself to save him. She can still only see him as Darth Vader, the icon of evil, until she reads her grandmother Shmi's journal entries about Anakin's young life as a slave and visits Tatooine to find out how she died at the hands of Tusken Raiders. Only then does she empathize with what the good man who was her father went through. Only then does it become understandable to her how he could have fallen onto the dark path he did. This is the journey the first-time viewer must go through for maximum emotional impact.

100. Machete Order (4 5 – 2 3 – 6) is one alternate *Star Wars* viewing order, proposed by blogger Rod Hilton in 2011. It begins with the original trilogy but interrupts the narrative after Episode 5 to go back in time for Episodes 2 and 3 as an extended flashback (skipping Episode 1 entirely due to its supposedly superfluous impact on the plot), then finishes with Episode 6. I have a hard time imagining a worse way to experience the story, both because of its interruption of the original trilogy after Episode 5 and its omission of Episode 1's essential mythological setup and the demonstration of child Anakin's original, pure characterization.

INTRODUCING THE ANAKINALOME

The unalome is a spiritual symbol originating in Buddhist iconography, representing the path to enlightenment or self-realization. To me, it broadly represents self-discovery and personal growth:

Stage 1. The spiral at the base represents the beginning of the journey, where things are more or less stable but quickly evolve to a higher point where grand new changes will be introduced, just like the stability of childhood:

Stage 2. Coming out of childhood, it becomes twisting, turning, exciting, and challenging, like the tumultuous times of adolescence. You constantly pivot off new experiences, heading in directions you couldn't have predicted, in search of a stable path ahead:

Stage 3. As the spiral straightens, it reflects how we begin to find clarity and direction through the mistakes we have made. We oscillate less wildly around a more defined path that, in an increasingly linear way, takes us where we are destined to go as stable adults. Our mistakes become less destructive and occur less frequently. This is how things go under ideal conditions when heroes like you, me, Luke, or Anakin learn the lessons they are supposed to. Some depictions feature the flowering of a lotus at the tip to represent apotheosis or the full embodiment of the inherent potential within:

The optimistic outline of the unalome ignores the possibility that outcomes do not align with ideal expectations in the real world. Fiction, too, including the archetypal Hero's Journey, is most often guilty of glossing over the bumps and expediting a protagonist's path toward their ideal destination. That's one of the many things that make *Star Wars* and the tragedy of Darth Vader noteworthy in human culture. It shows the opposite path that very few other stories have dared to explore in any detail. Someone like Anakin can climb for a time toward their ideal outcome, even almost reaching their stable peak, and then suddenly descend much lower than when they started, lower than anyone ever thought possible.

I had the idea to amend the traditional unalome to reflect the possibility of deviating from the ideal upward path, at first just by having the path make a sudden downward turn toward Hell (meaning the loss of consciousness, order, and authentic self) at the peak of its third stage. Someone may then remain the rest of their life there, or they may, as in the case of Anakin, use the perspective they gain from that time to correct the mistake they made and finally ascend up to Heaven (the reversal of the qualities of Hell):

My revised version of the traditional unalome, called the Anakinalome, alters the linear upward path of stage 3 to turn around on itself and begin an unexpected downward path, just as Anakin did at the midpoint of Episode 3:

What we see in the remaining films after Anakin's fall, Episodes 4, 5, and 6, is the slow recovery from that state back to the path he should have always been on as the Chosen One. It culminates with the final upward surge to Heaven he makes at the end of *Return of the Jedi* when he saves Luke and finally fulfills his authentic destiny in death:

The Anakinalome differs from the traditional unalome by depicting a journey that worsens before it improves. It's a reminder not to give up hope even when it seems like the worst has occurred and Hell has won. Heaven is always within reach.

The journey never looks the same for any two heroes on their paths. My dear friend, Elham Montazeri, was introduced to *Star Wars* for the first time when I asked her to help with this book's design. It wasn't necessary for her to have seen the movies, but she quickly found herself fascinated by the book's content as she read it for the first time. She insisted that she must see all six movies in rapid succession before beginning the design work on the cover and the Anakinalome to do it justice. Shortly thereafter, she began to understand my vision for the Anakinalome and proposed several alternative designs. There could be infinite variations because no two heroic paths toward self-actualization look the same or align perfectly with the ideal.

Here are ten of the variations Elham conjured. If you're artistically inclined, I hope you come up with your own, too:

ABOUT THE AUTHOR

Gregory V. Diehl (www.gregorydiehl.net) is a book producer, educator, and personal development mentor whose work centers on helping people question inherited assumptions and rediscover their authentic selves. He combines philosophical depth with practical insight, offering frameworks that challenge conventional thinking about learning, human potential, and heroic mythology applied in real life.

Raised in Southern California, Gregory left home at 18 and spent more than a decade traveling the world, immersing himself in diverse cultures and new ways of living. These experiences shaped his conviction that the root of social problems lies in self-understanding and a person's mental relationship with reality. He argues that lasting change begins with knowing who you really are and learning to perceive the world beyond the limits of comfort, commonality, and convention.

He now lives in rural Armenia, where he operates the Kalavan Retreat Center (www.kalavan.net), a social initiative dedicated to the realization of a single, powerful idea: ***You are not the person the world told you to be.*** Through educational workshops, lifestyle freedom, and Zen-inspired coaching, Gregory Invites visitors to Kalavan village to get away from "the real world," where they can step outside conditioned identities and remember their original face before they were born.